KB087731

적중 100

영어 기출 문제집

중 3

천재 | 이재영

Best Collection

구성과 특징

교과서의 주요 학습 내용을 중심으로 학습 영역별 특성에 맞춰 단계별로 다양한 학습 기회를 제공하여
단원별 학습능력 평가는 물론 중간 및 기말고사 시험 등에 완벽하게 대비할 수 있도록 내용을 구성

Words & Expressions

Step1   Key Words 단원별 핵심 단어 설명 및 풀이
         Key Expression 단원별 핵심 숙어 및 관용어 설명
         Word Power 반대 또는 비슷한 뜻 단어 배우기
         English Dictionary 영어로 배우는 영어 단어

Step2   실력평가 단원별 수시평가 대비 주관식, 객관식 문제풀이

Step3   서술형 대비 학업성취도 및 수행능력평가 대비 서술형 문제풀이

Conversation

Step1   핵심 의사소통 소통에 필요한 주요 표현 방법 요약
         핵심 Check 기본적인 표현 방법 및 활용능력 확인

Step2   대화문 익히기 교과서 대화문 심층 분석 및 확인

Step3   교과서 확인학습 빈칸 채우기를 통한 문장 완성 능력 확인

Step4   기본평가 시험대비 기초 학습 능력 평가

Step5   실력평가 단원별 수시평가 대비 주관식, 객관식 문제풀이

Step6   서술형 대비 학업성취도 및 수행능력평가 대비 서술형 문제풀이

Grammar

Step1   주요 문법 단원별 주요 문법 사항과 예문을 알기 쉽게 설명

         핵심 Check 기본 문법사항에 대한 이해 여부 확인

Step2   기본평가 시험대비 기초 학습 능력 평가

Step3   실력평가 단원별 수시평가 대비 주관식, 객관식 문제풀이

Step4   서술형 대비 학업성취도 및 수행능력평가 대비 서술형 문제풀이

Reading

Step1   구문 분석 단원별로 제시된 문장에 대한 구문별 분석과 내용 설명
         확인문제 문장에 대한 기본적인 이해와 인지능력 확인

Step2   확인학습A 빈칸 채우기를 통한 문장 완성 능력 확인

Step3   확인학습B 제시된 우리말을 영어로 완성하여 작문 능력 키우기

Step4   실력평가 단원별 수시평가 대비 주관식, 객관식 문제풀이

Step5   서술형 대비 학업성취도 및 수행능력평가 대비 서술형 문제풀이
         교과서 구석구석 교과서에 나오는 기타 문장까지 완벽 학습

Composition

|영역별 핵심문제|

단어 및 어휘, 대화문, 문법, 독해 등 각 영역별 기출문제의 출제 유형을 분석하여 실전에 대비하고 연습할 수 있도록 문제를 배열

|단원별 예상문제|

기출문제를 분석한 후 새로운 시험 출제 경향을 더하여 새롭게 출제될 수 있는 문제를 포함하여 시험에 완벽하게 대비할 수 있도록 준비

|서술형 실전 및 창의사고력 문제|

학교 시험에서 점차 늘어나는 서술형 시험에 집중 대비하고 고득점을 취득하는데 만전을 기하기 위한 학습 코너

|단원별 모의고사|

영역별, 단계별 학습을 모두 마친 후 실전 연습을 위한 모의고사

교과서 파헤치기

- **단어Test1~3** 영어 단어 우리말 쓰기, 우리말을 영어 단어로 쓰기, 영영풀이에 해당하는 단어와 우리말 쓰기
- **대화문Test1~2** 대화문 빈칸 완성 및 전체 대화문 쓰기
- **본문Test1~5** 빈칸 완성, 우리말 쓰기, 문장 배열연습, 영어 작문하기 복습 등 단계별 반복 학습을 통해 교과서 지문에 대한 완벽한 습득
- **구석구석지문Test1~2** 지문 빈칸 완성 및 전문 영어로 쓰기

Contents

Lesson 7

Watch Out

 의사소통 기능

- 당부하기
  A: Make sure you don't play with the knives.
  B: I'll keep that in mind.

- 부탁하기
  A: Can you do me a favor?
  B: Sure. What is it?

 언어 형식

- 분사구문
  I study math, **listening to** music.

- 조동사가 포함된 수동태
  The party **will be held** at 7 p.m.

Words & Expressions

Key Words

- **active** [ǽktiv] 형 활동 중인
- **area** [ɛ́əriə] 명 지역
- **ash** [æʃ] 명 재
- **chance** [tʃæns] 명 가능성, 기회
- **circle** [sə́:rkl] 동 둘러싸다
- **cold wave** 한파
- **crop** [krɑp] 명 농작물
- **destroy** [distrɔ́i] 동 파괴하다
- **discover** [diskʌ́vər] 동 발견하다
- **disturb** [distə́:rb] 동 방해하다
- **drought** [draut] 명 가뭄
- **dust** [dʌst] 명 먼지
- **earphone** [íərfòun] 명 이어폰
- **earthquake** [ə́:rθkweik] 명 지진
- **effect** [ifékt] 명 영향, 효과, 결과
- **entire** [intáiər] 형 전체의, 온
- **erupt** [irʌ́pt] 동 분출하다
- **eruption** [irʌ́pʃən] 명 분출
- **fantastic** [fæntǽstik] 형 환상적인
- **favor** [féivər] 명 친절, 부탁
- **flat** [flæt] 형 평평한
- **flood** [flʌd] 동 범람하다 명 홍수
- **heat** [hi:t] 동 데우다
- **helmet** [hélmit] 명 헬멧, 안전모
- **hit** [hit] 동 (태풍 등이) 덮치다, 엄습하다
- **hopeful** [hóupfəl] 형 희망적인
- **hot spring** 온천
- **hurricane** [hə́:rəkèin] 명 허리케인
- **issue** [íʃu:] 동 발표하다, 발행하다
- **Jupiter** [dʒú:pitər] 명 목성
- **landslide** [lǽndslaid] 명 산사태

- **lie** [lai] 동 위치해 있다
- **locate** [lóukeit] 동 ~의 위치를 찾아내다
- **Mars** [mɑ:rz] 명 화성
- **nearby** [nìərbái] 형 근처의 부 근처에
- **occur** [əkə́:r] 동 일어나다, 발생하다
- **overnight** [óuvərnait] 부 하룻밤 사이에, 하룻밤 동안
- **planet** [plǽnit] 명 행성
- **prevent** [privént] 동 막다, 예방하다
- **produce** [prədjú:s] 동 생산하다
- **rainfall** [réinfɔl] 명 강우, 강우량
- **relieve** [rilí:v] 동 완화하다, 줄이다
- **resource** [rí:sɔ:rs] 명 자원
- **ring** [riŋ] 명 고리, 반지
- **sandstorm** [sǽndstɔrm] 명 모래 폭풍
- **scenery** [sí:nəri] 명 경치, 풍경
- **soil** [sɔil] 명 토양
- **solar system** 태양계
- **spread** [spred] 동 퍼지다
- **sudden** [sʌ́dn] 형 갑작스러운
- **threaten** [θrétn] 동 위협하다
- **traffic** [trǽfik] 명 교통
- **tsunami** [tsunɑ́:mi] 명 해일
- **typhoon** [taifú:n] 명 태풍
- **underwater** [ʌndərwɔ́tər] 형 수중의
- **volcano** [vɑlkéinou] 명 화산
- **volume** [vɑ́lju:m] 명 부피, 용적
- **warning** [wɔ́:rniŋ] 명 주의, 경고
- **weather** [wéðər] 명 날씨
- **wildfire** [wɔ́ildfaiər] 명 산불
- **yellow dust** 명 황사

Key Expressions

- **do ~ a favor** ~의 부탁을 들어주다
- **do harm** 해를 입히다
- **get hurt** 다치다
- **get stuck in** ~에 갇히다
- **have an effect on** ~에 영향을 미치다
- **have ~ in common** ~을 공통점으로 가지다
- **in harmony with** ~와 조화를 이루어
- **keep ~ in mind** ~을 명심하다
- **millions of** 수백만의

- **make use of** ~을 이용하다
- **name after** ~을 따라 이름 짓다
- **on one's way back** ~으로 돌아오는 길에
- **prevent A from -ing** A가 ~하지 못하게 하다
- **put A in danger** A를 위험하게 하다
- **shoot ~ into ...** ~을 …으로 내뿜다
- **so far** 지금까지
- **take care of** ~을 돌보다, ~을 처리하다
- **take off** ~을 벗다

Word Power

※ 서로 비슷한 뜻을 가진 어휘

□ **chance** 가능성 – **possibility** 가능성
□ **effect** 영향 – **influence** 영향
□ **erupt** 분출하다 – **burst** 터뜨리다
□ **heat** 데우다 – **warm** 데우다
□ **produce** 생산하다 – **yield** 생산하다
□ **threaten** 위협하다 – **scare** 겁주다

□ **discover** 발견하다 – **detect** 탐지하다
□ **entire** 전체의, 온 – **whole** 전체의
□ **fantastic** 환상적인 – **wonderful** 훌륭한
□ **prevent** 막다 – **stop** 가로막다
□ **sudden** 갑작스러운 – **abrupt** 갑작스러운

※ 서로 반대의 뜻을 가진 어휘

□ **active** 활동 중인 ↔ **inactive** 활동하지 않는
□ **destroy** 파괴하다 ↔ **construct** 건축하다
□ **heat** 데우다 ↔ **cool** 식히다
□ **nearby** 근처의 ↔ **faraway** 멀리 떨어진

□ **cold wave** 한파 ↔ **heat wave** 혹서, 열기
□ **entire** 전체의, 온 ↔ **partial** 부분적인
□ **hopeful** 희망적인 ↔ **hopeless** 절망적인
□ **sudden** 갑작스러운 ↔ **expected** 예상된

※ 동사 → 명사

□ **destroy** 파괴하다 – **destruction** 파괴
□ **disturb** 방해하다 – **disturbance** 방해
□ **prevent** 막디 – **prevention** 예방
□ **threaten** 위협하다 – **threat** 위협

□ **discover** 발견하다 – **discovery** 발견
□ **erupt** 분출하다 – **eruption** 분출
□ **produce** 생산하다 – **production** 생산

※ 명사 → 형용사

□ **action** 행동 – **active** 활동 중인
□ **fantasy** 환상 – **fantastic** 환상적인
□ **hope** 희망 – **hopeful** 희망적인

□ **effect** 영향, 효과 – **effective** 효과적인
□ **favor** 친절 – **favorable** 우호적인
□ **volcano** 화산 – **volcanic** 화산의

English Dictionary

□ **active** 활동 중인
→ involved in a particular activity 특정한 활동에 몰두한

□ **ash** 재
→ the grey powder that remains after something has burnt 어떤 것이 불타고 난 후 남은 회색 가루

□ **circle** 둘러싸다
→ to make a line in the shape of a ring 둥근 모양으로 선을 만들다

□ **dust** 먼지
→ dry powder that consists of very small bits of earth or sand 흙이나 모래의 매우 작은 조각으로 구성된 마른 가루

□ **earthquake** 지진
→ a sudden shaking of Earth's surface 지구 표면의 갑작스러운 흔들림

□ **eruption** 분출
→ a sudden outbreak of something 무엇인가의 갑작스러운 발생

□ **flat** 평평한
→ even and smooth without curved or high parts 곡선이나 도드라지는 부분 없이 매끈하고 평평한

□ **planet** 행성
→ a large round object in space that moves around a star 별 주변을 도는 우주에 있는 크고 둥근 물체

□ **prevent** 막다, 예방하다
→ to keep something from happening 어떤 것이 발생하지 못하게 하다

□ **traffic** 교통
→ the movement of cars, ships or aircraft 차, 선박, 비행기의 움직임

□ **volcano** 화산
→ a mountain with a big hole at the top, through which lava is pushed up 꼭대기에 용암이 솟아나오는 구멍이 있는 산

서답형

01 다음 짝지어진 단어의 관계가 같도록 빈칸에 알맞은 말을 쓰시오.

action : active = effect : _____

02 다음 영영풀이가 가리키는 것을 고르시오.

a mountain with a big hole at the top, through which lava is pushed up

① volcano   ② earthquake
③ flood   ④ drought
⑤ tornado

03 다음 중 밑줄 친 부분의 뜻풀이가 바르지 <u>않은</u> 것은?

① People cleaned the <u>ashes</u> left by the forest fire. (재)
② Rice is the main <u>crop</u> of the country. (농작물)
③ The war is bad because it <u>destroys</u> everything. (건설하다)
④ Please do not <u>disturb</u> me when I am sleeping. (방해하다)
⑤ The desk was covered with <u>dust</u>. (먼지)

서답형

04 다음 우리말에 맞게 빈칸에 알맞은 말을 쓰시오.

(1) 그 나라의 모든 도시에 홍수가 났다.
➡ All the cities of the country have been _____.
(2) 도로 한복판에서 차 사고가 발생했다.
➡ The car accident _____ in the middle of the road.
(3) 그 여행객은 하룻밤 묵을 곳을 찾고 있다.
➡ The traveler is looking for a place to stay _____.

서답형

05 다음 문장의 빈칸에 들어갈 말을 〈보기〉에서 골라 쓰시오.

┌─ 보기 ┐
shot ~ into / solar system / on his way back / have ~ in common / do harm
└─────┘

(1) My dad bought a cake _____ _____ _____ _____ home.
(2) My brother and I _____ nothing _____ _____ .
(3) Mars and Jupiter belong to the same _____ _____ .
(4) Some animals _____ _____ to crops.
(5) The old truck _____ bad gas _____ the air.

중요

06 다음 빈칸 (A)~(C)에 공통으로 들어갈 말이 바르게 짝지어진 것은?

- I don't (A)_____ nothing in common with my younger brother.
- Colors (A)_____ an effect on our moods.
- There was a car accident, but anyone didn't (B)_____ hurt.
- We left earlier than usual, so we didn't (B)_____ stuck in the rush-hour traffic.
- Would you (C)_____ care of my pet for a week?
- You should (C)_____ off your hat in the classroom.

① make – take – get   ② make – get – take
③ have – get – take   ④ have – put – do
⑤ put – take – get

01 다음 짝지어진 단어의 관계가 같도록 빈칸에 알맞은 말을 쓰시오.

> sudden : expected = _____ : partial

02 다음 우리말에 맞게 빈칸에 알맞은 말을 쓰시오.

(1) 쌍둥이 언니와 나는 많은 것들을 공통적으로 가지고 있다.
➡ My twin sister and I _____ lots of things _____ _____.

(2) 우리는 자연과 조화를 이루며 살아야 한다.
➡ We should live _____ _____ _____ nature.

(3) Paul이라는 이름은 그의 아버지에게서 따온 것이다.
➡ Paul was _____ _____ his father.

03 다음 문장의 빈칸에 들어갈 말을 〈보기〉에서 골라 쓰시오.

> ┤ 보기 ├
> prevent / scenery / threaten / volume / warnings

(1) She stopped her car to enjoy the beautiful _____.
(2) The bad boys often _____ children in his neighborhood.
(3) If you want to _____ car accidents, do not use your phone while driving.
(4) They gave _____ about the dangers of smoking.
(5) Which of these bottles has the greater _____?

04 우리말과 일치하도록 주어진 단어를 모두 배열하여 영작하시오.

(1) 스트레칭은 목의 통증을 완화하는 데 좋은 방법이다.
(neck / stretching / way / pain / a / to / your / good / relieve / is)
➡ _____
_____

(2) 나의 가족은 겨울에 온천에 가는 것을 좋아한다.
(likes / to / my / in / hot / winter / family / springs / visit)
➡ _____
_____

(3) 세균이 공기 중에 퍼질 수 있다.
(the / can / through / germs / air / spread)
➡ _____
_____

05 다음 우리말에 맞게 주어진 단어를 사용하여 영작하시오.

(1) 자전거를 탈 때에는 헬멧을 착용해야 한다. (wear, ride)
➡ _____
_____

(2) 폭염 주의보가 발효되었다. (heatwave, warnings, were)
➡ _____
_____

(3) 이 앱은 당신의 아이의 위치를 찾아내도록 도와준다. (locate, app)
➡ _____
_____

(4) 도둑은 가게주인을 협박하고 현금을 훔쳤다. (the shopkeeper, stole, cash)
➡ _____
_____

Conversation

① 당부하기

> **A** Make sure you don't play with the knives. 절대로 칼을 가지고 놀지 않도록 해라.
>
> **B** I'll keep that in mind. 명심할게요.

■ 당부하는 의미로 상대방에게 '꼭 ~해라.'라고 말할 때는 'Make sure ~.'라고 한다. 'make sure'는 '~을 확실하게 하다'의 뜻으로 명령문으로 나타내게 되면 '확실하게 해라.'의 의미이다. 'be sure to ~'도 마찬가지로 '반드시 ~해라.'의 의미가 된다.

■ 'Make sure'는 'Make sure (that) 주어+동사 ~.', 'Make sure to부정사 ~.'의 형태로 쓰고, 상대방에게 '~하지 마라., ~할 것을 잊지 마라., ~할 것을 기억해라.'라고 당부할 때는 부정 명령문으로 'Don't+동사원형 ~.', 'Don't forget to+동사원형 ~.'으로 말할 수 있고 'Remember to+동사원형 ~.'으로 나타내기도 한다.

■ 상대방에게 권고하는 의미가 될 때는 '~하는 편이 더 낫다.'는 의미로 'You had better+동사원형 ~.'을 쓰게 된다. '~해야 한다'의 의미로 'be supposed to ~'도 일상적으로 많은 쓰는 표현이다.

당부하기

- Make sure to+동사원형 / (that) ~. 반드시 ~해라.
- Make certain that ~. 반드시 ~해라.
- Be sure to ~. 반드시 ~해라.
- Don't forget to ~. ~하는 것을 잊지 마라.
- Please remember to ~. ~할 것을 기억해 주세요.

핵심 Check

1. 다음 대화의 밑줄 친 우리말에 맞게 영작하시오.

(The phone rings.)

B: Hi, Mom.

W: Hi, Junho. Are you having a good time with Dad?

B: Yeah. Today we visited Dokdo.

W: That sounds cool. What are you going to do tomorrow?

B: We're going fishing on a boat.

W: Great. <u>반드시 구명조끼를 입도록 해라.</u>(a life jacket, make)

B: Okay, Mom. I'll keep that in mind.

➡ _____

② 부탁하기

> **A** Can you do me a favor? 부탁해도 됩니까?
> **B** Sure. What is it? 물론. 그게 무엇입니까?
>
> **A** Can you feed the dog? 개에게 먹이를 줄 수 있니?
> **B** No problem. 물론이지.

- 'Can you do me a favor?'는 상대에게 부탁을 하는 말로 '부탁 하나 해도 될까요?'의 의미이다. 조동사 can 대신 could, would 등을 사용하여 'Could you do me a favor?', 'Would you do me favor, please?'라고 할 수 있다.

- 부탁하는 말로 'Can I ask you a favor?'도 '부탁 하나 해도 될까요?'의 뜻이고, 'May I ask you a favor?' 또는 'May I ask for a favor?'라고 할 수도 있다. 'do A a favor'는 'A에게 부탁을 들어주다'의 의미이고, 'ask A a favor'는 'A에게 부탁하다'라는 뜻이다.

- '상대방에게 직설적으로 도움을 부탁을 할 때는 'Can you help me+동사원형 ~?', 'Can/Could you help me with+명사?(~ 좀 도와주시겠습니까?)'라고 할 수 있다. 이 표현은 'Do you mind helping me with ~?', 'Would you mind helping me ~?'라고 해도 같은 의도의 표현이 된다.

- 상대방에게 부탁을 하거나 허락을 요청할 때는 허락을 요청하는 조동사를 사용하여 'Can you ~?', 'May I ~?'라고 할 수 있고, 'Is it okay if I ~?' 등을 사용하여 구체적인 부탁의 내용을 말할 수 있다.

부탁하기

- Can you do me a favor? 부탁해도 될까요?
- Could/Would you do me a favor? 부탁해도 될까요?
- Can/May I ask you a favor? 부탁해도 될까요?
- Could/Would you ~ for me? ~ 좀 해 주시겠습니까?
- Could you help me with ~? ~ 좀 도와 주시겠습니까?

핵심 Check

2. 다음 대화를 가장 자연스러운 순서로 배열한 것은?

　(A) Sure. What is it?

　(B) No problem. Anything else?

　(C) Can you do me a favor?

　(D) Can you feed the dog?

　① (A) – (C) – (D) – (B)　　　② (C) – (A) – (D) – (B)
　③ (D) – (A) – (C) – (B)　　　④ (C) – (B) – (D) – (A)
　⑤ (A) – (B) – (D) – (C)

Listen - Listen & Answer Talk 1

M: Hi, this is Cha Gisang from the Weather Station. Here is today's weather. ❶Typhoon Doni is moving north and is going to ❷hit Jejudo tonight. A typhoon warning has been ❸issued. There will be lots of rainfall with a high chance of flooding in some areas. Please ❹stay inside because Typhoon Doni will come with strong winds. Also, please ❺make sure you keep listening to our reports. Thank you.

남: 안녕하세요, 기상대에서 차 기상입니다. 오늘 날씨를 말씀드리겠습니다. 태풍 도니가 북상 중이며 오늘 밤에 제주도를 강타할 예정입니다. 태풍주의보가 발효되었습니다. 많은 양의 비가 내릴 예정이고 일부 지역에서는 홍수의 가능성이 높습니다. 태풍 도니는 강한 바람을 동반하므로 실내에 머무십시오. 또, 보도를 계속 청취해 주시기를 당부 드립니다. 감사합니다.

❶ typhoon: 태풍
❷ hit: 강타하다
❸ issue: 발표하다, 발행하다
❹ 동사원형으로 시작하는 명령문이다.
❺ 'make sure+주어+동사: 꼭 ~ 해라, 반드시 ~해라'의 뜻으로 당부의 표현이다.

Check(√) True or False

(1) The man is talking about the weather forecast.　　　　　　　T ☐ F ☐

(2) Typhoon Doni is coming with heavy rain and snow from the north area.　　T ☐ F ☐

Listen - Listen & Answer Dialog 2

M: Sora, ❶can you do me a favor?

G: What is it, Dad?

M: A typhoon is coming tonight. Can you bring in the clothes from outside?

G: No problem. What about your bike?

M: I'll take care of ❷it after I finish the dishes.

G: Okay. Do you want me to call Grandma and tell ❸her about the typhoon?

M: Yes. Please tell ❸her to ❹stay home.

G: Okay, Dad.

남: 소라야, 부탁 좀 들어줄래?
여: 뭔데요, 아빠?
남: 오늘 밤 태풍이 온다는구나. 바깥에서 옷가지들을 들여와 주겠니?
여: 그럴게요. 아빠의 자전거는 어떻게 할까요?
남: 자전거는 설거지를 끝낸 후에 내가 처리하마.
여: 알겠어요. 할머니께 전화해서 태풍에 관해 말씀드릴까요?
남: 그래. 할머니께 집안에 계시라고 말씀드리렴.
여: 네, 아빠.

❶ 상대에게 부탁하는 말로 '부탁 하나 해도 될까요?'를 의미한다.
❷ it은 Dad's bike를 가리킨다.
❸ her는 모두 Grandma를 가리킨다.
❹ stay home: 집에 머물다

Check(√) True or False

(3) Dad is going to do dishes after bringing in his bike from outside.　　T ☐ F ☐

(4) The girl is going to call Grandma and ask her not to go outside.　　T ☐ F ☐

Listen - Listen More

B: Jimin, are you ❶going out?

G: Yeah. I'm going to buy some sandwiches at Choi's.

B: Are you walking there?

G: No. I'll ride my bike.

B: That's good. ❷Can you do me a favor?

G: Sure. What is it?

B: Can you buy chocolate ice cream for me ❸on your way back?

G: No problem.

B: Thanks. ❹Please make sure you wear a helmet and no ear phones!

G: Don't worry about that.

❶ go out: 외출하다

❷ 'Can you help me?' 또는 'Would you do me a favor?' 등으로 바꾸어 표현할 수 있다.

❸ on one's way back: 돌아오는 길에

❹ 당부하는 표현으로 'Be certain that ~.' 또는 'Remember that ~.' 등으로 바꾸어 표현할 수 있다.

 Wrap Up 5

(The phone rings.)

B: Hi, Mom.

W: Hi, Junho. Are you having a good time with Dad?

B: Yeah. Today we visited Dokdo.

W: That sounds cool. ❶What are you going to do tomorrow?

B: We're going fishing on a boat.

W: Great. Please make sure you wear ❷a life jacket.

B: Okay, Mom. I'll ❸keep ❹that in mind.

❶ 내일 계획을 묻는 표현으로 'What are you planning to do?' 등으로 바꾸어 표현할 수 있다.

❷ life jacket: 구명조끼

❸ keep ~ in mind: ~을 명심하다

❹ that은 구명조끼를 입어야 한다는 것을 가리킨다.

 Speak - Talk in pairs.

A: Can I start now?

B: ❶Wash your hands before you start.

A: Okay. No problem.

B: One more thing. Make sure you don't play with the ❷knives.

A: I'll keep ❸that in mind.

❶ 동사로 시작하는 명령문이다.

❷ knife의 복수형이다.

❸ that은 칼을 갖고 놀지 않겠다는 것을 뜻한다.

Wrap Up 6

W: ❶Can you do me a favor?

B: Sure, Grandma. What is it?

W: I want to go to the Tom Dylan concert on Christmas. Can you buy some tickets for me?

B: No problem. How many tickets do you want?

W: Two tickets, please.

❶ 상대에게 부탁을 하는 말로 'Can you give me a hand?' 등으로 바꾸어 표현할 수 있다.

● 다음 우리말과 일치하도록 빈칸에 알맞은 말을 쓰시오.

Listen - Listen & Answer Talk 1

M: Hi, this is Cha Gisang from the Weather Station. Here is today's weather. Typhoon Doni is moving north and is going to _____ Jejudo tonight. A typhoon _____ has been _____. There will be lots of _____ with a high chance of _____ in some areas. Please stay _____ because Typhoon Doni will come with strong winds. Also, please _____ _____ you keep listening to our reports. Thank you.

Listen - Listen & Answer Dialog 2

M: Sora, can you do me a _____?

G: What is it, Dad?

M: A _____ is coming tonight. Can you _____ _____ the clothes from outside?

G: _____ problem. What about your _____?

M: I'll take _____ of it after I finish the _____.

G: Okay. Do you want me to call Grandma and tell her about the _____?

M: Yes. Please tell her to _____ _____.

G: Okay, Dad.

Listen - Listen More

B: Jimin, are you going out?

G: Yeah. I'm going to buy some _____ at Choi's.

B: Are you walking there?

G: No. I'll _____ _____ _____.

B: That's _____. Can you do me _____ _____?

G: Sure. What is it?

B: Can you buy chocolate ice cream for me _____ _____ _____?

G: No _____.

B: Thanks. Please _____ _____ you _____ a helmet and _____ ear phones!

G: Don't _____ about that.

해석

남: 안녕하세요, 기상대에서 차기상입니다. 오늘 날씨를 말씀드리겠습니다. 태풍 도니가 북상 중이며 오늘 밤에 제주도를 강타할 예정입니다. 태풍 주의보가 발효되었습니다. 많은 양의 비가 내릴 예정이고 일부 지역에서는 홍수의 가능성이 높습니다. 태풍 도니는 강한 바람을 동반하므로 실내에 머무십시오. 또, 보도를 계속 청취해 주시기를 당부 드립니다. 감사합니다.

남: 소라야, 부탁 좀 들어줄래?
여: 뭔데요, 아빠?
남: 오늘 밤 태풍이 온다는구나. 바깥에서 옷가지들을 들여와 주겠니?
여: 그럴게요. 아빠의 자전거는 어떻게 할까요?
남: 자전거는 설거지를 끝낸 후에 내가 처리하마.
여: 알겠어요. 할머니께 전화해서 태풍에 관해 말씀드릴까요?
남: 그래. 할머니께 집안에 계시라고 말씀드리렴.
여: 네, 아빠.

남: 지민아, 외출하니?
여: 응. '최가네'에서 샌드위치 좀 사려고.
남: 그곳에 걸어서 갈 거니?
여: 아니. 자전거를 타고 갈 거야.
남: 잘됐다. 부탁 좀 들어줄래?
여: 그럼. 뭔데?
남: 돌아오는 길에 초콜릿 아이스크림 좀 사다 줄 수 있어?
여: 물론이야.
남: 고마워. 헬멧 꼭 쓰고, 이어폰은 안 돼!
여: 걱정하지 마.

Speak - Talk in pairs.

A: Can I start now?

B: _____ _____ _____ before you start.

A: Okay. No problem.

B: One _____ thing. Make sure _____ _____ _____ _____

_____ _____ .

A: I'll keep that in _____ .

Wrap Up 5

(The phone rings.)

B: Hi, Mom.

W: Hi, Junho. Are you _____ _____ _____ _____ with Dad?

B: Yeah. Today we visited Dokdo.

W: That sounds _____ . What are you _____ to do tomorrow?

B: We're going _____ on a boat.

W: Great. Please make sure you _____ _____ _____ _____ .

B: Okay, Mom. I'll _____ that _____ _____ .

Wrap Up 6

W: Can you _____ _____ _____ _____ _____ ?

B: Sure, Grandma. What is it?

W: I want to go to the Tom Dylan concert _____ _____ . Can you

buy some _____ for me?

B: No problem. How many _____ _____ _____ _____ ?

W: Two tickets, please.

[01~02] 다음 대화를 읽고 물음에 답하시오.

(The phone rings.)

Junho: Hi, Mom.

Mom: Hi, Junho. Are you having a good time with Dad?

Junho: Yeah. Today we ⓐ<u>visited</u> Dokdo.

Mom: That ⓑ<u>sounds</u> cool. What are you going to do tomorrow?

Junho: We're going fishing ⓒ<u>on</u> a boat.

Mom: Great. Please make sure you ⓓ<u>wearing</u> a life jacket.

Junho: Okay, Mom. I'll keep ⓔ<u>that</u> in mind.

01 위 대화의 밑줄 친 ⓐ~ⓔ 중 어법상 어색한 것을 찾아 바르게 고치시오.

➡ _____

02 위 대화를 읽고 대답할 수 <u>없는</u> 것은?

① Where did Junho visit?

② With whom did Junho visit Dokdo?

③ What is Junho planning to do tomorrow?

④ What does Mom advise to Junho?

⑤ What should Dad keep in mind?

[03~04] 다음 대화를 읽고 물음에 답하시오.

Grandma: Can you do me a favor?

Jack: Sure, Grandma. What is it?

Grandma: I want to go to the Tom Dylan concert on Christmas. Can you buy some tickets for me?

Jack: No problem. How many tickets do you want?

Grandma: Two tickets, please.

03 Where does Grandma want to go on Christmas?

➡ _____

04 What does Grandma want Jack to do?

➡ _____

[01~03] 다음 대화를 읽고 물음에 답하시오.

Girl: Can I start now?

Man: Wash your hands before you start.

Girl: Okay. No problem.

Man: One more thing. Make sure you don't play with the knives.

Girl: I'll keep that in mind.

01 위 대화가 일어나는 장소로 가장 적절한 것은?

① hospital   ② post office

③ kitchen   ④ airport

⑤ grocery store

서답형

02 What does the man ask the girl to do first?

➡ _____

서답형

03 남자가 여자에게 하지 말도록 당부한 것을 10자 내외의 우리말로 쓰시오.

➡ _____

[04~05] 다음 대화를 읽고 물음에 답하시오.

Dad: Sora, (A)can you do me a favor?

Sora: What is it, Dad?

Dad: A typhoon is coming tonight. Can you bring in the clothes from outside?

Sora: No problem. What about your bike?

Dad: I'll take care of it after I finish the dishes.

Sora: Okay. Do you want me to call Grandma and tell her about the typhoon?

Dad: Yes. Please tell her to stay home.

Sora: Okay, Dad.

04 위 대화의 밑줄 친 (A)와 바꾸어 쓰기에 어색한 것은?

① would you do me a favor?

② can you help me?

③ can you give me a hand?

④ may I ask you a favor?

⑤ what can I do for you?

05 위 대화를 읽고 대답할 수 없는 것은?

① What does Dad ask Sora to do?

② Who will take care of the bike?

③ How's the weather tonight?

④ What will Sora tell her grandmother about?

⑤ What is Sora going to bring to her grandmother?

[06~08] 다음 대화를 읽고 물음에 답하시오.

M: Hi, this is Cha Gisang from the Weather Station. Here is today's weather. Typhoon Doni is moving north and is going to hit Jejudo tonight. A typhoon warning has been issued. There will be lots of rainfall with a high chance of flooding in some areas. Please stay inside because Typhoon Doni will come with strong winds. Also, (A)please make sure you keep listening to our reports. Thank you.

서답형

06 위 대화에서 다음의 영영풀이가 뜻하는 것을 찾아 쓰시오.

a violent tropical storm with very strong winds

➡ _____

07 위 대화의 밑줄 친 (A)와 바꾸어 쓰기에 <u>어색한</u> 것은?

① make certain that you should keep listening to our reports

② don't forget to keep listening to our reports

③ remember to keep listening to our reports

④ be sure to keep listening to our reports

⑤ I'm not certain that you should keep listening to our reports

08 위 대화의 내용과 일치하지 <u>않는</u> 것은?

① 태풍 도니가 북상 중이다.

② 태풍은 오늘 밤에 제주도를 강타할 예정이다.

③ 태풍주의보가 해제되었다.

④ 많은 양의 비가 내릴 예정이고 일부 지역에서는 홍수의 가능성이 높다.

⑤ 태풍 도니는 강한 바람을 동반하므로 실내에 머물 것을 당부한다.

[09~11] 다음 대화를 읽고 물음에 답하시오.

Brian: Jimin, are you going out?

Jimin: Yeah. I'm going to buy some sandwiches at Choi's. (A)

Brian: Are you walking there?

Jimin: No. I'll ride my bike. (B)

Brian: That's good. (C)

Jimin: Sure. What is it?

Brian: Can you buy chocolate ice cream for me on your way back?

Jimin: No problem. (D)

Brian: Thanks. Please make sure you wear a helmet and no ear phones! (E)

Jimin: Don't worry about that.

09 위 대화의 (A)~(E) 중 주어진 문장이 들어가기에 적절한 곳은?

> Can you do me a favor?

① (A)　② (B)　③ (C)　④ (D)　⑤ (E)

10 Choose all the places that Jimin is going to visit.

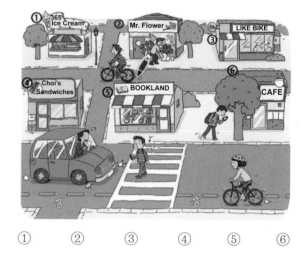

① ② ③ ④ ⑤ ⑥

11 위 대화를 읽고 대답할 수 <u>없는</u> 것은?

① Where is Jimin going?

② What is Jimin going to buy?

③ What does Brian ask Jimin to do?

④ What shouldn't Jimin wear when she rides her bike?

⑤ How can Brian help Jimin?

12 다음 중 짝지어진 대화가 <u>어색한</u> 것을 고르시오.

① A: Can you do me a favor?
　B: Sure. What is it?

② A: Can I ask you a favor?
　B: Sure. What can I do for you?

③ A: Could you take out the trash?
　B: No problem. I'll do that for you.

④ A: Would you do me a favor?
　B: I'm sorry to hear that. Anything else?

⑤ A: Can you help me? Please take me to the flower shop.
　B: Umm. I can take you to the bus stop.

01 다음 대화가 자연스럽게 이어지도록 순서대로 배열하시오.

> (A) Two tickets, please.
> (B) Can you do me a favor?
> (C) Sure, Grandma. What is it?
> (D) No problem. How many tickets do you want?
> (E) I want to go to the Tom Dylan concert on Christmas. Can you buy some tickets for me?

➡ _____

02 다음 대화의 내용과 일치하도록 빈칸을 완성하시오.

> Dad: Sora, can you do me a favor?
> Sora: What is it, Dad?
> Dad: A typhoon is coming tonight. Can you bring in the clothes from outside?
> Sora: No problem. What about your bike?
> Dad: I'll take care of it after I finish the dishes.
> Sora: Okay. Do you want me to call Grandma and tell her about the typhoon?
> Dad: Yes. Please tell her to stay home.
> Sora: Okay, Dad.
>
> ↓
>
> Sora: Hello, this is Sora.
> Grandma: Hi, Sweety. What's up?
> Sora: Grandma, you should ___(A)___ because ___(B)___.
> Grandma: Oh, I see. Thank you for letting me know that.
> Sora: You're welcome.

(A) _____

(B) _____

[03~05] 다음 글을 읽고 물음에 답하시오.

> M: Hi, this is Cha Gisang from the Weather Station. Here is today's weather. Typhoon Doni is moving north and is going to hit Jejudo tonight. A typhoon warning has been issued. There will be lots of rainfall with a high chance of flooding in some areas. Please stay inside because Typhoon Doni will come with strong winds. Also, please make sure you keep listening to our reports. Thank you.

03 When is Typhoon Doni going to hit Jejudo?

➡ _____

04 What will Typhoon Doni cause in some areas?

➡ _____

05 What does the man ask the listeners to do?

➡ _____

_____

06 다음 대화가 자연스럽게 이어지도록 순서대로 배열하시오.

> (The phone rings.)
> Junho: Hi, Mom.
> Mom: Hi, Junho. Are you having a good time with Dad?
> (A) Okay, Mom. I'll keep that in mind.
> (B) We're going fishing on a boat.
> (C) Yeah. Today we visited Dokdo.
> (D) Great. Please make sure you wear a life jacket.
> (E) That sounds cool. What are you going to do tomorrow?

➡ _____

Grammar

1 분사구문

> • I study math, **listening** to music. 나는 음악을 들으면서 수학을 공부한다.

■ 분사가 이끄는 구를 분사구문이라고 하며, 이유, 조건, 시간, 동시동작, 양보 등의 뜻을 나타낸다. 분사구문은 '접속사+주어+동사'로 이루어진 부사절의 주어가 주절의 주어와 일치할 때 접속사와 주어를 생략하고 동사를 분사(동사원형+-ing)로 만들어 부사구로 표현한 것이다.

- While I was walking along the street, I met Mr. White.
  → **Walking** along the street, I met Mr. White. (시간)

■ 부사절과 주절의 주어가 다를 때는 부사절의 주어를 생략하지 않고 사용하며 이것을 독립분사구문이라고 한다. 일반인이 주어일 경우에는 생략한다. (비인칭 독립분사구문)

- As it was getting dark, we soon turned back.
  → It **being** getting dark, we soon turned back. 어두워지기 시작하였으므로 이내 우리는 돌아왔다.

■ 분사구문의 부정은 분사 앞에 'not'이나 'never'를 쓴다.

- She had to leave early because she didn't have much time.
  → **Not having** much time, she had to leave early. 그녀는 시간이 촉박해서 빨리 떠나야 했다.

■ 분사구문의 의미를 분명히 하기 위해 분사 앞에 접속사를 쓰는 경우도 있다. 이 경우는 부사절에서 '주어+be동사'를 생략한 것과 같은 형태가 된다.

- While **taking** this medicine, avoid alcohol. 이 약을 복용하는 동안 술은 피해라.

■ 부사절의 시제가 주절보다 앞선 경우에는 완료분사구문(having+과거분사)으로 쓴다.

- After I had been sick, I realized how precious health is.
  = **Having been** sick, I realized how precious health is. 아프고 난 후, 나는 건강의 소중함을 알았다.

■ 분사구문에서 Being이나 Having been은 대부분 생략하지만, 보어가 명사일 경우나 분사가 아닌 경우에 보통 접속사 없이 being을 생략하지 않는다.

- Though she was lonely, she was good-humored.
  → Though (**being**) lonely, she was good-humored. 그녀는 외로웠음에도 불구하고 유머 감각이 넘쳤다.

■ 과거분사로 시작되는 분사구문은 being이 생략된 것으로 수동의 의미를 갖는다.

- (Being) **Seen** from above, hurricanes look peaceful. 상공에서 봤을 때 허리케인들은 평온해 보인다.

핵심 Check

1. 다음 괄호 안에서 알맞은 말을 고르시오.

(1) (Live / Living) next door, I seldom see her.

(2) (Being / To be) rich, he could buy such a big house.

② 조동사가 포함된 수동태

> • The party **will be held** at 7 p.m. 파티는 오후 7시에 열릴 것이다.

■ 수동태는 행위자보다는 행위의 대상에 중점을 두고 말할 때 쓰며, 조동사가 있는 문장의 수동태는 '조동사+be+과거분사'의 형태로 나타낸다.

- You must keep accurate records. 너는 정확한 기록을 간직해야 한다.

  = Accurate records **must be kept** by you. 정확한 기록이 너에 의해 간직되어야 한다.

■ 부정문은 '조동사+not+be+과거분사'의 형태로, 의문문은 '조동사+주어+be+과거분사 ～?'의 형태로 쓴다.

- The value of regular exercise **should not be underestimated**. 규칙적인 운동의 가치를 과소평가하면 안 된다.

- How **can** it **be said** that people are not paying taxes out of force?
  사람들은 효력을 잃은 세금을 지불하지 않는다고 어떻게 말할 수 있을까?

cf. 1. 수동태 구문에서 행위자가 일반인이거나 강조할 필요가 없을 때에는 'by+행위자'를 생략하고 쓸 수 있다.

- The textbooks **will be used** in schools nationwide beginning next year.
  그 교과서들은 내년부터 전국의 학교에서 사용될 것이다.

2. 수동태로 쓰지 않는 동사

자동사는 목적어가 없으므로 수동태로 쓸 수 없으며 '상태'나 '소유'를 나타내는 타동사도 수동태로 쓰이지 않음에 주의해야 한다.

- The accident **happened** late last year. 그 사고는 작년 말에 일어났다.
  The accident was happened late last year. (×)

- The scorpion **has** a sting in its tail. 전갈은 꼬리에 독침이 있다.
  A sting is had in its tail by the scorpion. (×)

핵심 Check

2. 다음 우리말과 일치하도록 주어진 어휘를 이용하여 빈칸에 알맞게 쓰시오.

(1) 그 법을 어떻게 개정할 것인지 숙고할 필요가 있다. (might, reform)

➡ We need to consider how the law _____ _____ _____.

(2) 그녀의 허락 없이는 아무것도 할 수 없을 것이다. (could, do)

➡ Nothing _____ _____ _____ without her say-so.

01 다음 빈칸에 들어갈 말로 알맞은 것은?

> _____ hungry, he ate much.

① Being   ② Been   ③ Am
④ Was   ⑤ Be

02 다음 괄호 안에서 알맞은 말을 고르시오.

(1) (Feel / Feeling) sick, I went to the doctor.
(2) She stared blankly into space, (knowing not / not knowing) what to say next.
(3) The chair (will be delivered / will deliver) on Thursday.
(4) Costs (should be kept / should be keep) to a minimum.

03 다음 우리말에 맞게 빈칸에 알맞은 것은?

> 텔레비전을 보다가 그는 잠이 들었다.
> = _____ television, he fell asleep.

① Watch   ② Watches   ③ Watched
④ To watch   ⑤ Watching

04 다음 문장을 수동태로 고쳤을 때 알맞은 것은?

> We can see germs through a microscope.

① Germs can see us through a microscope.
② Germs are seen through a microscope.
③ Germs can be seen through a microscope.
④ Germs be seen through a microscope.
⑤ Germs can seen through a microscope.

01 다음 중 어법상 어색한 문장은?

① After dinner, we sat talking on the veranda.

② The boys and girls danced, singing together.

③ Every Friday evening, we dance together, listen to music.

④ He was covered with dust while walking along the road.

⑤ Turning to the left, you will find the police station.

02 다음 대화의 빈칸에 들어갈 말로 알맞은 것은?

> M: Did you finish the work?
>
> B: No. Not yet.
>
> M: Why? Do you have any problems?
>
> B: Yes. They gave no indication of how the work _____.

① does
② is done
③ should do
④ should done
⑤ should be done

03 다음 빈칸에 알맞은 말이 바르게 짝지어진 것은?

> • Not _____ his phone number, I couldn't call him.
>
> • Creativity can _____.

① knowing – teach
② knowing – be taught
③ know – teach
④ knew – be taught
⑤ knew – be teach

04 다음 문장의 밑줄 친 부분 중 어법상 어색한 것은?

> I always give ⓐmyself allowances, ⓑknow that things ⓒmay not always ⓓgo as ⓔplanned.

① ⓐ
② ⓑ
③ ⓒ
④ ⓓ
⑤ ⓔ

서답형

05 다음 괄호 안에서 알맞은 말을 고르시오.

(1) As usual, up to five books (can be borrowed / can borrow) at a time for two weeks.

(2) Some vitamins (can be not / cannot be) manufactured by our bodies.

(3) Slowly, an image began to (appear / be appeared) on the screen.

(4) Many changes (took place / were taken place) between the two world wars.

(5) (Finish / Finishing) dinner, he went out to walk his dog.

(6) While (wait / waiting) for a bus, she met her best friend.

(7) He took the last Wednesday off, (feeling not / not feeling) well.

(8) (Being / It being) a sunny day, she went swimming.

06 다음 중 어법상 바르지 <u>않은</u> 것은?

① The work should finished by 7 p.m. by us.
② Safety rules must be followed by everyone.
③ Many herbs can be grown indoors.
④ This essay will have to be completely rewritten.
⑤ The highway will be closed this Wednesday.

07 주어진 두 문장을 한 문장으로 바꿀 때 옳지 <u>않은</u> 것은?

> • They saw the dog.
> • The sheep gathered together.

① The sheep gathered together as they saw the dog.
② Seeing the dog, the sheep gathered together.
③ When seeing the dog, the sheep gathered together.
④ When they saw the dog, the sheep gathered together.
⑤ When saw the dog, the sheep gathered together.

서답형

08 다음 두 문장을 한 문장으로 바꿔 쓸 때 빈칸에 들어갈 한 단어를 쓰시오.

> • He was walking around the park.
> • He met his neighbor Ms. Marple.
>
> ➡ _____ around the park, he met his neighbor Ms. Marple.

[09~10] 다음 우리말을 바르게 영작한 것을 고르시오.

09

> 동물들이 오락거리로 이용되어서는 안 된다.

① Animals should not use for entertainment.
② Animals should not be use for entertainment.
③ Animals should not be used for entertainment.
④ Animals should be not for entertainment.
⑤ Animals should be not used for entertainment.

10

> 매우 추웠기 때문에, 그녀는 따뜻한 차 한 잔을 마셨다.

① Because very cold, she drank a cup of hot tea.
② Because she very cold, she drank a cup of hot tea.
③ Being she felt very cold, she drank a cup of hot tea.
④ Feeling very cold, she drank a cup of hot tea.
⑤ Feeling she very cold, she drank a cup of hot tea.

서답형

11 다음 괄호 안의 어휘를 바르게 배열하시오.

(1) This book (be, read, can) by children.
　　➡ _____

(2) Such rude manners (be, not, should, accepted).
　　➡ _____

12 밑줄 친 부분의 쓰임이 주어진 문장과 같은 것은?

> Feeling tired, she went to bed early.

① She wouldn't change it, knowing it was wrong.
② Being tired, every player went home right after the game.
③ Receiving payment, I will send the book to you.
④ I study math, listening to music.
⑤ Seeing him, give him this note.

13 다음 문장을 수동태로 고쳤을 때 올바른 것은?

> We should keep the meeting room clean.

① The meeting room should keep clcan by us.
② The meeting room is kept clean by us.
③ The meeting room be kept clean by us.
④ The meeting room should kept clean by us.
⑤ The meeting room should be kept clean by us.

서답형

14 다음 문장에서 생략할 수 있는 것을 찾아 쓰시오.

(1) John broke his arm while he was building his house.

➡ _____

(2) Although she was tired, she continued to work on her report.

➡ _____

(3) I'm sure you were very good-looking when you were young.

➡ _____

15 다음 우리말에 맞도록 빈칸에 들어갈 알맞은 것은?

> 내년 봄에 학교 구내 식당이 지어질 것이다.
> = A school cafeteria _____ next spring.

① builds
② will build
③ will built
④ will be built
⑤ will be build

[16~17] 다음 우리말을 참고하여 주어진 문장의 **틀린** 부분을 찾아 바르게 고친 것을 고르시오.

16

> 나는 돈을 잃어버렸기 때문에 그 시계를 살 수 없다.
> = Lose the money, I can't buy the watch.

① Having lost the money, I can't buy the watch.
② Losing the money, I can't buy the watch.
③ As losing the money, I can't buy the watch.
④ Lost the money, I can't buy the watch.
⑤ Though lost the money, I can't buy the watch.

 17

> 날씨가 좋다면, 나는 수영하러 갈 것이다.
> = Being fine, I'll go swimming.

① Fine, I'll go swimming.
② Being fine the weather, I'll go swimming.
③ The weather being fine, I'll go swimming.
④ As the weather fine, I'll go swimming.
⑤ The weather fine, I'll go swimming.

01 다음 주어진 문장을 분사구문으로 바꿔 쓰시오.

(1) Because she got up late, she was late for school yesterday.

➡ _____

_____

(2) The girl got off the bus, and said goodbye to her friend.

➡ _____

_____

(3) If you climb to the top of the hill, you can see the garden well.

➡ _____

_____

(4) Although she studied hard, she failed the exam.

➡ _____

_____

(5) Since I didn't know the way to the theater, I asked the girl sitting next to me to tell me the way.

➡ _____

_____

(6) If it is fine tomorrow, I'll go hiking Dobong Mountain.

➡ _____

_____

(7) As she had lost her job, she had to leave the office.

➡ _____

_____

(8) As she is interested in history, she likes her history class.

➡ _____

_____

02 주어진 문장을 수동태로 바꿔 쓰시오. 바꿔 쓸 수 <u>없는</u> 것은 '불가'라고 쓰고 그 이유를 쓰시오.

(1) You should return new books in a week.

➡ _____

_____

(2) People will love this song for a long time.

➡ _____

_____

(3) We have to slow down the population growth.

➡ _____

_____

(4) She may doubt the sincerity of his decision.

➡ _____

_____

(5) You resemble your mother very closely.

➡ _____

_____

(6) The airline has an excellent safety record.

➡ _____

_____

03 다음 문장에서 어법상 어색한 부분을 분사구문을 이용하여 바르게 고치시오. (생략하지 말 것.)

(1) Embarrassing to wear the clothes to work, she wore them only at home.

_____ ➡ _____

(2) Meeting him several times, she can remember him.

_____ ➡ _____

04 다음 그림을 보고, 주어진 어휘를 이용하여 빈칸을 알맞게 채우시오.

The burned skin _____ with running water. (must, cool)

05 다음 그림을 보고, 주어진 어휘를 이용하여 빈칸을 알맞게 채우시오.

Mike fell down the steps, _____ his arm. (break)

06 다음 우리말에 맞게 주어진 어구를 바르게 배열하시오.

(1) 기차역에 도착한 후에 Mike는 그의 친구들을 찾기 시작했다. (Mike, his friends, the train station, arriving, look, began, to, for, at)

➡ _____

_____

(2) 어찌할 바를 몰라 그녀는 나에게 조언을 구했다. (she, my advice, knowing, asked, what, do, not, for, to)

➡ _____

_____

(3) 이 지역에서는 더 많은 금이 발견될 수 있다. (region, gold, this, be, can, more, found, in)

➡ _____

_____

(4) 조리실은 항상 청결하게 유지되어야 한다. (the cooking room, all times, be, clean, kept, should, at)

➡ _____

_____

07 다음 문장에서 어법상 <u>어색한</u> 것을 바르게 고쳐 다시 쓰시오.

(1) Knives must keep in a safe place.

➡ _____

_____

(2) The department denies responsibility for what was occurred.

➡ _____

_____

(3) Arrived home, he cleaned the whole house.

➡ _____

_____

(4) Being chilly outside, I wanted to stay home.

➡ _____

_____

(5) Writing in haste, the book has many mistakes.

➡ _____

_____

Reading

교과서

The Power of Volcanoes

What do Jejudo, Sicily, and Hawaii have in common? They are islands, of course. In fact, they are all islands made from volcanic eruptions. Volcanoes are very powerful, so they are named after Vulcan, the Roman god of fire. They can make big islands appear or destroy entire cities like Pompeii. Therefore, they should be studied and understood.

Nobody knows for sure how many volcanoes there are in the world. According to scientists, there are about 1,500 active volcanoes above sea level. Many more are underwater, and they are hard to locate. Still, scientists have discovered a large number of them so far.

Many of the volcanoes on Earth are located along the Ring of Fire that circles the Pacific Ocean. The ring is about 40,000 kilometers long, and it is home to around 75% of the world's active volcanoes. Indonesia alone has over 120 active volcanoes since the country lies on the Ring of Fire. This ring is also the area where most of the world's earthquakes occur.

volcano 화산
have ~ in common ~을 공통적으로 가지다
eruption 분출
name after ~을 따서 이름 짓다
destroy 파괴하다
entire 전체의, 온
active 활동 중인
underwater 수중의
locate ~의 위치를 찾아내다
discover 발견하다
ring 고리, 반지
circle 둘러싸다
lie 위치해 있다
earthquake 지진

📎 확인문제

● 다음 문장이 본문의 내용과 일치하면 T, 일치하지 않으면 F를 쓰시오.

1 Jejudo, Sicily, and Hawaii are all islands made from volcanic eruptions. ☐

2 According to scientists, there are about 1,500 active volcanoes underwater. ☐

3 Many of the volcanoes on Earth are located along the Ring of Fire that circles the Pacific Ocean. ☐

A Sudden Volcano

<u>Working on a cornfield one day in 1943</u>, farmers in Mexico found
= While they were working on a cornfield one day in 1943

something surprising. A volcano appeared overnight on a flat cornfield.
-thing이나 -body로 끝나는 대명사는 형용사가 뒤에서 수식

Residents <u>watched the volcano grow</u> over 100 meters tall within
지각동사 watch+목적어+목적보어(동사원형 grow)

a week. The volcano, called Paricutin, kept growing, and it finally

stopped growing at 424 meters in 1952.

You may think volcanoes <u>can be found</u> only on Earth. However, they
조동사가 포함된 수동태: 조동사+be+과거분사

<u>have been discovered</u> on other planets, too, such as Mars and Jupiter.
현재완료 수동태: have been+과거분사

In fact, "Olympus Mons" on Mars is <u>the largest known</u> volcano in the
가장 크다고 알려진

solar system. Its volume is about <u>100 times greater than</u> <u>that</u> of Mauna
~ times+비교급+than A: A보다 ~ 배 더 …한 = 100 times as great as = the volume

Loa, the largest volcano on Earth.
the largest volcano on Earth는 Mauna Loa와 동격

<u>Being very powerful and dangerous</u>, volcanoes do harm to people in
= Because volcanoes are very powerful and dangerous

many ways. Sometimes people get hurt, or they may lose their houses.

<u>Crops may be destroyed</u>, and <u>air traffic can be threatened</u>. Volcanoes
조동사가 포함된 수동태: 조동사+be+과거분사   조동사가 포함된 수동태: 조동사+be+과거분사

can also have serious effects on world weather. A volcanic eruption

shoots lots of ash and dust into the air, <u>preventing</u> some of the sunlight
= and it prevents(부대상황)

<u>from reaching</u> Earth and thus <u>disturbing</u> usual weather patterns.
prevent A from -ing: A가 ~하는 것을 막다   = and thus disturbs(부대상황)

sudden 갑작스러운
overnight 하룻밤 사이에
flat 평평한
planet 행성
Mars 화성
Jupiter 목성
solar system 태양계
volume 부피
do harm 해를 입히다
get hurt 다치다
crop 농작물
traffic 교통
threaten 위협하다
effect 영향, 효과, 결과
shoot ~ into … ~을 …으로 내뿜다
ash 재
dust 먼지
prevent 막다, 방해하다

 확인문제

● 다음 문장이 본문의 내용과 일치하면 T, 일치하지 않으면 F를 쓰시오.

1 Volcanoes have been discovered on other planets, too, such as Mars and Jupiter. ☐

2 The volume of Mauna Loa, the largest volcano on Earth, is about 100 times greater than that of "Olympus Mons" on Mars. ☐

A Deadly Volcano

Mt. Tambora, an active volcano on the island of Sumbawa, Indonesia, erupted in 1815. The eruption killed more than 10,000 residents. It also caused an unusually cold summer around the world the following year.

What volcanoes do is not always bad for humans, however. The soil
선행사를 포함하는 관계대명사   '언제나 ~인 것은 아닌'이라는 의미로 부분 부정
near a volcano is good for farming. Volcanoes are also a great tourist attraction. Looking for fantastic scenery, millions of tourists visit
= Because millions of tourists are looking for fantastic scenery
Mt. Halla in Jejudo, Mt. Etna in Sicily, or Diamond Head in Hawaii every year. Volcanoes can be used to produce electricity, too. Iceland,
조동사가 포함된 수동태: 조동사+be+과거분사 to부정사의 부사적 용법(목적)
for example, actively turns its volcanoes' heat energy into electricity. Today people around the world are studying ways to live in greater
to부정사의 형용사적 용법
harmony with volcanoes, and they are hopeful that more ways will be found soon.

human 인간
soil 토양
fantastic 환상적인
scenery 경치
millions of 수백만의
produce 생산하다
electricity 전기
in harmony with ~와 조화를 이루어
hopeful 희망적인

확인문제

● 다음 문장이 본문의 내용과 일치하면 T, 일치하지 <u>않으면</u> F를 쓰시오.

1 Because volcanoes are very powerful and dangerous, they do harm to people in many ways ☐

2 What volcanoes do is always bad for humans. ☐

● 우리말을 참고하여 빈칸에 알맞은 말을 쓰시오.

1 The _____ of Volcanoes

2 What do Jejudo, Sicily, and Hawaii _____ _____ _____?

3 They are islands, _____ _____.

4 In fact, they are all islands made from _____ _____.

5 Volcanoes are very powerful, so they _____ _____ _____ Vulcan, the Roman god of fire.

6 They can _____ _____ _____ _____ or destroy entire cities like Pompeii.

7 Therefore, they _____ _____ _____ _____.

8 Nobody knows for sure _____ _____ _____ _____ in the world.

9 _____ _____ scientists, there are about 1,500 active volcanoes _____ _____ _____.

10 Many more are underwater, and they are _____ _____ _____.

11 Still, scientists have discovered _____ _____ them so far.

12 Many of the volcanoes on Earth _____ _____ along the Ring of Fire that circles the Pacific Ocean.

13 The ring is about 40,000 kilometers long, and it is _____ _____ around 75% of the world's active volcanoes.

14 Indonesia _____ has over 120 active volcanoes since the country _____ _____ the Ring of Fire.

15 This ring is also the area _____ most of the world's earthquakes _____.

16 A _____ Volcano

17 Working on a cornfield one day in 1943, farmers in Mexico found _____ _____.

18 A volcano _____ _____ on a flat cornfield.

19 Residents watched the volcano _____ over 100 meters tall within a week.

20 The volcano, called Paricutin, _____ _____, and it finally _____ _____ at 424 meters in 1952.

1 화산의 힘

2 제주도, 시칠리아, 하와이의 공통점은 무엇일까?

3 물론, 그것들은 섬이다.

4 사실, 그것들은 모두 화산 분출에 의해 형성된 섬이다.

5 화산은 매우 강력한 힘을 가지고 있어서 로마의 불의 신, 불카누스에게서 이름을 따왔다.

6 화산은 큰 섬이 생겨나게 하거나 폼페이 같은 도시 전체를 파멸시킬 수도 있다.

7 그러므로 화산은 연구되고, 이해되어야 한다.

8 세계에 얼마나 많은 화산이 있는지 누구도 정확히 알지 못한다.

9 과학자들에 따르면, 해수면 위에 대략 1,500개의 활화산이 있다.

10 더 많은 화산이 해저에 존재하는데, 그것들은 정확한 위치를 파악하기가 어렵다.

11 그럼에도 불구하고, 과학자들은 지금까지 그중 많은 수를 발견했다.

12 지구상에 있는 많은 화산들은 태평양을 둘러싸는 '불의 고리(환태평양조산대)'를 따라 위치한다.

13 그 고리는 길이가 약 40,000km에 달하며, 전 세계 활화산의 약 75%가 여기에 있다.

14 인도네시아에만 120개가 넘는 활화산이 있는데, 이 나라가 '불의 고리'에 위치하고 있기 때문이다.

15 이 고리는 또한 전 세계 지진의 대부분이 발생하는 곳이다.

16 갑작스럽게 생겨난 화산

17 1943년 어느 날 옥수수 밭에서 일을 하다가 멕시코의 농부들이 놀라운 것을 발견했다.

18 밤사이에 평평한 옥수수 밭 위로 화산이 생겨난 것이다.

19 주민들은 그 화산이 일주일이 못 되는 사이 100m 넘게 자라는 것을 지켜보았다.

20 'Paricutin(파리쿠틴)'이라고 불리는 이 화산은 계속 자라났고, 1952년에 424m로 드디어 성장을 멈추었다.

21 You may think volcanoes _____ _____ _____ only on Earth.

22 However, they _____ _____ _____ on other planets, too, such as Mars and Jupiter.

23 In fact, "Olympus Mons" on Mars is _____ _____ _____ volcano in the solar system.

24 Its volume is about _____ _____ _____ _____ _____ _____ Mauna Loa, the largest volcano on Earth.

25 Being very powerful and dangerous, volcanoes _____ _____ _____ people in many ways.

26 Sometimes people _____ _____, or they may lose their houses.

27 Crops _____ _____ _____, and air traffic _____ _____ _____.

28 Volcanoes can also _____ _____ _____ _____ world weather.

29 A volcanic eruption _____ lots of ash and dust _____ the air, _____ some of the sunlight _____ _____ Earth and thus _____ usual weather patterns.

30 A _____ Volcano

31 Mt. Tambora, an active volcano on the island of Sumbawa, Indonesia, _____ in 1815.

32 The _____ killed more than 10,000 residents.

33 It also caused an _____ cold summer around the world the following year.

34 _____ _____ _____ is _____ _____ bad for humans, however.

35 The soil near a volcano _____ _____ _____ farming.

36 Volcanoes are also a great _____ _____.

37 _____ _____ fantastic scenery, millions of tourists visit Mt. Halla in Jejudo, Mt. Etna in Sicily, or Diamond Head in Hawaii every year.

38 Volcanoes _____ _____ _____ to produce electricity, too.

39 Iceland, for example, actively _____ its volcanoes' heat energy _____ electricity.

40 Today people around the world are studying ways to live in _____ _____ _____ volcanoes, and they are hopeful that more ways will be found soon.

---

21 화산이 지구에만 존재한다고 생각할지 모른다.

22 그러나 화산은 화성이나 목성 같은 다른 행성에서도 발견되어 왔다.

23 사실 화성에 있는 Olympus Mons(올림푸스 몬스)가 태양계에서 가장 크다고 알려진 화산이다.

24 그것의 부피는 지구에서 가장 큰 화산 Mauna Loa(마우나로아)의 부피보다 약 100배 더 크다.

25 매우 강력하고 위험하기 때문에, 화산은 여러 면에서 사람들에게 해를 끼친다.

26 때로는 사람들이 다치기도 하고, 집을 잃기도 한다.

27 작물이 파괴되거나, 항공 교통이 위협받을 수도 있다.

28 화산은 또한 세계 날씨에 심각한 영향을 미치기도 한다.

29 화산 분출은 다량의 화산재와 먼지를 공중으로 내뿜어, 태양 광선의 일부가 지구에 도달하는 것을 방해하고 그리하여 정상적인 기상 패턴을 깨뜨린다.

30 목숨을 앗아 가는 화산

31 인도네시아 Sumbawa(숨바와) 섬에 위치한 활화산, Tambora(탐보라) 산이 1815년에 분출했다.

32 분출은 주민 1만 명 이상을 죽음에 이르게 했다.

33 또한 이듬해 전 세계에 비정상적으로 추운 여름을 초래했다.

34 그러나 화산이 인류에게 항상 나쁜 것만은 아니다.

35 화산 인근의 토양은 농사에 좋다.

36 화산은 또한 매우 훌륭한 관광명소이다.

37 환상적인 경관을 찾아 매년 수백만 명의 여행객들이 제주도의 한라산, 시칠리아의 Etna(에트나) 산, 하와이의 Diamond Head(다이아몬드헤드)를 방문한다.

38 화산은 또한 전기를 생산하는 데에도 이용될 수 있다.

39 예를 들어, 아이슬란드는 적극적으로 화산의 열에너지를 전기로 바꾼다.

40 오늘날 전 세계에서 사람들이 화산과 더 조화롭게 살 방법을 연구하고 있으며, 더 많은 방법이 곧 발견될 것으로 기대하고 있다.

● 우리말을 참고하여 본문을 영작하시오.

1 화산의 힘
➡ _____

2 제주도, 시칠리아, 하와이의 공통점은 무엇일까?
➡ _____

3 물론, 그것들은 섬이다.
➡ _____

4 사실, 그것들은 모두 화산 분출에 의해 형성된 섬이다.
➡ _____

5 화산은 매우 강력한 힘을 가지고 있어서 로마의 불의 신, 불카누스에게서 이름을 따왔다.
➡ _____

6 화산은 큰 섬이 생겨나게 하거나 폼페이 같은 도시 전체를 파멸시킬 수도 있다.
➡ _____

7 그러므로 화산은 연구되고, 이해되어야 한다.
➡ _____

8 세계에 얼마나 많은 화산이 있는지 누구도 정확히 알지 못한다.
➡ _____

9 과학자들에 따르면, 해수면 위에 대략 1,500개의 활화산이 있다.
➡ _____

10 더 많은 화산이 해저에 존재하는데, 그것들은 정확한 위치를 파악하기가 어렵다.
➡ _____

11 그럼에도 불구하고, 과학자들은 지금까지 그중 많은 수를 발견했다.
➡ _____

12 지구상에 있는 많은 화산들은 태평양을 둘러싸는 '불의 고리(환태평양조산대)'를 따라 위치한다.
➡ _____

13 그 고리는 길이가 약 40,000km에 달하며, 전 세계 활화산의 약 75%가 여기에 있다.
➡ _____

14 인도네시아에만 120개가 넘는 활화산이 있는데, 이 나라가 '불의 고리'에 위치하고 있기 때문이다.
➡ _____

15 이 고리는 또한 전 세계 지진의 대부분이 발생하는 곳이다.
➡ _____

16 갑작스럽게 생겨난 화산
➡ _____

17 1943년 어느 날 옥수수 밭에서 일을 하다가 멕시코의 농부들이 놀라운 것을 발견했다.
➡ _____

18 밤사이에 평평한 옥수수 밭 위로 화산이 생겨난 것이다.
➡ _____

19 주민들은 그 화산이 일주일이 못 되는 사이 100m 넘게 자라는 것을 지켜보았다.
➡ _____

20 'Paricutin(파리쿠틴)'이라 불리는 이 화산은 계속 자라났고, 1952년에 424m로 드디어 성장을 멈추었다.
➡ _____

21 화산이 지구에만 존재한다고 생각할지 모른다.
➡ _____

22 그러나 화산은 화성이나 목성 같은 다른 행성에서도 발견되어 왔다.
➡ _____

23 사실 화성에 있는 Olympus Mons(올림푸스 몬스)가 태양계에서 가장 크다고 알려진 화산이다.
➡ _____

24 그것의 부피는 지구에서 가장 큰 화산 Mauna Loa(마우나 로아)의 부피보다 약 100배 더 크다.
➡ _____

25 매우 강력하고 위험하기 때문에, 화산은 여러 면에서 사람들에게 해를 끼친다.
➡ _____

26 때로는 사람들이 다치기도 하고, 집을 잃기도 한다.
➡ _____

27 작물이 파괴되거나, 항공 교통이 위협받을 수도 있다.
➡ _____

28 화산은 또한 세계 날씨에 심각한 영향을 미치기도 한다.
➡ _____

29 화산 분출은 다량의 화산재와 먼지를 공중으로 내뿜어, 태양 광선의 일부가 지구에 도달하는 것을 방해하고 그리하여 정상적인 기상 패턴을 깨트린다.
➡ _____

30 목숨을 앗아 가는 화산
➡ _____

31 인도네시아 Sumbawa(숨바와) 섬에 위치한 활화산, Tambora(탐보라) 산이 1815년에 분출했다.
➡ _____

32 분출은 주민 1만 명 이상을 죽음에 이르게 했다.
➡ _____

33 또한 이듬해 전 세계에 비정상적으로 추운 여름을 초래했다.
➡ _____

34 그러나 화산이 인류에게 항상 나쁜 것만은 아니다.
➡ _____

35 화산 인근의 토양은 농사에 좋다.
➡ _____

36 화산은 또한 매우 훌륭한 관광 명소이다.
➡ _____

37 환상적인 경관을 찾아 매년 수백만 명의 여행객들이 제주도의 한라산, 시칠리아의 Etna(에트나) 산, 하와이의 Diamond Head(다이아몬드헤드)를 방문한다.
➡ _____

38 화산은 또한 전기를 생산하는 데에도 이용될 수 있다.
➡ _____

39 예를 들어, 아이슬란드는 적극적으로 화산의 열에너지를 전기로 바꾼다.
➡ _____

40 오늘날 전 세계에서 사람들이 화산과 더 조화롭게 살 방법을 연구하고 있으며, 더 많은 방법이 곧 발견될 것으로 기대하고 있다.
➡ _____

[01~03] 다음 글을 읽고 물음에 답하시오.

What do Jejudo, Sicily, and Hawaii have in common? ⓐThey are islands, of course. In fact, ⓑthey are all islands made from volcanic eruptions. Volcanoes are very powerful, so ⓒthey are named after Vulcan, the Roman god of fire. ⓓThey can make big islands appear or destroy entire cities like Pompeii. ___(A)___, ⓔthey should be studied and understood.

01 위 글의 빈칸 (A)에 들어갈 알맞은 말을 고르시오.

① However   ② In addition
③ In other words   ④ For example
⑤ Therefore

02 밑줄 친 ⓐ~ⓔ 중에서 가리키는 대상이 같은 것을 고르시오.

① ⓐ와 ⓑ   ② ⓐ와 ⓒ
③ ⓐ와 ⓓ   ④ ⓑ와 ⓒ
⑤ ⓑ와 ⓔ

서답형

03 본문의 내용과 일치하도록 다음 빈칸에 알맞은 단어를 본문에서 찾아 쓰시오.

> Jejudo, Sicily, and Hawaii are all islands which are made from _____ .

[04~06] 다음 글을 읽고 물음에 답하시오.

Nobody knows for sure how many volcanoes there are in the world. ⓐ According as scientists, there are about 1,500 active volcanoes above sea level. Many more are underwater, and they are hard ⓑto locate. Still, scientists have discovered a large number of them so far.

04 위 글의 제목으로 알맞은 것을 고르시오.

① What's the Origin of the Name of Volcanoes?
② How Many Volcanoes Are There in the World?
③ There Are Many Active Volcanoes above Sea Level
④ Underwater Volcanoes Are Hard to Locate
⑤ How Amazing the Achievement of Scientists Are!

서답형

05 위 글의 밑줄 친 ⓐ에서 어법상 틀린 부분을 찾아 고치시오.

_____ ➡ _____

06 아래 〈보기〉에서 위 글의 밑줄 친 ⓑto locate와 to부정사의 용법이 같은 것의 개수를 고르시오.

> ┤ 보기 ├
> ① He is too busy to go to the movies.
> ② It is very dangerous to play on the street.
> ③ I was surprised to find a bomb in the box.
> ④ The subway is a great way to get around Seoul.
> ⑤ I don't know how to drive a car.

① 1개   ② 2개   ③ 3개   ④ 4개   ⑤ 5개

[07~08] 다음 글을 읽고 물음에 답하시오.

A Sudden Volcano

ⓐWorking on a cornfield one day in 1943, farmers in Mexico found something surprising. A volcano appeared overnight on a flat cornfield. Residents watched the volcano grow over 100 meters tall within a week. ⓑThe volcano, called Paricutin, kept growing, and it finally stopped to grow at 424 meters in 1952.

서답형

07 위 글의 밑줄 친 분사구문 ⓐ를 부사절로 고치시오.

➡ _____

_____

_____

서답형

08 위 글의 밑줄 친 ⓑ에서 어법상 틀린 부분을 찾아 고치시오.

_____ ➡ _____

[09~11] 다음 글을 읽고 물음에 답하시오.

You may think volcanoes can be found only on Earth. However, they have been discovered on other planets, too, such as Mars and Jupiter. In fact, "Olympus Mons" on Mars is the largest known volcano in the solar system. ⓐIts volume is about 100 times greater than ⓑthat of Mauna Loa, the largest volcano on Earth.

서답형

09 위 글의 밑줄 친 ⓐIts가 가리키는 것을 본문에서 찾아 쓰시오.

➡ _____

10 위 글의 밑줄 친 ⓑthat과 문법적 쓰임이 같은 것을 고르시오.

① Look at that man over there.
② That's a nice dress.
③ This year's fashion is quite different from that of last year.
④ He is the greatest novelist that has ever lived.
⑤ Are you sure she's that young?

서답형

11 본문의 내용과 일치하도록 다음 빈칸 (A)와 (B)에 알맞은 단어를 쓰시오.

"Olympus Mons" is the largest known volcano (A)_____ _____ _____ _____ and "Mauna Loa" is the largest volcano (B)_____ _____.

[12~14] 다음 글을 읽고 물음에 답하시오.

ⓐ _____

Mt. Tambora, an active volcano on the island of Sumbawa, Indonesia, erupted in 1815. The eruption killed more than 10,000 residents. ⓑIt also caused an unusually cold summer around the world the following year.

12 위 글의 빈칸 ⓐ에 들어갈 제목으로 가장 알맞은 것을 고르시오.

① The Definition of an Active Volcano
② A Deadly Volcano
③ Volcanoes on Sumbawa, Indonesia
④ The Volume of the Mt. Tambora
⑤ the Largest Active Volcano on Earth

13 위 글의 밑줄 친 ⓑ이 가리키는 것을 본문에서 찾아 쓰시오.

➡ _____

14 위 글을 읽고 알 수 없는 것을 고르시오.

① Where is Mt. Tambora?
② When did Mt. Tambora erupt?
③ How many residents did the eruption of Mt. Tambora kill?
④ When Mt. Tambora erupted in 1815, how long did it erupt?
⑤ How was the weather around the world in the summer of 1816?

[15~17] 다음 글을 읽고 물음에 답하시오.

ⓐBeing very powerful and dangerous, volcanoes do harm to people in many ways. Sometimes people get hurt, or they may lose their houses. Crops may be destroyed, and air traffic can be threatened. Volcanoes can also have serious effects on world weather. A volcanic eruption shoots lots of ash and dust into the air, ⓑ태양 광선의 일부가 지구에 도달하는 것을 방해하고 그리하여 정상적인 기상 패턴을 깨뜨리며.

15 위 글의 밑줄 친 ⓐ와 분사구문의 의미가 같은 것을 모두 고르시오.

① Having no money, I had to go home on foot.
② Feeling sick, I had to take the test.
③ Drinking lots of water, you will get healthy.
④ Not feeling hungry, she didn't have lunch.
⑤ Waiting for her, I read the fashion magazine.

16 위 글의 밑줄 친 ⓑ의 우리말에 맞게 주어진 어휘를 알맞게 배열하시오.

> disturbing / from / some of the sunlight / preventing / and thus / usual weather patterns / reaching Earth

➡ _____

_____

17 위 글의 주제로 알맞은 것을 고르시오.

① the measures to reduce global warming due to greenhouse effect

② climate change caused by the eruption of volcanoes

③ the harmful effects of volcanoes on human life

④ the most powerful volcano in history

⑤ the abnormal weather patterns of the world

[18~19] 다음 글을 읽고 물음에 답하시오.

What volcanoes do is not always bad for humans, however. (①) The soil near a volcano is good for farming. (②) Looking for fantastic scenery, millions of tourists visit Mt. Halla in Jejudo, Mt. Etna in Sicily, or Diamond Head in Hawaii every year. (③) Volcanoes can be used to produce electricity, too. (④) Iceland, ___ⓐ___, actively turns its volcanoes' heat energy into electricity. (⑤) Today people around the world are studying ways to live in greater harmony with volcanoes, and they are hopeful that more ways will be found soon.

18 위 글의 빈칸 ⓐ에 들어갈 알맞은 말을 고르시오.

① in addition   ② as a result

③ however   ④ on the other hand

⑤ for example

19 위 글의 흐름으로 보아, 주어진 문장이 들어가기에 가장 적절한 곳은?

> Volcanoes are also a great tourist attraction.

①   ②   ③   ④   ⑤

[20~22] 다음 글을 읽고 물음에 답하시오.

What do Jejudo, Sicily, and Hawaii have in common? (①) They are islands, of course. (②) In fact, they are all islands made from volcanic eruptions. (③) Volcanoes are very powerful, so they are named after Vulcan, the Roman god of fire. (④) Therefore, they should be studied and understood. (⑤)

Nobody knows for sure how many volcanoes there are in the world. According to scientists, there are about 1,500 active volcanoes above sea level. Many more are underwater, and they are hard to locate. Still, scientists ____ⓐ____ a large number of them so far.

서답형

20 위 글의 빈칸 ⓐ에 discover를 알맞은 형태로 쓰시오.

➡ _____

21 위 글의 흐름으로 보아, 주어진 문장이 들어가기에 가장 적절한 곳은?

> They can make big islands appear or destroy entire cities like Pompeii.

①   ②   ③   ④   ⑤

중요

22 According to the passage, which is NOT true?

① Jejudo, Sicily, and Hawaii are all islands made from volcanic eruptions.
② Volcanoes are named after Vulcan, the Roman god of fire.
③ We should study and understand volcanoes.
④ Nobody surely knows the exact number of volcanoes in the world.
⑤ According to scientists, there are about 1,500 active volcanoes underwater.

[23~24] 다음 글을 읽고 물음에 답하시오.

A Sudden Volcano

Working on a cornfield one day in 1943, farmers in Mexico found something (A)[surprising / surprised]. A volcano appeared overnight on a flat cornfield. Residents watched the volcano (B)[grow / to grow] over 100 meters tall within a week. The volcano, (C)[calling / called] Paricutin, kept growing, and it finally stopped growing at 424 meters in 1952.

서답형

23 위 글의 괄호 (A)~(C)에서 어법상 알맞은 낱말을 골라 쓰시오.

(A) _____ (B) _____ (C) _____

24 According to the passage, which is NOT true?

① One day farmers in Mexico found something surprising in 1943.
② Paricutin appeared on a flat cornfield during the night.
③ The inhabitants watched Paricutin grow more than 100 meters tall within a week.
④ Paricutin kept growing for over 10 years.
⑤ Paricutin is a 424-meter-high volcano.

[01~03] 다음 글을 읽고 물음에 답하시오.

What do Jejudo, Sicily, and Hawaii have in common? They are islands, of course. (A)In fact, they are all islands made from volcanic _____ⓐ_____. Volcanoes are very powerful, so they are named after Vulcan, the Roman god of fire. They can make big islands appear or destroy entire cities like Pompeii. Therefore, they should be studied and understood.

01 주어진 영영풀이를 참고하여 빈칸 ⓐ에 철자 e로 시작하는 단어를 쓰시오.

> the sudden occurrences of a violent discharge of steam and volcanic material

➡ _____

02 위 글의 밑줄 친 (A)In fact와 바꿔 쓸 수 있는 말을 쓰시오.

➡ _____

03 Why should volcanoes be studied and understood? Answer in English beginning with "Because".

➡ _____

_____

[04~06] 다음 글을 읽고 물음에 답하시오.

Many of the volcanoes on Earth are located along the Ring of Fire that circles the Pacific Ocean. The ring is about 40,000 kilometers long, and ⓐit is home to around ⓑ75% of the world's active volcanoes. Indonesia alone has over 120 active volcanoes since the country lies on the Ring of Fire. This ring is also the area where most of the world's earthquakes occur.

04 위 글의 밑줄 친 ⓐit이 가리키는 것을 본문에서 찾아 쓰시오.

➡ _____

05 위 글의 밑줄 친 ⓑ75%를 분수로 읽는 법을 쓰시오.

➡ _____

06 How many active volcanoes are there in Indonesia? Answer in English in a full sentence. (8 words)

➡ _____

[07~09] 다음 글을 읽고 물음에 답하시오.

You may think volcanoes can be found only on Earth. However, they have been discovered on (A)[another / other] planets, too, such as Mars and Jupiter. In fact, "Olympus Mons" on Mars (B)[are / is] the largest (C)[knowing / known] volcano in the solar system. ⓐIts volume is about 100 times greater than Mauna Loa, the largest volcano on Earth.

07 위 글의 괄호 (A)~(C)에서 어법상 알맞은 낱말을 골라 쓰시오.

(A) _____ (B) _____ (C) _____

08 위 글의 밑줄 친 ⓐ에서 어법상 **틀린** 부분을 찾아 고치시오.

_____ ➡ _____

09 Which is larger, Olympus Mons or Mauna Loa? Answer in English. (2 words)

➡ _____

[10~13] 다음 글을 읽고 물음에 답하시오.

(A)화산이 하는 것이 인류에게 항상 나쁜 것만은 아니다, however. The soil near a volcano is good for farming. Volcanoes are also a great tourist attraction. Looking for fantastic scenery, millions of tourists visit Mt. Halla in Jejudo, Mt. Etna in Sicily, or Diamond Head in Hawaii every year. Volcanoes can __ⓐ__ to produce electricity, too. Iceland, for example, actively turns its volcanoes' heat energy into electricity. Today people around the world are studying ways to live in greater harmony with volcanoes, and they are hopeful that more ways will be found soon.

10 위 글의 밑줄 친 (A)의 우리말에 맞게 주어진 어휘를 이용하여 9 단어로 영작하시오.

what, always, for humans

➡ _____

11 위 글의 빈칸 ⓐ에 use를 알맞은 형태로 쓰시오.

➡ _____

12 위 글을 읽고 화산의 좋은 점 세 가지를 우리말로 쓰시오.

(1) _____
(2) _____
(3) _____

13 다음 문장에서 위 글의 내용과 **다른** 부분을 찾아서 고치시오.

Iceland actively turns its volcanoes' explosive power into electricity.

_____ ➡ _____

[14~16] 다음 글을 읽고 물음에 답하시오.

You may think volcanoes can be found only on Earth. However, they have been discovered on other planets, too, ⓐsuch as Mars and Jupiter. In fact, "Olympus Mons" on Mars is the largest known volcano in the solar system. Its volume is about ⓑ100 times greater than that of Mauna Loa, the largest volcano on Earth.

14 위 글의 밑줄 친 ⓐsuch as와 바꿔 쓸 수 있는 한 단어를 쓰시오.

➡ _____

15 위 글의 밑줄 친 ⓑ를 다음과 같이 바꿔 쓸 때 빈칸에 들어갈 알맞은 말을 세 단어로 쓰시오.

100 times _____ _____ _____

16 본문의 내용과 일치하도록 다음 빈칸에 알맞은 단어를 쓰시오.

Volcanoes can be found not only on Earth but also on _____ _____.

해석

My Speaking Portfolio Step 1

a. The electricity is out.

b. The pan caught on fire.
   불이 붙었다

c. I got stuck in the elevator.
   (엘리베이터 등에) 갇혔다

d. I burned my finger in hot water.

e. I fell down the steps and broke my arm.
   넘어졌다

구문해설 • electricity 전기 • burn 데우다, 화상을 입다

a. 정전됐어요.

b. 프라이팬에 불이 붙었어요.

c. 나는 엘리베이터에 갇혔어요.

d. 나는 뜨거운 물에 손을 데었어요.

e. 나는 계단에서 넘어져서 팔이 부러졌어요.

After You Read Details

The name "volcano" comes from the Roman god of fire. – Mila

75% of the world's active volcanoes are located along the Ring of Fire. – James
부분을 나타내는 말은 다음에 나오는 명사의 수에 동사를 일치시킨다. is(✕)

The volcano Paricutin in Mexico stopped growing. – Lucy
                              stop+~ing: ~하기를 멈추다

The eruption of Mt. Tambora brought about an unusually cold summer in
                              bring about: ~을 초래하다
1816. – David

구문해설 • active: 활동 중인 • locate: ~의 위치를 찾아내다 • ring: 고리, 반지 • eruption: 분출

"화산"이라는 이름은 로마의 불의 신에게서 이름을 따왔다. – Mila

전 세계 활화산의 75%는 '불의 고리(환태평양조산대)'를 따라 위치한다. – James

멕시코의 Paricutin 화산은 성장을 멈추었다. – Lucy

Tambora산의 분출은 1816년에 비정상적으로 추운 여름을 초래했다. – David

My Writing Portfolio

The Perfect Storm

I saw the movie *The Perfect Storm* last weekend. The movie came out in 2000,
                                                           연도 앞에 전치사 in
and it was directed by the German director Wolfgang Petersen. It is about a
        수동태   ~에 관한
big storm in the Atlantic Ocean that put a fishing boat in danger. I liked the
                              주격 관계대명사
movie because the scenes were exciting and very realistic. Also, I liked the
                          감정동사가 감정을 유발하는 경우 현재분사
good acting of the leading actor George Clooney. From the movie, I learned

that natural disasters like storms can be very dangerous.
명사절 접속사   ~ 같은(전치사)

구문해설 • storm: 폭풍(우) • direct: (영화·연극 따위를) 감독하다 • the Atlantic Ocean: 대서양
• scene: 장면 • realistic: 현실적인, 사실적인 • leading actor: 주연 배우
• natural disaster: 자연재해

퍼펙트 스톰

나는 지난 주말에 영화 '퍼펙트 스톰'을 봤다. 그 영화는 2000년에 개봉했고, 독일 감독 Wolfgang Petersen이 연출했다. 그것은 어선을 위험에 빠뜨린 대서양의 거대한 폭풍에 관한 것이다. 나는 장면들이 흥미진진하고 매우 사실적이었기 때문에 이 영화가 좋았다. 또한, 나는 주연 배우 George Clooney의 훌륭한 연기도 마음에 들었다. 이 영화를 통해 나는 폭풍과 같은 자연재해가 매우 위험할 수 있다는 것을 배웠다.

영역별 핵심문제

01 다음 짝지어진 단어의 관계가 같도록 빈칸에 알맞은 말을 쓰시오.

> destroy : destruction = discover : _____

02 다음 중 밑줄 친 부분의 뜻풀이가 바르지 <u>않은</u> 것은?

① A big <u>typhoon</u> is coming to Korea. (태풍)

② A powerful earthquake <u>hit</u> Indonesia last summer. (덮쳤다, 엄습했다)

③ A yellow dust <u>warning</u> was issued this morning. (경고)

④ The government <u>issued</u> a statement on current economic problems. (경고했다)

⑤ The <u>rainfall</u> has been below average this year. (강우량)

03 다음 우리말을 주어진 단어를 이용하여 영작하시오.

(1) 다른 행성에 생명체가 있을 수도 있다. (there, may)

  ➡ _____

(2) 올 여름에는 호우가 예상된다. (heavy)

  ➡ _____

(3) 우리 태양계에는 8개의 행성이 있다. (are, there)

  ➡ _____

04 다음 주어진 문장의 밑줄 친 volume과 같은 의미로 쓰인 것은?

> I will explain how to calculate the <u>volume</u> of this box.

① Kathy gave me her latest <u>volume</u> of poetry.

② Please turn the <u>volume</u> down.

③ Sugar is sold by weight, not <u>volume</u>.

④ I used to listen to rock music at full <u>volume</u>.

⑤ The <u>volume</u> control of a CD player is broken down.

05 우리말과 일치하도록 주어진 어구를 배열하여 영작하시오.

(1) 집에 있는 모든 것들이 화재 후에 재로 변하였다.
  (the fire / the house / everything / into / in / ash / after / turned)

  ➡ _____
  _____

(2) 방바닥이 먼지로 덮여 있었다.
  (the room / with / the floor / covered / dust / was / of)

  ➡ _____

(3) 올해 농부들은 풍작을 기대한다.
  (this / a / farmers / have / expect / crop / year / good / to)

  ➡ _____

06 다음 주어진 문장의 밑줄 친 issue와 같은 의미로 쓰인 것은?

> A tornado warnings have been <u>issued</u>.

① We <u>issue</u> a monthly newsletter.

② In my plan, money is not an <u>issue</u>.

③ This is a big <u>issue</u>, so we need more time to think about it.

④ She usually writes about health <u>issues</u>.

⑤ You're just avoiding the <u>issue</u>.

Conversation

[07~08] 다음 글을 읽고 물음에 답하시오.

M: Hi, this is Cha Gisang from the Weather Station. Here is today's weather. Typhoon Doni is ⓐ<u>moving</u> north and is going to hit Jejudo tonight. A typhoon ⓑ<u>warning</u> has been issued. There will be lots of rainfall with a high chance of ⓒ<u>flooding</u> in some areas. Please stay ⓓ<u>outside</u> because Typhoon Doni will come with strong winds. Also, please make sure you keep ⓔ <u>listening</u> to our reports. Thank you.

07 위 글의 밑줄 친 ⓐ~ⓔ에서 내용의 흐름상 어색한 곳을 찾아 바르게 고치시오.

➡ _____

08 위 글의 내용과 일치하는 것은?

① Typhoon Doni is moving south.

② Typhoon Doni is coming with heavy snow.

③ Cha Gisang is talking about tomorrow's weather.

④ Typhoon Doni will bring strong winds and lots of rainfall.

⑤ People are asked to watch the news about Jejudo.

[09~11] 다음 대화를 읽고 물음에 답하시오.

(*The phone rings.*)

Junho: Hi, Mom.

Mom: Hi, Junho. Are you having a good time with Dad?

Junho: Yeah. Today we visited Dokdo.

Mom: That sounds cool. What are you going to do tomorrow?

Junho: We're going fishing on a boat.

Mom: Great. Please make sure you wear a _____(A)_____.

Junho: Okay, Mom. _____(B)_____

09 위 대화의 빈칸 (A)에 '구명조끼'를 나타내는 표현을 쓰시오.

➡ _____

10 위 대화의 빈칸 (B)에 들어갈 말로 적절한 것은?

① I'll keep that in mind.

② Thank you for your great efforts.

③ I'm sorry, but I can't.

④ Of course not.

⑤ No, not at all.

11 위 대화에서 알 수 있는 준호의 기분으로 적절한 것은?

① worried   ② nervous

③ excited   ④ disappointed

⑤ frightened

[12~13] 다음 대화를 읽고 물음에 답하시오.

Grandma: (A)<u>Can you do me a favor?</u> (hand, give)

Jack: Sure, Grandma. What is it?

Grandma: I want to go to the Tom Dylan concert on Christmas. Can you buy some tickets for me?

Jack: No problem. How many tickets do you want?

Grandma: Two tickets, please.

12 위 대화의 밑줄 친 (A)와 의도가 같도록 주어진 단어를 사용하여 다시 쓰시오.

➡ _____

13 위 대화의 내용과 일치하지 <u>않는</u> 것은?

① 할머니는 Jack에게 부탁할 것이 있다.

② 할머니는 Tom Dylan의 콘서트에 가고 싶어 하신다.

③ 할머니는 Jack에게 콘서트 표를 구매해 줄 것을 부탁하였다.

④ 할머니는 두 장의 표를 구매하기를 원하신다.

⑤ 할머니는 Jack과 함께 크리스마스에 콘서트에 가고 싶어 하신다.

14 다음 중 짝지어진 대화가 <u>어색한</u> 것을 고르시오.

① A: Remember that you don't taste or smell chemicals.
   B: OK. I will.

② A: Make sure you should take off your shoes before entering the room.
   B: Never mind. Cheer up!

③ A: Be sure you wear a helmet when you ride your bike.
   B: Sure, but now I'm going out to hike.

④ A: Make sure you are patient and kind.
   B: Okay. I'll keep that in mind.

⑤ A: Make certain that you don't run.
   B: Sure. No problem.

Grammar

15 다음 중 어법상 <u>어색한</u> 문장을 고르시오.

① A flying car will be developed in the near future.

② The work should be finished by 7 p.m.

③ Lions and tigers are belonged to the cat family.

④ Today people around the world are studying ways to live in greater harmony with volcanoes, and they are hopeful that more ways will be found soon.

⑤ Phones must be turned off.

16 다음 문장을 바꾸어 쓸 때 가장 적절한 것은?

> Getting up late, I rode my bike to school.

① I got up late, for I rode my bike to school.

② I rode my bike to school, and I got up late.

③ I got up late, or I rode my bike to school.

④ If I got up late, I rode my bike to school.

⑤ Because I got up late, I rode my bike to school.

17 수동태로 바꾼 문장 중 <u>틀린</u> 것은?

① We have to take him to hospital to get treated.
   → He has to be taken to hospital to get treated.

② My uncle will pick up John.
   → John is picked up by my uncle.

③ They cannot fix my bike today.
   → My bike cannot be fixed today by them.

④ Should you clean the shoes quickly?
   → Should the shoes be cleaned quickly by you?

⑤ People may use art as a vehicle for advertisement.
   → Art may be used as a vehicle for advertisement.

18 다음 중 어법상 올바른 문장을 고르시오.

① Ridden in a flying car, you will be able to go places faster.

② Having not much work to do, I have time to see a movie.

③ The sun rose, we made wishes.

④ Singing and dance together, we had a great time.

⑤ Having appeared overnight, Paricutin is a sudden volcano.

19 다음 그림을 보고, 주어진 어휘를 이용하여 빈칸을 알맞게 채우시오.

_____ out, Emily stopped studying math. (the electricity)

20 다음 빈칸에 알맞은 말이 순서대로 짝지어진 것은?

- He made dinner, _____ a baseball game.
- The energy inside the earth _____ in different ways.

① watches – can be felt
② watches – can feel
③ watching – can be felt
④ watching – can is felt
⑤ to watch – is can felt

Reading

[21~23] 다음 글을 읽고 물음에 답하시오.

Nobody knows for sure how many volcanoes there are in the world. According to scientists, there are about 1,500 active volcanoes above sea level. Many more are underwater, and they are hard to locate. ⓐStill, scientists ⓑhave discovered a large number of them ⓒso far.

21 위 글의 밑줄 친 ⓐStill과 같은 의미로 쓰인 것을 고르시오.

① I wrote to them last month and I'm still waiting for a reply.
② The next day was still warmer.
③ The weather was cold and wet. Still, we had a great time.
④ Keep still while I brush your hair.
⑤ It was, and still is, my favourite movie.

22 위 글의 밑줄 친 ⓑhave discovered와 현재완료 용법이 같은 것을 모두 고르시오.

① She has just come.
② How long have you studied English?
③ He has lost his watch.
④ He has watched the movie twice.
⑤ She has been sick since last Friday.

23 위 글의 밑줄 친 ⓒso far와 바꿔 쓸 수 있는 말을 두 단어로 쓰시오.

➡ _____

[24~25] 다음 글을 읽고 물음에 답하시오.

ⓐ_____

Working on a cornfield one day in 1943, farmers in Mexico found something surprising. A volcano appeared overnight on a flat cornfield. Residents watched the volcano grow over 100 meters tall within a week. The volcano, called Paricutin, kept ____ⓑ____, and it finally stopped growing at 424 meters in 1952.

24 위 글의 빈칸 ⓐ에 들어갈 제목으로 가장 알맞은 것을 고르시오.

① The Origin of a Volcano
② The Proper Condition for Volcanic Formation
③ A Sudden Volcano
④ The Reason Paricutin Kept Growing
⑤ The Highest Volcano in the World

25 위 글의 빈칸 ⓑ에 grow를 알맞은 형태로 쓰시오.

➡ _____

[26~28] 다음 글을 읽고 물음에 답하시오.

ⓐBeing very powerful and dangerous, volcanoes do harm ___①___ people ___②___ many ways. Sometimes people get hurt, or they may lose their houses. Crops may be destroyed, and air traffic can be threatened. Volcanoes can also have serious effects ___③___ world weather. A volcanic eruption shoots lots of ash and dust ___④___ the air, preventing some of the sunlight ___⑤___ reaching Earth and thus disturbing usual weather patterns.

26 위 글의 빈칸 ①~⑤에 들어갈 전치사로 옳지 않은 것은?

① to   ② in
③ on   ④ into
⑤ with

27 위 글의 밑줄 친 분사구문 ⓐ를 부사절로 고치시오.

➡ _____

28 위 글에서 설명하고 있는 화산이 끼치는 해에 속하지 않는 것을 고르시오.

① 사람들을 다치게 하고 집을 잃게 한다.
② 작물을 파괴하고 항공 교통을 위협한다.
③ 세계의 날씨에 심각한 영향을 미친다.
④ 다량의 용암을 분출시킨다.
⑤ 정상적인 기상 패턴을 깨뜨린다.

[29~30] 다음 글을 읽고 물음에 답하시오.

I saw the movie *The Perfect Storm* last weekend. The movie came out in 2000, and it was directed by the German director Wolfgang Petersen. It is about a big storm in the Atlantic Ocean that put a fishing boat in danger. I liked the movie because the scenes were exciting and very realistic. Also, I liked the good acting of the leading actor George Clooney. From the movie, I learned that natural disasters like storms can be very dangerous.

29 위 글의 종류로 알맞은 것을 고르시오.

① article   ② review   ③ essay
④ summary   ⑤ book report

30 위 글을 읽고 알 수 없는 것을 고르시오.

① What is the title of the movie?
② Who is the director?
③ When did the movie come out?
④ What is the movie about?
⑤ With whom did the writer see the movie?

01 다음 영영풀이가 가리키는 것을 고르시오.

출제율 95%

> a sudden shaking of Earth's surface

① ash   ② earthquake
③ eruption   ④ dust
⑤ planet

02 다음 우리말에 맞게 빈칸에 알맞은 말을 쓰시오.

출제율 90%

(1) 지진은 도시에 있는 집과 건물의 60%를 파괴했다.
⇒ The _____ _____ 60% of houses and buildings in the city.

(2) 신체 활동이 뇌에 미치는 효과는 굉장하다.
⇒ The _____ of _____ exercise on the brain is great.

(3) 섬에 도착했을 때, 화산이 분출하기 시작했다.
⇒ When we arrived at the island, the _____ started to _____.

[03~04] 다음 글을 읽고 물음에 답하시오.

M: Hi, this is Cha Gisang from the Weather Station. Here is today's weather. Typhoon Doni is moving north and is going to hit Jejudo tonight. A typhoon warning has been (A)[issuing / issued]. There will be lots of rainfall with a high chance of flooding in some areas. Please stay inside (B)[because / because of] Typhoon Doni will come with strong winds. Also, please make sure you keep (C)[to listen / listening] to our reports. Thank you.

03 위 글을 읽고 (A)~(C)에 알맞은 말이 바르게 짝지어진 것은?

출제율 90%

	(A)	(B)	(C)
①	issuing	because	to listen
②	issuing	because of	listening
③	issued	because	listening
④	issued	because of	listening
⑤	issued	because	to listen

04 위 글을 읽고 대답할 수 없는 것은?

출제율 100%

① What does Cha Gisang do?
② Where is a typhoon moving toward?
③ What has been issued?
④ What does Cha Gisang ask to do?
⑤ When will it stop raining?

[05~06] 다음 대화를 읽고 물음에 답하시오.

(*The phone rings.*)
Junho: Hi, Mom.
Mom: Hi, Junho. Are you having a good time with Dad?
Junho: Yeah. Today we visited Dokdo.
Mom: That sounds cool. What are you going to do tomorrow?
Junho: We're going fishing on a boat.
Mom: Great. Please make sure you wear a life jacket.
Junho: Okay, Mom. I'll keep that in mind.

05 What did Junho do with his father today?

출제율 95%

⇒ _____

06 What should Junho make sure when he goes fishing?

출제율 90%

⇒ _____

Brian: Jimin, are you going ⓐ<u>out</u>?

Jimin: Yeah. I'm going to buy ⓑ<u>some</u> sandwiches at Choi's.

Brian: Are you walking there?

Jimin: No. I'll ride my bike.

Brian: That's good. Can you do me ⓒ<u>a favor</u>?

Jimin: Sure. What is it?

Brian: Can you buy chocolate ice cream for me ⓓ<u>on</u> your way back?

Jimin: No problem.

Brian: Thanks. Please make sure you ⓔ<u>to wear</u> a helmet and no ear phones!

Jimin: Don't worry about that.

출제율 90%

07 위 대화의 밑줄 친 ⓐ~ⓔ 중 어법상 어색한 것을 찾아 바르게 고치시오.

➡ _____

출제율 95%

08 위 대화의 내용과 일치하지 <u>않는</u> 것은?

① 지민이는 샌드위치를 사러 외출한다.

② 지민이는 자전거를 타고 '최가네'에 갈 것이다.

③ Brian은 지민이에게 돌아오는 길에 초콜릿 아이스크림을 사다 줄 것을 부탁하였다.

④ Brian은 지민이에게 헬멧을 쓰고 이어폰을 낄 것을 당부하였다.

⑤ 지민이는 Brian에게 걱정하지 말라고 안심시켰다.

Brian: Sora, (A)부탁 좀 들어줄래? (favor, can)

Sora: What is it, Dad?

Dad: A typhoon is coming tonight. Can you bring in the clothes from outside?

Sora: No problem. What about your bike?

Dad: I'll take care of it after I finish the dishes.

Sora: Okay. Do you want me to call Grandma and tell her about the typhoon?

Dad: Yes. Please tell her to stay home.

Sora: Okay, Dad.

출제율 90%

09 위 대화의 밑줄 친 (A)의 우리말을 주어진 단어들을 사용하여 영작하시오.

➡ _____

출제율 100%

10 위 대화의 내용과 일치하지 <u>않는</u> 것은?

① 오늘 밤 태풍이 온다.

② 아빠는 소라에게 옷가지들을 바깥으로 가져다 줄 것을 요청했다.

③ 자전거는 아빠가 설거지를 한 후 처리할 것이다.

④ 아빠는 소라가 할머니에게 전화하기를 원하신다.

⑤ 소라는 할머니에게 집안에 계시라고 말씀드릴 것이다.

출제율 95%

11 다음 그림을 보고, 주어진 어휘를 이용하여 빈칸을 알맞게 채우시오.

When the pan caught on fire, what _____ ? (be, should)

12 다음 중 어법상 어색한 문장을 고르시오. *출제율 100%*

① This book must be returned by Nov. 30.
② They produce heat energy that is turned can into electricity.
③ The project will be completed soon.
④ The disease may be infected.
⑤ Foods should be kept cool.

13 다음 주어진 문장을 분사구문을 써서 바꿔 쓰시오. *출제율 95%*

> While he was listening to music, he read the novel he had bought the other day.

➡ _____

_____

14 다음 ⓐ~ⓗ 중 어법상 옳은 것을 모두 고르시오. *출제율 90%*

> ⓐ Felt tired, I went to bed early.
> ⓑ Having not enough time, I was unable to finish my homework in time.
> ⓒ Being Sunday, most shops were closed.
> ⓓ The airplane was flying in the sky, making a big noise.
> ⓔ A new school uniform must design soon.
> ⓕ You may think volcanoes can be found only on Earth.
> ⓖ The matter will discuss tomorrow.
> ⓗ The news will known to the classmates soon.

➡ _____

[15~17] 다음 글을 읽고 물음에 답하시오.

> Many of the volcanoes on Earth are located along the Ring of Fire that circles the Pacific Ocean. The ring is about 40,000 kilometers long, and it is home to ⓐaround 75% of the world's active volcanoes. Indonesia alone has over 120 active volcanoes since the country lies on the Ring of Fire. ⓑThis ring is also the area where most of the world's earthquakes occurs.

15 위 글의 밑줄 친 ⓐaround와 같은 의미로 쓰인 것을 고르시오. *출제율 90%*

① I could hear laughter all around.
② He arrived around five o'clock.
③ He put his arms around her.
④ We were all running around trying to get ready in time.
⑤ I can't arrange everything around your timetable!

16 위 글의 밑줄 친 ⓑ에서 어법상 틀린 부분을 찾아 고치시오. *출제율 90%*

_____ ➡ _____

17 Which question CANNOT be answered after reading the passage? *출제율 100%*

① Where are many of the volcanoes on Earth located?
② How long is the Ring of Fire that circles the Pacific Ocean?
③ How often do the active volcanoes erupt in Indonesia?
④ Why are there many active volcanoes in Indonesia?
⑤ Where do most of the world's earthquakes occur?

[18~19] 다음 글을 읽고 물음에 답하시오.

You may think volcanoes can be found only on Earth. ____ⓐ____, they have been discovered on other planets, too, such as Mars and Jupiter. ____ⓑ____, "Olympus Mons" on Mars is the largest known volcano in the solar system. Its volume is about 100 times greater than that of Mauna Loa, the largest volcano on Earth

출제율 100%

18 위 글의 빈칸 ⓐ와 ⓑ에 들어갈 말이 바르게 짝지어진 것은?

① However – Therefore
② In addition – In fact
③ In fact – However
④ For example – On the other hand
⑤ However – In fact

출제율 95%

19 According to the passage, which is NOT true?

① Volcanoes can be found only on Earth.
② "Olympus Mons" is on Mars.
③ "Olympus Mons" is the largest known volcano in the solar system.
④ "Mauna Loa" is not so large as "Olympus Mons".
⑤ "Mauna Loa" is the largest volcano on Earth.

[20~21] 다음 글을 읽고 물음에 답하시오.

____ⓐ____ volcanoes do is not always bad for humans, however. The soil near a volcano is good for farming. Volcanoes are also a great tourist attraction. Looking for fantastic scenery, millions of tourists visit Mt. Halla in Jejudo, Mt. Etna in Sicily, or Diamond Head in Hawaii every year. ⓑVolcanoes can use to produce electricity, too. Iceland, for example, actively turns its volcanoes' heat energy into electricity.

출제율 90%

20 위 글의 빈칸 ⓐ에 들어갈 알맞은 말을 고르시오.

① How   ② Which   ③ That
④ What   ⑤ Why

출제율 90%

21 위 글의 밑줄 친 ⓑ에서 어법상 어색한 것을 고치시오.

_____ ➡ _____

[22~23] 다음 글을 읽고 물음에 답하시오.

The energy inside the earth can be felt in different ways. First, we can see this energy in volcanoes. (①) Another way to feel the earth's power is to visit a hot spring. (②) ⓐThis is a spring of water which is usually heated by volcanic activity. (③) People say that hot spring do us good. (④) They help relieve stress and can bring on a good night's sleep. (⑤) The earth's energy is both amazing and helpful.

출제율 90%

22 위 글의 흐름으로 보아, 주어진 문장이 들어가기에 가장 적절한 곳은?

As the hot rock comes out of the earth, it changes the ground and makes hills and mountains.

①   ②   ③   ④   ⑤

출제율 95%

23 위 글의 밑줄 친 ⓐThis가 가리키는 것을 본문에서 찾아 쓰시오.

➡ _____

[01~03] 다음 대화를 읽고 물음에 답하시오.

> Brian: Jimin, are you going out?
> Jimin: Yeah. I'm going to buy some sandwiches at Choi's.
> Brian: Are you walking there?
> Jimin: No. I'll ride my bike.
> Brian: That's good. Can you do me a favor?
> Jimin: Sure. What is it?
> Brian: Can you buy chocolate ice cream for me on your way back?
> Jimin: No problem.
> Brian: Thanks. Please make sure you wear a helmet and no ear phones!
> Jimin: Don't worry about that.

01 Where is Jimin going now and why? (Answer with 9 words.)

➡ _____

02 What does Brian ask Jimin to do?

➡ _____

_____

03 What should Jimin keep in mind?

➡ _____

_____

04 분사구문은 부사절로, 부사절은 분사구문으로 바꿔 쓰시오.

(1) Walking home after school, Tom found a soccer ball on the street.

➡ _____

_____

(2) Sleeping on the bus, I missed my stop.

➡ _____

_____

(3) He started to cry as he admitted his fault.

➡ _____

_____

(4) As it was not so cold outside, she went out without a coat.

➡ _____

_____

05 다음 우리말을 괄호 안에 주어진 어휘를 활용하여 영작하시오.

(1) 그녀는 부모님께 손을 흔들며 집을 떠났다.
(leave, wave, at)

➡ _____

(2) 나는 피곤해서 평소보다 일찍 집에 왔다.
(feel, early, usual)

➡ _____

(3) 이 프로젝트는 오늘까지 마무리될 수 없다.
(this project, finish, by)

➡ _____

(4) 연주회는 다음 주에 열릴 것이다.
(the concert, hold)

➡ _____

06 다음 문장을 수동태는 능동태로, 능동태는 수동태로 바꾸어 쓰시오.

(1) School rules must be followed by all students.

➡ _____

(2) The project should be finished tonight.

➡ _____

(3) Who will solve the problem?

➡ _____

(4) You can add eggs and cheese according to your taste.

➡ _____

_____

[07~09] 다음 글을 읽고 물음에 답하시오.

ⓐ세계에 얼마나 많은 화산이 있는지 누구도 정확히 알지 못한다. According to scientists, there are about ⓑ1,500 active volcanoes above sea level. Many more are underwater, and ⓒ they are hard to locate. Still, scientists have discovered a large number of them so far.

07 위 글의 밑줄 친 ⓐ의 우리말에 맞게 주어진 어휘를 알맞게 배열하시오.

how many volcanoes / are / knows / in the world / for sure / nobody / there

➡ _____

_____

08 위 글의 밑줄 친 ⓑ1,500을 영어로 읽는 법을 쓰시오.

➡ _____

09 위 글의 밑줄 친 ⓒ를 다음과 같이 바꿔 쓸 때 빈칸에 들어갈 알맞은 말을 한 단어를 쓰시오.

it is hard to locate _____

[10~12] 다음 글을 읽고 물음에 답하시오.

Being very powerful and dangerous, volcanoes do harm to people in many ways. Sometimes people get hurt, or they may lose their houses. Crops may be destroyed, and air traffic can be threatened. ⓐVolcanoes can also have serious effects on world weather. A volcanic eruption shoots lots of ash and dust into the air, ⓑpreventing some of the sunlight from reaching Earth and thus disturbing usual weather patterns.

10 위 글의 밑줄 친 ⓐ를 다음과 같이 바꿔 쓸 때 빈칸에 공통으로 들어갈 알맞은 한 단어를 쓰시오.

• Volcanoes can also have serious _____ s on world weather.
• Volcanoes can also _____ world weather seriously.

11 위 글의 밑줄 친 분사구문 ⓑ를 절로 고치시오.

and _____ _____ some of the sunlight from reaching Earth and thus _____ usual weather patterns

12 본문의 내용과 일치하도록 다음 빈칸 (A)와 (B)에 알맞은 단어를 쓰시오.

Volcanoes can hurt people and destroy (A)_____ as well as houses. They can also threaten (B)_____ _____ and change world weather.

창의사고력 서술형 문제

01 다음 대화의 내용과 일치하도록 빈칸을 완성하시오.

> **Brian:** Jimin, are you going out?
>
> **Jimin:** Yeah. I'm going to buy some sandwiches at Choi's.
>
> **Brian:** Are you walking there?
>
> **Jimin:** No. I'll ride my bike.
>
> **Brian:** That's good. Can you do me a favor?
>
> **Jimin:** Sure. What is it?
>
> **Brian:** Can you buy chocolate ice cream for me on your way back?
>
> **Jimin:** No problem.
>
> **Brian:** Thanks. Please make sure you wear a helmet and no ear phones!
>
> **Jimin:** Don't worry about that.

▼

> Jimin is going to Choi's by (A)_____ to buy (B)_____. Brian asks her to (C)_____ for him on her way back. Brian reminds her that she should (D)_____.

02 다음 내용을 바탕으로 영화 'The Perfect Storm'의 감상문을 쓰시오.

> • What is the title of the movie? – *The Perfect Storm*
> • Who is the director? – Wolfgang Petersen
> • When did the movie come out? – 2000
> • What is the movie about? – a big storm in the Atlantic Ocean that put a fishing boat in danger
> • What do you like about the movie? – • exciting and realistic scenes • the good acting of the leading actor
> • What did you learn from the movie? – natural disasters can be very dangerous

> The Perfect Storm
>
> I saw the movie (A)_____ last weekend. The movie came out (B)_____, and it was directed by the German director (C)_____. It is about (D)_____. I liked the movie because the scenes were exciting and very realistic. Also, I liked the (E)_____ of the leading actor George Clooney. From the movie, I learned that (F)_____ like storms can be very dangerous.

단원별 모의고사

01 다음 영영풀이가 가리키는 것은?

> a large round object in space that moves around a star

① Mars　　　　② planet
③ Jupiter　　　④ eruption
⑤ typhoon

02 다음 주어진 어휘 중 성격이 나머지와 다른 것은?

① typhoon　　　② earthquake
③ snowstorm　　④ heat wave
⑤ solar system

03 다음 문장의 빈칸에 들어갈 말을 〈보기〉에서 골라 쓰시오.

> ┌──── 보기 ────
> favor / volcano / chance / flooding / area

(1) Sodam Park is closed today because of _____.
(2) There is little _____ of rain tomorrow morning.
(3) I am familiar with this _____.
(4) I want to ask you a _____.
(5) _____s are major tourist attractions in the region.

[04~05] 다음 대화를 읽고 물음에 답하시오.

Grandma: Can you do me a favor?
Jack: Sure, Grandma. What is it?
Grandma: I want to go to the Tom Dylan concert on Christmas. Can you buy some tickets for me?
Jack: No problem. _____(A)_____ (want, many)
Grandma: Two tickets, please.

04 위 대화의 빈칸 (A)에 들어갈 질문을 주어진 단어를 사용하여 영작하시오.

➡ _____

05 위 대화의 내용과 일치하지 않는 것은?

① Grandma needs Jack's help.
② Grandma wants to enjoy the Tom Dylan concert on Christmas.
③ Grandma wants Jack to buy tickets for her.
④ Grandma needs two tickets of the Tom Dylan concert.
⑤ Grandma is in favor of Jack's plan for Christmas.

[06~08] 다음 대화를 읽고 물음에 답하시오.

Dad: Sora, can you do me a favor?
Sora: What is it, Dad?
Dad: A typhoon is coming tonight. Can you bring in the clothes from outside?
Sora: No problem. What about your bike?
Dad: I'll take care of it after I finish the dishes.
Sora: Okay. Do you want me to call Grandma and tell her about the typhoon?
Dad: Yes. Please tell her to stay home.
Sora: Okay, Dad.

06 What does Dad want Sora to do?

➡ _____
_____

07 What is Dad going to do after washing the dishes?

➡ _____

08 What will Sora tell her grandma to do?

➡ _____

09 다음 대화가 자연스럽게 이어지도록 순서대로 배열하시오.

> Dad: Jimin, are you going out?
>
> Jimin: Yeah. I'm going to buy some sandwiches at Choi's.
>
> Brian: Are you walking there?
>
> (A) No problem.
>
> (B) No. I'll ride my bike.
>
> (C) Sure. What is it?
>
> (D) That's good. Can you do me a favor?
>
> (E) Can you buy chocolate ice cream for me on your way back?

➡ _____

[10~11] 다음 대화를 읽고 물음에 답하시오.

> (*The phone rings.*)
>
> Junho: Hi, Mom.
>
> Mom: Hi, Junho. Are you having a good time with Dad?
>
> Junho: Yeah. Today we visited Dokdo.
>
> Mom: That sounds cool. What are you going to do tomorrow?
>
> Junho: We're going fishing on a boat.
>
> Mom: Great. (A)Please make sure you wear a life jacket.
>
> Junho: Okay, Mom. I'll keep that in mind.

10 위 대화의 밑줄 친 (A)와 바꾸어 쓰기에 어색한 것은?

① Don't forget to wear a life jacket.

② Please remember that you should wear a life jacket.

③ Be sure to wear a life jacket.

④ I'm wondering if you wear a life jacket.

⑤ Please make certain that you should wear a life jacket.

11 위 대화의 내용과 일치하지 않는 것은?

① 준호는 아빠와 좋은 시간을 보내고 있다.

② 준호는 아빠와 독도를 방문했다.

③ 준호는 내일 낚시를 갈 것이다.

④ 엄마는 준호에게 구명조끼를 입을 것을 당부했다.

⑤ 준호는 내일 부모님과 함께 보트를 탈 것이다.

12 다음 대화가 자연스럽게 이어지도록 순서대로 배열하시오.

> Dad: Sora, can you do me a favor?
>
> Sora: What is it, Dad?
>
> (A) I'll take care of it after I finish the dishes.
>
> (B) No problem. What about your bike?
>
> (C) Yes. Please tell her to stay home.
>
> (D) Okay. Do you want me to call Grandma and tell her about the typhoon?
>
> (E) A typhoon is coming tonight. Can you bring in the clothes from outside?
>
> Sora: Okay, Dad.

➡ _____

13 다음 두 문장의 의미가 같도록 빈칸을 완성하시오.

(1) We can use volcanoes to produce electricity.

= Volcanoes _____ to produce electricity.

(2) We should not allow young children to use smartphones.

= Young children _____ to use smartphones.

(3) They will build a tourist information center next year.

= A tourist information center _____ _____ next year.

14 다음 중 어법상 옳은 문장을 고르시오. (2개)

① Walked down the street, Sora met her PE teacher.

② Working on a cornfield one day in 1943, farmers in Mexico found something surprising.

③ Very powerful and dangerous, volcanoes do harm to people in many ways.

④ Homework should be handed in by Friday.

⑤ Therefore, they should study and understood.

15 다음 우리말을 주어진 어휘를 이용하여 영작하시오.

(1) 피자가 30분 내로 배달될 것이다.
(the pizza, deliver, within, 8 단어)
➡ _____

(2) 그 문제는 즉시 해결되어야 한다.
(the problem, should, now, solve, 7 단어)
➡ _____

(3) Dana는 시장을 향해 걷다가 우연히 역사 선생님을 만났다. (to the market, her history teacher, come across, 10 단어)
➡ _____
_____

(4) 추위를 느껴서 Susan은 그녀의 코트를 입었다.
(her coat, cold, put, 7 단어)
➡ _____

16 Which is grammatically WRONG? Select ALL.

① This medicine must taken after meal.

② The library will be closed during lunch break to encourage students to go outdoors and play sports.

③ Finding his mom, the little boy quickly ran to her.

④ Tina sat back on the sofa, closed her eyes.

⑤ A volcanic eruption shoots lots of ash and dust into the air, preventing some of the sunlight from reaching Earth and thus disturbing usual weather patterns.

17 다음 문장에서 어법상 어색한 것을 바르게 고쳐 다시 쓰시오.

(1) Food and drinks must not brought into the library.
➡ _____
_____

(2) The computer should fix Mr. Hinkle.
➡ _____

(3) Tiring after the game, the players took a rest for a while.
➡ _____

(4) Having not any money, I borrowed some from my older brother.
➡ _____
_____

[18~19] 다음 글을 읽고 물음에 답하시오.

Many of the volcanoes on Earth are located along the Ring of Fire that circles the Pacific Ocean. The ring is about 40,000 kilometers long, and it is home to around 75% of the world's active volcanoes. Indonesia alone has over 120 active volcanoes (A)since the country lies on the Ring of Fire. This ring is also the area _____ⓐ_____ most of the world's earthquakes occur.

18 위 글의 빈칸 ⓐ에 들어갈 알맞은 말을 고르시오.

① which   ② when   ③ why
④ where   ⑤ how

19 위 글의 밑줄 친 (A)since와 같은 의미로 쓰인 것을 고르시오.

① She hasn't phoned me since she went to Berlin.
② I did it since he told me to.
③ How long is it since we last went there?
④ I've been busy since I came here.
⑤ It's twenty years since she came up to Seoul.

[20~21] 다음 글을 읽고 물음에 답하시오.

What volcanoes do is not always bad for humans, however. The soil near a volcano is good (A)[at / for] farming. Volcanoes are also a great tourist attraction. Looking for fantastic scenery, millions of tourists visit Mt. Halla in Jejudo, Mt. Etna in Sicily, or Diamond Head in Hawaii every year. Volcanoes can be used to (B)[produce / producing] electricity, too. Iceland, for example, actively turns its volcanoes' heat energy into electricity. Today people around the world are studying ways to live in greater (C)[conflict / harmony] with volcanoes, and they are hopeful that more ways will be found soon.

20 위 글의 괄호 (A)~(C)에서 문맥이나 어법상 알맞은 낱말을 골라 쓰시오.

(A) _____ (B) _____ (C) _____

21 According to the passage, which is NOT true?

① What volcanoes do is sometimes good for humans.
② The soil near a volcano is suitable for farming.
③ It's impossible to produce electricity by using volcanoes.
④ Iceland actively turns its volcanoes' heat energy into electricity.
⑤ People are hopeful that more ways will be found soon.

[22~23] 다음 글을 읽고 물음에 답하시오.

A Sudden Volcano

Working on a cornfield one day in 1943, farmers in Mexico found something surprising. A volcano appeared overnight on a flat cornfield. ⓐ주민들은 그 화산이 일주일도 못 되는 사이에 100미터 넘게 자라는 것을 지켜보았다. The volcano, called Paricutin, kept growing, and it ⓑfinally stopped growing at 424 meters in 1952.

22 위 글의 밑줄 친 ⓐ의 우리말에 맞게 주어진 어휘를 이용하여 12 단어로 영작하시오.

residents, watched, grow, over, within

➡ _____

_____

23 위 글의 밑줄 친 ⓑfinally와 바꿔 쓸 수 없는 말을 고르시오.

① all at once ② eventually ③ at last
④ in the end   ⑤ in the long run

Lesson 8

All Your Dreams Are Worth Chasing

🎙 의사소통 기능

- 후회 표현하기

  A: I should have saved food for the winter.
  B: Don't worry. I'll share my food with you.

- 수정하기

  A: People in Brazil speak Spanish, right?
  B: I'm afraid you're mistaken. They speak Portuguese.

🎙 언어 형식

- 조동사+have p.p.

  They **must have been** hungry.

- 관계대명사의 계속적 용법

  My favorite writer is Ken Kuller, **who** lives in New York.

Words & Expressions

Key Words

- □ **achieve**[ətʃíːv] 통 이루다, 달성[성취]하다
- □ **activity**[æktívəti] 명 활동, 행동
- □ **audition**[ɔːdíʃən] 명 오디션 통 오디션을 보다
- □ **banner**[bǽnər] 명 현수막
- □ **batting title** 타격왕
- □ **calm**[kaːm] 형 침착한, 냉정한
- □ **capital**[kǽpətl] 명 수도
- □ **challenging**[tʃǽlindʒiŋ] 형 도전적인
- □ **chase**[tʃeis] 통 쫓다, 추적하다
- □ **cheerful**[tʃíərfəl] 형 기분 좋은, 즐거운
- □ **completely**[kəmplíːtli] 부 완전히, 전적으로
- □ **confident**[kánfədənt] 형 확신하는, 자신만만한
- □ **connect**[kənékt] 통 연결하다
- □ **create**[kriéit] 통 만들다, 창조하다
- □ **decision**[disíʒən] 명 결정, 판단
- □ **delighted**[diláitid] 형 아주 기뻐하는
- □ **express**[iksprés] 통 표현하다
- □ **found**[faund] 통 설립하다
- □ **imagination**[imædʒənéiʃən] 명 상상, 상상력
- □ **impatient**[impéiʃənt] 형 짜증 난, 참지 못하는
- □ **improve**[imprúːv] 통 향상시키다, 개선하다
- □ **include**[inklúːd] 통 포함하다
- □ **join**[dʒɔin] 통 결합하다, 합류하다, 가담하다
- □ **league**[liːg] 명 리그, 연맹
- □ **lifelong**[laiflɔŋ] 형 일생[평생]의

- □ **Mars**[maːrz] 명 화성
- □ **mistaken**[mistéikən] 형 잘못 알고 있는
- □ **offer**[ɔ́ːfər] 명 제의, 제안
- □ **opportunity**[ɑ̀pərtʃúːnəti] 명 기회
- □ **pick**[pik] 통 뽑다, 고르다
- □ **practice**[prǽktis] 통 연습하다, 훈련하다
- □ **protection**[prətékʃən] 명 보호
- □ **quite**[kwait] 부 꽤, 상당히
- □ **read**[riːd] 통 ~라고 적혀 있다
- □ **regret**[rigrét] 통 후회하다
- □ **repair**[ripέər] 통 수리하다
- □ **rest**[rest] 명 나머지, 휴식
- □ **right**[rait] 부 바로
- □ **rule**[ruːl] 명 규칙
- □ **save**[seiv] 통 구하다, 절약하다, 저축하다
- □ **scared**[skɛərd] 형 무서워하는, 겁먹은
- □ **serious**[síəriəs] 형 심각한, 진지한
- □ **share**[ʃɛər] 통 공유하다
- □ **skill**[skil] 명 기량, 기술
- □ **stuck**[stʌk] 형 갇힌, (~에 빠져) 꼼짝 못 하는
- □ **suit**[suːt] 명 정장
- □ **tryout**[traiaut] 명 심사, 테스트
- □ **worried**[wɔ́ːrid] 형 난처한, 걱정[근심]스러운
- □ **worth**[wəːrθ] 형 ~할 가치가 있는

Key Expressions

- □ **animal doctor** 수의사
- □ **apply for** ~에 지원하다, ~을 신청하다
- □ **be ashamed of** ~을 부끄러워하다
- □ **break down** 고장나다
- □ **break out** 발발[발생]하다
- □ **deal with** ~을 다루다
- □ **do one's hair** 머리를 손질하다
- □ **even if** 비록 ~일지도
- □ **get off** (자동차 등에서) 내리다
- □ **go after** ~을 추구하다, ~을 얻기 위해 노력하다
- □ **go by** 지나가다, 흐르다
- □ **hang out with** ~와 시간을 보내다
- □ **How come?** 왜 그렇지?, 어쩌다 그렇게 됐니?

- □ **I'd[I would] say ~.** 내 생각에 ~인 것 같다.
- □ **may[might] have p.p.** ~했을지도 모른다
- □ **must have p.p.** ~했음에 틀림없다
- □ **not ~ anymore** 더 이상 ~ 않다
- □ **over and over** 반복해서
- □ **prepare for** ~을 준비하다
- □ **set one's alarm** 알람을 맞추다
- □ **should have p.p.** ~했어야 한다
- □ **spend+시간+-ing** ~하면서 시간을 보내다
- □ **too ~ to부정사** ~하기에 너무 …하다
- □ **traffic jam** 교통 체증
- □ **used to** (과거에) ~이었다[했다]
- □ **You can make it!** 넌 해낼 수 있어!

Word Power

※ 서로 비슷한 뜻을 가진 어휘

- □ **achieve** 이루다, 달성[성취]하다 – **accomplish** 이루다, 성취하다
- □ **decision** 결정, 판단 – **determination** 결심, 결단(력)
- □ **improve** 향상시키다, 개선하다 – **enhance** 향상시키다
- □ **offer** 제의, 제안 – **proposal** 제안, 제의
- □ **practice** 연습하다, 훈련하다 – **exercise** 연습하다
- □ **regret** 후회하다 – **repent** 후회하다
- □ **save** 구하다 – **rescue** 구조하다

- □ **completely** 완전히, 전적으로 – **entirely** 완전히
- □ **found** 설립하다 – **establish** 설립하다
- □ **include** 포함하다 – **contain** 포함하다
- □ **opportunity** 기회 – **chance** 기회
- □ **join** 결합하다 – **connect** 잇다, 연결하다
- □ **repair** 수리하다 – **fix** 수리하다
- □ **worth** ~할 가치가 있는 – **worthy** 가치 있는

※ 서로 반대의 뜻을 가진 어휘

- □ **impatient** 참지 못하는 ↔ **patient** 인내심이 강한
- □ **include** 포함하다 ↔ **exclude** 제외[배제]하다
- □ **save** 구하다, 절약하다 ↔ **waste** 낭비하다

- □ **improve** 향상시키다 ↔ **worsen** 악화시키다
- □ **join** 결합하다 ↔ **divide** 나누다, 분할하다 **separate** 분리하다
- □ **worth** ~할 가치가 있는 ↔ **worthless** 가치 없는

※ 감정을 나타내는 형용사

- □ **ashamed** 부끄러이 여기는
- □ **calm** 침착한, 냉정한
- □ **cheerful** 기분 좋은, 즐거운
- □ **confident** 확신하는, 자신만만한
- □ **curious** 호기심 있는

- □ **delighted** 아주 기뻐하는
- □ **disappointed** 실망한
- □ **embarrassed** 난처한
- □ **gloomy** 우울한
- □ **jealous** 질투심이 많은

- □ **lonely** 외로운, 고독한
- □ **regretful** 후회하는
- □ **relieved** 안도하는
- □ **scared** 무서워하는, 겁먹은
- □ **worried** 난처한, 걱정[근심]스러운

English Dictionary

- □ **banner** 현수막
  → a long piece of cloth with words written on it
  위에 글씨가 쓰여진 긴 천 조각

- □ **be ashamed of** ~을 부끄러워하다
  → to feel embarrassed and guilty about something you did 당신이 한 일에 대해 난처하거나 죄스러움을 느끼다

- □ **create** 만들다, 창조하다
  → to make something new 무언가 새로운 것을 만들다

- □ **challenging** 도전적인
  → difficult in a way that is usually enjoyable
  보통 즐길 수 없는 방식으로 어려운

- □ **connect** 연결하다
  → to join together 함께 연결하다

- □ **decision** 결정, 판단
  → the act of making up one's mind 결정하는 행위

- □ **found** 설립하다
  → to establish 설립하다

- □ **go after** ~을 추구하다, ~을 얻기 위해 노력하다
  → to pursue or run after 추구하거나 뒤쫓다

- □ **include** 포함하다
  → to have something as part of a group or total
  단체나 전체의 일부로 어떤 것을 갖다

- □ **league** 리그, 연맹
  → a group of sports teams that play against each other
  서로 상대하여 경기하는 스포츠 팀의 단체

- □ **opportunity** 기회
  → chance for doing something
  어떤 것을 할 기회

- □ **over and over** 반복해서
  → repeatedly 반복해서

- □ **read** ~라고 적혀 있다
  → to have or give information 정보를 갖거나 주다

- □ **regret** 후회하다
  → to feel sorry about something that you did in the past
  과거에 한 것에 대해 미안함을 느끼다

- □ **rest** 나머지
  → the part that is left 남아 있는 부분

- □ **serious** 심각한, 진지한
  → acting or speaking sincerely and without joking
  농담하지 않고 진심으로 행하거나 말하는

- □ **suit** 정장
  → a set of clothes usually consisting of a jacket and pants or skirt
  보통 재킷과 바지나 치마로 이루어진 한 벌의 옷

- □ **tryout** 심사, 테스트
  → a test of the potential of someone
  누군가의 가능성을 점검하는 것

- □ **worth** ~할 가치가 있는
  → good or important enough for something
  어떤 것에 대해 좋거나 충분히 중요한

서답형

01 다음 짝지어진 단어의 관계가 같도록 빈칸에 알맞은 말을 쓰시오.

> achieve : accomplish = entirely : _____

02 다음 영영풀이가 가리키는 것을 고르시오.

> to pursue or run after

① go after   ② break down

③ break out   ④ get off

⑤ be ashamed of

03 다음 중 밑줄 친 부분의 뜻풀이가 바르지 <u>않은</u> 것은?

① If I'm not <u>mistaken</u>, this book belongs to Henry. (잘못 알고 있는)

② You should <u>prepare for</u> the trip well in advance. (~을 준비하다)

③ She made up her mind to <u>apply for</u> the job. (~에 적응하다)

④ Wait until the paint has <u>completely</u> dried. (완전히)

⑤ There are many ways to <u>express</u> sad feelings. (표현하다)

서답형

04 다음 우리말을 주어진 어휘를 이용하여 영작하시오.

(1) 하버드 대학교는 1636년에 설립되었다.
(Harvard University, found)
➡ _____

(2) 그 작가의 소설은 여러 번 읽을 가치가 있다.
(over, read, worth)
➡ _____

서답형

05 다음 문장의 빈칸에 들어갈 말을 〈보기〉에서 골라 쓰시오. (필요하면 어형을 변화할 것)

> ─┤ 보기 ├─
> be ashamed of / deal with / do her hair /
> hang out with / go by

(1) As time _____, things got more dangerous.

(2) He has some unfinished business to _____.

(3) You should _____ yourself for telling such lies.

(4) Tell her to go and _____ and nails.

(5) He's very friendly and really fun to _____.

06 다음 빈칸 (A)~(B)에 각각 공통으로 들어갈 말이 바르게 짝지어진 것은?

> • We had gone about fifty miles when the car (A)_____ down.
> • They had escaped to America shortly before the war (A)_____ out in 1939.
> • I think we should (B)_____ after an increase in production this year.
> • Days (B)_____ by, and his father does not come, but Alex decides to wait.

① made – go   ② made – get

③ broke – go   ④ broke – get

⑤ put – do

01 다음 짝지어진 단어의 관계가 같도록 빈칸에 알맞은 말을 쓰시오.

> lend : borrow = _____ : exclude

02 다음 우리말에 맞게 빈칸에 알맞은 말을 쓰시오.

(1) 네가 정말 원하는 직업을 추구해라.

➡ _____ _____ the job you really want.

(2) 그녀는 시험에서 부정행위를 한 것을 부끄럽게 생각했다.

➡ She _____ _____ _____ herself for cheating on the test.

(3) 그는 그녀가 그 상황을 처리할 것으로 믿어도 된다는 것을 알고 있었다.

➡ He knew he could depend upon her to _____ _____ the situation.

03 다음 문장의 빈칸에 들어갈 말을 〈보기〉에서 골라 쓰시오.

> ┌─ 보기 ┌─
> impatient / opportunity / offer /
> read / include

(1) The price of pizza does not _____ the delivery fee.

(2) Don't be _____ with the children.

(3) The sign on the bench _____s "Wet Paint."

(4) Traveling abroad can give you a good _____ to learn about other cultures.

(5) Rex is considering job _____s from several companies.

04 우리말과 일치하도록 주어진 어구를 배열하여 영작하시오.

(1) 그 책은 당신의 상상력을 넓히는 데에 도움이 될 것이다. (you / your / the book / imagination / will / expand / help)

➡ _____

_____

(2) 그녀는 자신의 관심사를 추구해서 동물원 사육사가 되었다. (she / she / a zookeeper / became / was / going / interested / what / in / by / after)

➡ _____

_____

(3) 그는 도전 의식을 북돋우고 보람이 있는 일을 찾고 있다. (he / job / rewarding / challenging / looking / is / and / a / for)

➡ _____

_____

05 다음 우리말에 맞게 주어진 어구를 사용하여 영작하시오.

(1) 원숭이들은 놀거나 서로를 뒤쫓을 때 웃는다. (chase, play, each other)

➡ _____

(2) 우리 가게의 모든 샌드위치 가격은 음료를 포함한다. (the price, drinks, store, include)

➡ _____

_____

(3) 그 병원은 가난한 사람들을 치료하기 위해 설립되었다. (treat, poor, found)

➡ _____

_____

Conversation

① 후회 표현하기

> **A** I should have saved food for the winter. 나는 겨울용 식량을 저장해 놨어야 해.
>
> **B** Don't worry. I'll share my food with you. 걱정하지 마. 내가 내 식량을 나눠 줄게.

■ 과거의 일에 대한 안타까움이나 후회를 나타낼 때 should have+p.p.로 표현한다. should have p.p.는 '~했어야 했는데 (하지 못했다)'는 의미이고, should not have p.p.는 '~하지 말았어야 했는데 (했다)'는 뜻이다. 'I ought to have+p.p.', 'I had to ~, but I didn't.', 'I regret ~.', 'It would have been better if ~', 'I'm very sorry for ~', 'It's a pity that ~.' 등으로 유감이나 후회를 나타낼 수도 있다.

- I should have gone to bed early. 나는 일찍 잤어야 했어.
- I shouldn't have spent so much money on buying pens. 나는 펜을 사는 데 그렇게 많은 돈을 쓰지 말았어야 했어.

■ 'I should have+p.p. ~.'는 'I ought to have+p.p.', 'I'm sorry I didn't[wasn't] ~.' 또는 'I regret I didn't[wasn't] ~.' 등으로 바꿔 쓸 수 있다.

- I should have studied math harder.
  = I ought to have studied math harder. 나는 수학을 더 열심히 공부했어야 했는데.
  = I'm sorry I didn't study math harder. 나는 수학을 더 열심히 공부하지 않은 것이 유감이다.
  = I regret I didn't study math harder. 나는 수학을 더 열심히 공부하지 않은 것을 후회한다.

유사 표현

- You could have told me before. 당신이 전에 내게 말을 해 줄 수도 있었잖아요.
- I wish I could give up smoking. 난 담배를 끊을 수 있으면 좋겠어.
- I really regret not listening to her. 그녀의 말을 듣지 않은 걸 정말 후회해.

핵심 Check

1. 다음 대화의 밑줄 친 우리말을 주어진 단어를 포함하여 영작하시오.

   A: I got up late this morning. <u>알람을 맞췄어야 했어.</u> (set, alarm)

   B: I'm sorry to hear that.

   ➡ _____

② 상대방의 말 수정하기

A People in Brazil speak Spanish, right? 브라질 사람들은 스페인어를 사용해. 그렇지?

B I'm afraid you're mistaken. They speak Portuguese.
미안하지만 네가 잘못 아는 거야. 그들은 포르투칼어를 사용해.

■ 상대방의 말을 수정하기 위해서 'That's not right[true].', 'I don't think that's right.', 'That's wrong.', 'You're mistaken.' 등의 표현을 사용한다.

· **A:** Shanghai is the biggest city in China. 상해가 중국에서 가장 큰 도시야.

B: That's not true. Beijing is the biggest one in China. 사실이 아니야. 중국에서 가장 큰 도시는 북경이야.

■ 상대방의 말이 잘못되어서 수정하고 싶을 때, 앞에 'I'm sorry, but ~.', 'I'm afraid ~.' 등을 붙여 좀 더 부드럽게 말할 수 있다.

· **A:** Vincent van Gogh was French, wasn't he? Vincent van Gogh는 프랑스 사람이었지, 그렇지 않니?

B: I'm afraid you're mistaken. He was Dutch. 네가 잘못 생각하는 거야. 그는 네덜란드 사람이야.

상대방의 말 수정하기

· I'm sorry, but ~ 미안하지만, ~

· I'm afraid ~ 미안하지만, ~

핵심 Check

2. 다음 대화의 빈칸에 적절하지 <u>않은</u> 것은?

G: What made you late?

B: Well, I got up early. But it took me some time to do my hair.

G: Oh, I see. We're stuck in a heavy traffic jam. We should get off and run.

B: No, ＿＿＿＿＿＿＿. The traffic is starting to move again. Let's stay on.

G: Okay. I just hope we're not terribly late.

① you're mistaken

② we shouldn't have got off

③ that's not right

④ I don't think that's right

⑤ that's wrong

Listen - Listen & Answer Dialog 1

B: Hi, Sora. What are you doing?

G: I'm drawing cartoons. I'm preparing for the exam for Mana Animation High School.

B: Oh, ❶are you? When is the exam?

G: On Friday, so I only have two days ❷left.

B: How's ❸it going?

G: ❹It's not easy to draw what I want to express. ❺I should have practiced more.

B: Don't worry! ❻You can make it!

G: Thanks.

남: 안녕, 소라야. 뭘 하고 있니?

여: 만화를 그리고 있어. 마나 애니메이션 고등학교 입학시험을 준비하고 있어.

남: 아, 그래? 시험이 언제야?

여: 금요일. 그래서 이틀밖에 안 남았어.

남: 어떻게 되고 있니?

여: 내가 표현하고 싶은 것을 그리기가 쉽지 않아. 나는 더 연습했어야 해.

남: 걱정하지 마! 넌 해낼 수 있어!

여: 고마워.

❶ preparing for the exam ~ 이하가 생략되어 있다. ❷ 과거분사로 two days를 수식하고 있다. ❸ 비인칭 주어이다.
❹ 가주어 It, 진주어로 to부정사가 쓰이고 있다. 의문사 what에 이끌리는 절이 draw의 목적어로 쓰이고 있다.
❺ should have p.p.'는 '~했어야 한다'는 의미로 과거의 행동이나 사실에 관한 추측이나 후회를 나타낸다.
❻ You can make it!: 넌 해낼 수 있어!

Check(√) True or False

(1) Sora has two days left for the exam.　　　　　　　　　　　　　　T ☐ F ☐

(2) Sora doesn't think it difficult to draw what she wants to express.　　T ☐ F ☐

Listen - Listen & Answer Dialog 2

M: Nice to meet you, Sora. Did you do well on the drawing exam?

G: I'm not sure, but I did my best.

M: Okay. Let's start the interview. ❶What made you apply for Mana Animation High School?

G: Well, ❷I've really loved drawing cartoons since I was a little child.

M: So, ❸you want to be a cartoon artist?

G: ❹That's not quite right. I want to be a game designer.

M: I see. ❺What do you think is the most important skill a game designer needs?

G: ❻I'd say imagination. A good designer should create a completely new world in a game.

M: Sounds good.

남: 소라 학생, 만나서 반가워요. 소묘 시험은 잘 봤나요?

여: 잘 모르겠지만 최선을 다했습니다.

남: 알겠어요. 면접을 시작합시다. 왜 마나 애니메이션 고등학교에 지원했나요?

여: 음. 저는 어렸을 때부터 만화 그리는 것을 정말 좋아했습니다.

남: 그렇다면, 만화가가 되고 싶나요?

여: 꼭 그렇지는 않습니다. 저는 게임 디자이너가 되고 싶습니다.

남: 그렇군요. 게임 디자이너에게 필요한 가장 중요한 기량이 무엇이라고 생각하나요?

여: 상상력이라고 말씀드리겠습니다. 훌륭한 게임 디자이너는 게임 속에서 완전히 새로운 세계를 창조해야 하거든요.

남: 좋습니다.

❶ 'Why did you apply for ~?'로 바꿔 쓸 수 있다. ❷ 현재완료의 계속 용법이다.
❸ 구어체에서 평서문의 어순으로 의문문을 대신하고 있다. ❹ 상대방의 말을 수정해 주고 있다.
❺ think 동사로 인해 간접의문문의 의문사가 문두에 쓰이고 있는 문장이다.
❻ I'd[I would] say ~.: 내 생각에 ~인 것 같다.

Check(√) True or False

(3) Sora is not sure if she did well on the drawing exam.　　　　　　T ☐ F ☐

(4) Sora thinks the most important skill in a game is imagination.　　T ☐ F ☐

Get Ready

A: We need 100 candles.

B: ❶That's not quite right. We need 101 candles.

A: ❷We should have prepared 110 candles.

❶ 상대방의 말을 수정하려고 쓴 문장이다.
❷ 'We ought to have prepared 110 candles.'와 같은 말이다.

Listen - Listen More

G: Hi, Jiho.

B: Hi, Amber. It's nice to see you on the bus.

G: Yeah, but I'm afraid we're going to be late.

B: Yeah. I hate to be late for the school festival.

G: Me, too. ❶I should have set my alarm. I forgot.

B: I understand. ❷That happens a lot to me when I'm tired, too.

G: How about you? ❸What made you late?

B: Well, I got up early. But it took me some time to do my hair.

G: Oh, I see. We're stuck in a heavy traffic jam. We should get off and run.

B: ❹No, you're mistaken. The traffic is starting to move again. Let's stay on.

G: Okay. I just hope we're not terribly late.

❶ 'should have p.p.'는 '~했어야 한다'는 의미로 과거의 행동이나 사실에 관한 추측이나 후회를 나타낸다.
❷ happens는 자동사이므로 수동태로 쓰이지 않고 a lot은 부사구로 쓰였다.
❸ 'Why were you late?'와 같은 말이다.
❹ 상대방의 말을 수정할 때 쓰는 표현이다.

Speak - Talk in pairs.

A: ❶What's the matter?

B: I feel hungry. ❷I should have saved food for the winter.

A: Don't worry. ❸I'll share my food with you.

B: Thanks.

❶ What's up?, What's the problem? 등으로 바꿔 쓸 수 있다.
❷ 과거에 대한 후회를 나타낸다.
❸ share A with B: A를 B와 공유하다

My Speaking Portfolio

G1: I didn't study English hard. I should have practiced more ❶to improve my speaking skills.

B1: I hung out with only a few close friends. ❷I regret that I didn't make more friends.

G1: ❸I should have read more books. ❹I'm afraid that I won't have time for reading when I go to high school.

B1: I ❺spent too much time on my cell phone. I should have played basketball more often.

❶ 부사적 용법으로 '목적'을 나타낸다.
❷ 'I regret that ~'으로 과거에 대한 후회를 나타낸다.
❸ 'should have p.p.'로 과거에 대한 후회를 나타낸다.
❹ 미래의 일에 대한 걱정을 표현하고 있다.
❺ spend+시간/돈+on ~ing: ~에 시간이나 돈을 쓰다

Wrap Up 6

B: What do you want to do when you grow up?

G: I want to work with robots.

B: Are you interested in making robots?

G: ❶No, that's not quite right. I want to repair robots.

B: I see. But why?

G: Because I think it'll be a good job in the future.

❶ 상대방의 말을 수정할 때 쓰는 표현이다.'

Wrap Up 7

G: My computer has viruses.

B: ❶How come?

G: I opened an e-mail from a stranger. ❷I shouldn't have done that.

B: ❸If I were you, I'd get help from a computer service center right now.

❶ 'How come?'은 이어지는 어순이 평서문의 어순임에 주의해야 한다. 즉, 뒤에 'your computer has viruses'가 생략되어 있다.
❷ 'I shouldn't have p.p.'로 하지 말았어야 하는 일을 한 것에 대한 후회를 나타내고 있다.
❸ 가정법 과거로 현재 사실에 대해 반대되는 일에 대해 가정하고 있다.

● 다음 우리말과 일치하도록 빈칸에 알맞은 말을 쓰시오.

Listen - Listen & Answer Dialog 1

B: Hi, Sora. _____ are you doing?

G: I'm drawing cartoons. I'm preparing _____ the exam for Mana Animation High School.

B: Oh, _____ you? _____ is the exam?

G: _____ Friday, so I only have two days _____.

B: _____ it _____?

G: _____'s not easy _____ _____ _____ I want to express. I _____ _____ _____ more.

B: Don't worry! You can _____ _____!

G: Thanks.

남: 안녕, 소라야. 뭘 하고 있니?
여: 만화를 그리고 있어. 마나 애니메이션 고등학교 입학시험을 준비하고 있어.
남: 아, 그래? 시험이 언제야?
여: 금요일. 그래서 이틀밖에 안 남았어.
남: 어떻게 되고 있니?
여: 내가 표현하고 싶은 것을 그리기가 쉽지 않아. 나는 더 연습했어야 해.
남: 걱정하지 마! 넌 해낼 수 있어!
여: 고마워.

Listen - Listen & Answer Dialog 2

M: Nice _____ _____ you, Sora. Did you _____ _____ _____ the drawing exam?

G: I'm not _____, but I _____ _____ _____.

M: Okay. Let's start the interview. _____ _____ you apply _____ Mana Animation High School?

G: Well, I'_____ really _____ drawing cartoons _____ I was a little child.

M: So, you want to be a cartoon artist?

G: That's not _____ _____. I want to be a game designer.

M: I see. _____ do you _____ is the most important skill a game designer needs?

G: _____ _____ imagination. A good designer should create a _____ new world in a game.

M: Sounds good.

남: 소라 학생, 만나서 반가워요. 소묘 시험은 잘 봤나요?
여: 잘 모르겠지만 최선을 다했습니다.
남: 알겠어요. 면접을 시작합시다. 왜 마나 애니메이션 고등학교에 지원했나요?
여: 음, 저는 어렸을 때부터 만화 그리는 것을 정말 좋아했습니다.
남: 그렇다면, 만화가가 되고 싶나요?
여: 꼭 그렇지는 않습니다. 저는 게임 디자이너가 되고 싶습니다.
남: 그렇군요. 게임 디자이너에게 필요한 가장 중요한 기량이 무엇이라고 생각하나요?
여: 상상력이라고 말씀드리겠습니다. 훌륭한 게임 디자이너는 게임 속에서 완전히 새로운 세계를 창조해야 하거든요.
남: 좋습니다.

Speak - Talk in pairs.

A: What's the matter?

B: I feel hungry. I should have _____ food for the winter.

A: Don't worry. I'll _____ my food _____ you.

B: Thanks.

A: 무슨 일이야?
B: 배가 고파. 나는 겨울용 식량을 저장해 놨어야 해.
A: 걱정하지 마. 내가 내 식량을 나눠 줄게.
B: 고마워.

Listen - Listen More

G: Hi, Jiho.

B: Hi, Amber. It's nice _____ _____ you on the bus.

G: Yeah, but _____ _____ we're going to be late.

B: Yeah. I _____ _____ _____ late for the school festival.

G: Me, too. I _____ _____ _____ my alarm. I forgot.

B: I understand. That _____ _____ _____ to me when I'm _____, too.

G: How about you? _____ _____ you late?

B: Well, I got up early. But it took me some time to _____ _____ _____.

G: Oh, I see. _____ _____ _____ a heavy traffic jam. We should _____ _____ and run.

B: No, _____ _____. The traffic is starting to move again. Let's _____ _____.

G: Okay. I just hope we're not _____ late.

여: 지호야. 안녕.
남: Amber. 안녕. 버스에서 너를 보다니 반갑다.
여: 맞아. 그런데 걱정스럽게도 우리가 늦을 것 같아.
남: 그러게. 학교 축제에 늦고 싶지 않은데.
여: 나도 그래. 알람을 맞출걸. 내가 깜빡했어.
남: 이해해. 나도 피곤할 때 그런 일이 많이 일어나.
여: 너는? 무슨 일로 늦었어?
남: 음. 난 일찍 일어났어. 그런데 머리를 손질하느라 시간이 좀 걸렸어.
여: 아, 그렇구나. 우리 교통 체증에 갇혔어. 버스에서 내려서 뛰어가자.
남: 아니, 네가 잘못 생각하는 거야. 차들이 다시 움직이기 시작해. 내리지 말자.
여: 알았어. 너무 늦지 않기를 바랄 뿐이야.

Wrap Up 6

B: What do you want to do _____ you grow up?

G: I want to work _____ robots.

B: Are you interested in _____ robots?

G: No, _____ not _____ _____. I want to repair robots.

B: I see. But _____?

G: Because I _____ it'll be a good job in the future.

남: 너는 커서 무엇을 하고 싶니?
여: 나는 로봇과 관련된 일을 하고 싶어.
남: 로봇 제작하는 것에 관심 있니?
여: 아니, 꼭 그렇지는 않아. 나는 로봇을 수리하고 싶어.
남: 그렇구나. 그런데 왜?
여: 그것이 미래에 좋은 직업이 될 거라고 생각하기 때문이야.

Wrap Up 7

G: My computer has viruses.

B: _____ come?

G: I opened an e-mail from a stranger. I _____ _____ _____ that.

B: If I _____ _____, _____ _____ help from a computer service center right now.

여: 내 컴퓨터가 바이러스에 걸렸어.
남: 어쩌다가 그랬니?
여: 모르는 사람에게서 온 이메일을 열었지. 그러지 말았어야 해.
남: 내가 너라면, 지금 바로 컴퓨터 서비스 센터에서 도움을 받겠어.

[01~02] 다음 대화를 읽고 물음에 답하시오.

B: Hi, Sora. What are you doing?

G: I'm drawing cartoons. I'm ⓐ<u>preparing for</u> the exam for Mana Animation High School.

B: Oh, ⓑ<u>are you</u>? When is the exam?

G: On Friday, so I only have two days ⓒ<u>left</u>.

B: How's it going?

G: It's not easy to draw what I want to express. ⓓ<u>I must have practiced more.</u>

B: Don't worry! ⓔ<u>You can make it!</u>

G: Thanks.

01 위 대화의 밑줄 친 ⓐ~ⓔ 중 흐름상 어색한 것을 찾아 바르게 고치시오.

➡ _____

02 위 대화를 읽고 대답할 수 <u>없는</u> 것은?

① What is Sora doing?

② When is the exam for Mana Animation High School?

③ How many days does Sora have for the exam?

④ Is it easy for Sora to draw what she wants to express?

⑤ Why does Sora want to attend Mana Animation High School?

[03~04] 다음 대화를 읽고 물음에 답하시오.

B: What do you want to do when you grow up?

G: I want to work with robots.

B: Are you interested in making robots?

G: No, that's not quite right. I want to repair robots.

B: I see. But why?

G: Because I think it'll be a good job in the future.

03 What does the girl want to do when she grows up?

➡ _____

04 Why does the girl want to repair robots?

➡ _____

[01~03] 다음 대화를 읽고 물음에 답하시오.

M: Nice to meet you, Sora. Did you do well on the drawing exam?

G: I'm not sure, but I did my best.

M: Okay. Let's start the interview. What made you apply for Mana Animation High School?

G: Well, I've really loved drawing cartoons since I was a little child.

M: So, you want to be a cartoon artist?

G: _____ (A) _____ I want to be a game designer.

M: I see. What do you think is the most important skill a game designer needs?

G: (B)상상력이라고 말씀드리겠습니다. A good designer should create a completely new world in a game.

M: Sounds good.

01 위 대화의 빈칸 (A)에 알맞은 것은?

① It's true.
② Of course.
③ You can say that again.
④ How did you know?
⑤ That's not quite right.

02 위 대화에 나오는 M과 G의 관계로 적절한 것은?

① teacher – student
② doctor – patient
③ interviewer – interviewee
④ customer – clerk
⑤ star – fan

서답형

03 위 대화의 밑줄 친 (B)의 우리말을 3 단어로 영작하시오.

➡ _____

[04~06] 다음 대화를 읽고 물음에 답하시오.

G: Hi, Jiho.

B: Hi, Amber. It's nice to see you on the bus.

G: Yeah, but I'm afraid we're going to be late.

B: Yeah. I hate to be late for the school festival.

G: Me, too. (A)I should have set my alarm. I forgot.

B: I understand. That happens a lot to me when I'm tired, too.

G: How about you? What made you late?

B: Well, I got up early. But it took me some time to do my hair.

G: Oh, I see. We're stuck in a heavy traffic jam. We should get off and run.

B: No, you're mistaken. The traffic is starting to move again. Let's stay on.

G: Okay. I just hope we're not terribly late.

04 위 대화의 밑줄 친 (A)와 바꾸어 쓰기에 어색한 것은?

① I ought to have set my alarm.
② I may have set my alarm.
③ I'm sorry I didn't set my alarm.
④ I wish I could have set my alarm.
⑤ I regret I didn't set my alarm.

05 위 대화를 읽고 대답할 수 없는 것은?

① Why is Amber late?
② Where do Jiho and Amber meet?
③ What did Amber forget to do last night?
④ How late are Jiho and Amber?
⑤ Why is Jiho late?

06 위 대화에서 다음의 영영풀이가 뜻하는 것을 찾아 쓰시오.

> difficult to move from one position to another

➡ _____

[07~08] 다음 글을 읽고 물음에 답하시오.

G1: I didn't study English hard. I should have practiced more to improve my speaking skills.

B1: I hung out with only a few close friends. I (A)[regret / wonder] that I didn't make more friends.

B2: I should have read more books. I'm (B) [afraid / sure] that I won't have time for reading when I go to high school.

G2: I spent too much time (C)[at / on] my cell phone. I should have played basketball more often.

07 위 글의 괄호 (A)~(C)에서 알맞은 것을 바르게 짝지은 것을 고르시오.

	(A)	(B)	(C)
①	regret	afraid	at
②	regret	sure	on
③	regret	afraid	on
④	wonder	sure	at
⑤	wonder	afraid	at

08 위 글의 내용과 일치하지 <u>않는</u> 것은?

① G1은 말하기 실력을 키우기 위해 열심히 영어 공부를 하지 않은 것을 후회하고 있다.

② B1은 친구 몇 명하고만 어울렸다.

③ B1은 많은 친구를 사귀지 않은 것을 후회한다.

④ B2는 고등학교에 가면 책을 읽을 시간이 없을까 봐 걱정한다.

⑤ G2는 휴대 전화에 많은 시간을 쓰고 싶어 한다.

09 다음 중 짝지어진 대화가 <u>어색한</u> 것을 고르시오.

① A: That's not quite right. I want to be a game designer.
  B: I'm sorry to hear that.

② A: I fell down on the stairs. I shouldn't have run down the stairs.
  B: I'm sorry to hear that.

③ A: I should have saved food for the winter.
  B: Don't worry. I'll share my food with you.

④ A: We're stuck in a heavy traffic jam. We should get off and run.
  B: No, you're mistaken. The traffic is starting to move again.

⑤ A: Mauna Loa is the largest known volcano in the solar system.
  B: I'm afraid you're mistaken. "Olympus Mons" on Mars is the largest known volcano in the solar system.

[10~11] 다음 대화를 읽고 물음에 답하시오.

G: My computer has viruses.

B: (A)How come?

G: I opened an e-mail from a stranger. I shouldn't have done (B)that.

B: If I were you, I'd get help from a computer service center right now.

10 위 대화의 밑줄 친 (A)를 완전한 문장으로 쓰시오.

➡ _____

11 위 대화를 읽고 밑줄 친 (B)that이 가리키는 것을 우리말로 쓰시오.

➡ _____

[01~04] 다음 대화를 읽고 물음에 답하시오.

B: What do you want to do when you grow up?
(A) No, (a)that's not quite right. I want to repair robots.
(B) I want to work with robots.
(C) Are you interested in making robots?
(D) Because I think it'll be a good job in the future.
(E) I see. But (b)why?

01 주어진 글에 대화가 자연스럽게 이어지도록 순서대로 배열하시오.

➡ _____

02 위 대화의 내용과 일치하도록 빈칸 (A)와 (B)에 알맞은 말을 쓰시오.

G wants to (A)_____ robots because she thinks it'll be (B)_____ _____ _____ in the future.

03 위 대화의 밑줄 친 (a)와 같은 뜻의 말을 주어진 어휘를 이용하여 쓰시오.

mistaken, afraid

➡ _____

04 위 대화의 밑줄 친 (b)why 다음에 생략되어 있는 말을 쓰시오.

➡ _____

[05~07] 다음 대화를 읽고 물음에 답하시오.

B: Hi, Sora. What are you doing?
G: I'm drawing cartoons. I'm preparing for the exam for Mana Animation High School.
B: Oh, are you? When is the exam?
G: On Friday, so I only have two days left.
B: How's it going?
G: It's not easy to draw what I want to express. I should have practiced more.
B: Don't worry! You can make it!
G: Thanks.

05 What does Sora regret?

➡ _____

06 When does Sora have the exam for Mana Animation High School? Answer in English with 6 words.

➡ _____

07 What is difficult for Sora?

➡ _____
_____

08 다음 대화가 자연스럽게 이어지도록 순서대로 배열하시오.

(A) Thanks.
(B) I feel hungry. I should have saved food for the winter.
(C) What's the matter?
(D) Don't worry. I'll share my food with you.

➡ _____

Grammar

1 조동사+have p.p.

> • They **must have been** hungry. 그들은 배고팠던 것이 틀림없다.

■ 형태: 조동사+have p.p.
  의미: 과거의 행동이나 사실에 관한 추측이나 후회 등을 나타낸다.

(1) must have p.p.: ~했음이 틀림없다 (강한 추측)

  • That dress **must have cost** a bomb! 저 드레스는 돈이 엄청 들었을 거야!

(2) may[might] have p.p.: ~했을지도 모른다 (약한 추측)

  • He **may have missed** his train. 그가 기차를 놓쳤는지도 모른다.

  • She was worried that he **might have met** with an accident.
    그녀는 그가 사고를 당했을지도 모른다고 걱정했다.

(3) should[ought to] have p.p.: ~했어야 한다(그런데 하지 못했다) (후회)

  • I **should have told** you the truth. 내가 너에게 진실을 말했어야 한다.

  • You **ought to have come** to the meeting. 네가 그 모임에 왔더라면 좋았을 걸 그랬어.

(4) should not[ought not to] have p.p.: ~하지 않았어야 했는데(그런데 했다) (후회)

  • This error **should not have happened**. 이 실수는 일어나서는 안 될 일이었습니다.

  • You **ought not to have done** that. 너는 그렇게 해서는 안 되었었다.

(5) cannot have p.p.: ~했을 리가 없다(강한 부정의 추측) (↔ must have p.p.)

  • He **cannot have said** so. 그가 그렇게 말했을 리가 없다.

(6) could have p.p.: ~했을 수도 있었는데[있었다] (과거와 관련된 가능성)

  • The accident **could have been avoided**. 그 사고는 방지할 수도 있었을 것이다.

(7) would have p.p.: ~했을 텐데[했을 것이다] (과거와 관련된 가정이나 상상, 과거의 의지)

  • He was so desperate for a job that he **would have done** anything.
    그는 일자리가 너무도 절실히 필요해서 무슨 일이라도 했을 것이다.

핵심 Check

1. 다음 괄호 안에서 알맞은 단어를 고르시오.

(1) I gained some weight. I _____ _____ _____ so much fast food. (should, eat)

(2) He looks fatter than before. He _____ _____ _____ on several kilos. (put)

② 관계대명사의 계속적 용법

> • My favorite writer is Ken Kuller, **who** lives in New York.
> 내가 가장 좋아하는 작가는 Ken Kuller인데, 그는 뉴욕에 산다.

■ 형태: 콤마(,) + who/which
쓰임: 관계대명사절이 선행사를 보충해서 설명하는 역할을 한다.

■ 관계대명사의 계속적 용법은 관계대명사 앞에 콤마(,)를 붙인 형태로 선행사를 보충해서 설명한다. 제한적 용법과 마찬가지로 선행사가 사람이면 who, 사물이면 which를 쓴다. 제한적 용법은 관계사가 이끄는 절부터 해석하고, 계속적 용법은 앞에서부터 해석한다.

• Ben has two sons **who** are doctors. Ben은 의사인 아들이 둘 있다. (제한적 용법 → 아들이 둘인지 더 있는지 모름.)

• Ben has two sons, **who** are doctors. Ben은 아들이 둘인데, 그들은 의사이다. (계속적 용법 → 아들이 둘만 있음.)

■ 계속적 용법의 관계대명사는 '접속사(and, but, for, though 등)+대명사'로 고쳐 쓸 수 있다.

• I began to read the book, **which** was very exciting.

= I began to read the book, **and it** was very exciting.
나는 그 책을 읽기 시작했는데 그것은 손에 땀을 쥐게 했다.

■ 관계대명사 that과 what은 계속적 용법으로 사용할 수 없으며, 관계대명사가 계속적 용법으로 쓰였을 때는 생략하지 않는다.

• Thank you for your invitation, **which** I am very pleased to accept. (O)

• Thank you for your invitation, that I am very pleased to accept. (X)
초대해 주셔서 고맙습니다. 기쁜 마음으로 응하겠습니다.

■ which는 선행사로 구나 절을 가질 수도 있다.

• The movie slowly brings them together, **which** I love.
그 영화는 그들을 천천히 함께 하게 만들죠. 저는 그것을 좋아해요.

핵심 Check

2. 다음 빈칸에 알맞은 관계대명사를 쓰시오.

(1) The policeman arrested a criminal, _____ had been hiding in the forest.

(2) The letter contains a number of typing errors, _____ I must correct.

(3) I had very strong ambitions about acting, _____ I still have.

01 다음 빈칸에 알맞은 것은?

> Mr. Decker, _____ is a teacher, works at an elementary school.

① who   ② which   ③ how
④ that   ⑤ what

02 다음 괄호 안에서 알맞은 말을 고르시오.

(1) He (must / should) have spread the news. Everyone knows it.

(2) Jinsu got up late this morning. He (must / might) have been late for school.

(3) I didn't pass the audition. I (should / may) have practiced more for the audition.

03 다음 두 문장을 한 문장으로 바꾸어 쓸 때 알맞게 표현한 것을 고르시오.

> • My favorite writer is Ken Kuller.
> • The writer lives in New York.

① My favorite writer, which lives in New York, is Ken Kuller.
② My favorite writer, what lives in New York is Ken Kuller.
③ My favorite writer, who lives in New York, is Ken Kuller.
④ My favorite writer, whom lives in New York, is Ken Kuller.
⑤ My favorite writer, that lives in New York, is Ken Kuller.

04 다음 우리말에 맞게 주어진 어휘를 바르게 배열하시오.

(1) 너는 너무 많이 먹지 말았어야 한다.

(you, so, eaten, shouldn't, much, have)

➡ _____

(2) 나는 방학 중에 너의 집을 방문할 예정인데, 방학은 내일 시작한다.

(I'll, you, the vacation, tomorrow, visit, begins, which, during)

➡ _____

01 다음 중 어법상 <u>어색한</u> 것은?

① I ran into an old gentleman, who looked just like my grandfather.

② My dad painted the door pink, that is my favorite color.

③ Josh likes to eat tacos, which are a traditional Mexican dish.

④ Rose Austin, whom I saw on the subway, is a famous singer.

⑤ The Sydney Opera House, which is designed by Jørn Utzon, is in Australia.

중요

02 다음 중 어법상 <u>어색한</u> 것은?

① He should have brushed his teeth.

② They may have liked to draw something on the wall.

③ I should have build it with stronger material.

④ I shouldn't have played online games so much.

⑤ She must have loved the sport very much.

03 다음 빈칸에 알맞은 말이 바르게 짝지어진 것은?

• I should _____ nicer to my teachers and classmates.
• My grandmother, _____ lives in Busan, has 13 grandchildren.
---

① have been – who

② have been – that

③ have be – which

④ have be – that

⑤ be – what

서답형

04 다음 괄호 안에서 알맞은 말을 고르시오.

(1) My hero is King Sejong, (who / that) invented Hangeul.

(2) He painted his room blue, (who / which) is his favorite color.

(3) Tom visited her, (that / which) made him feel good.

(4) There were fish bones. They (must / should) have eaten fish in the cave.

(5) I got a bad grade in math. I (must / should) have studied harder.

(6) We went back home thinking that our pet dog (might / should) have already returned home.

05 다음 주어진 문장과 의미가 같은 것은?

I'm sure that they had a good time at the party.
---

① They should have had a good time at the party.

② They can have had a good time at the party.

③ They cannot have had a good time at the party.

④ They must have a good time at the party.

⑤ They must have had a good time at the party.

중요

 다음 밑줄 친 부분을 바꿔 쓸 때, 의미상 가장 적절한 것은?

This is *The Potato Eaters*, <u>which</u> was painted by Vincent van Gogh in 1885.
---

① for it   ② but it   ③ or it

④ and it   ⑤ because it

07 Which is suitable for the blank?

> Linda was late for school again. She _____ have been late so often.

① can't   ② may   ③ must
④ shouldn't   ⑤ ought to

서답형

08 다음 빈칸에 알맞은 관계대명사를 쓰시오.

(1) He said nothing, _____ made her angry.

(2) He likes painting pictures very much, _____ is his number-one free time activity.

(3) I'd like to introduce my friend Mike, _____ wants to be an artist in the future.

(4) Did they climb up the Eiffel Tower, _____ is in Paris?

09 다음 우리말을 바르게 영작한 것을 고르시오.

> 나는 시카고에 갔어야 했다.

① I must have gone to Chicago.
② I should have gone to Chicago.
③ I may have gone to Chicago.
④ I can have gone to Chicago.
⑤ I would have gone to Chicago.

10 다음 문장의 밑줄 친 부분 중 어법상 어색한 것은?

> The robber ⓐstole a car, ⓑthat a woman ⓒparked ⓓoutside ⓔher house.

① ⓐ   ② ⓑ   ③ ⓒ   ④ ⓓ   ⑤ ⓔ

11 다음 빈칸에 들어갈 말로 알맞은 것을 고르시오.

> I felt sleepy all day. I _____ late last night.

① must have stayed
② can't have stayed
③ shouldn't have stayed
④ should have stayed
⑤ ought to have stayed

서답형

12 계속적 용법의 관계대명사를 사용하여 주어진 두 문장을 한 문장으로 바꾸시오.

> • My dad gave me a birthday present.
> • I got much happiness from it.

➡ _____

_____

13 다음 대화의 빈칸에 들어갈 말을 고르시오.

> A: Mike lost his smartphone again.
> B: Oh, that's too bad.
> A: _____

① He must be more careful.
② He should have been more careful.
③ He ought not to have been more careful.
④ You can't have been more careful.
⑤ You may have been more careful.

14 다음 밑줄 친 부분을 바꿔 쓸 때, 빈칸에 적절한 말을 쓰시오.

> He'd dyed his hair, <u>but it</u> was almost unheard-of in the 1960s.
> = He'd dyed his hair, _____ was almost unheard-of in the 1960s.

15 다음 빈칸에 알맞은 말이 순서대로 바르게 짝지어진 것을 고르시오.

> • Look at the letters. They _____ have had their own alphabet.
> • He _____ have smoked so much. He has lung cancer now.

① must – must
② must – should not
③ should – must
④ should – should not
⑤ cannot – might

16 다음 각 문장에서 어법상 <u>어색한</u> 부분을 하나씩 찾아서 알맞게 고치시오.

(1) Yesterday I called my aunt, which lives in Mexico.

➡ _____

(2) Tom also showed me a book, that had Ken Kuller's autograph on it.

➡ _____
_____

(3) You should have not broken the rule.

➡ _____

(4) They must have leave some messages with their own letters.

➡ _____
_____

17 다음 중 어법상 옳은 문장을 고르시오.

① He went to the Lost and Found, that was open until 6:00 p.m.
② John is a movie star, who often come to Korea.
③ Mozart was a composer, whom wrote a large amount of good music.
④ My sister likes this book, which has many colorful pictures.
⑤ He said nothing, who made her get angry.

18 다음 우리말과 의미가 같도록 빈칸에 들어갈 말로 알맞은 것을 고르시오.

> Smith 씨는 전에 그 영화를 봤음에 틀림없다.
> = Mr. Smith _____ the movie before.

① should have seen
② must have seen
③ cannot have seen
④ might have seen
⑤ may have seen

19 우리말 의미에 맞도록, 괄호 안의 어구를 알맞게 배열하시오.

(1) Molly 씨는 손녀 이름을 'Daisy'라고 지었는데, 그것은 꽃 이름이다. (Ms. Molly, Daisy, flower, the name, named, is, her granddaughter, which, a, of)

➡ _____
_____

(2) 그 작가는 소설 집필을 마쳤을지도 모른다. (the writer, his novel, might, finished, have)

➡ _____
_____

01 다음 빈칸에 알맞은 관계대명사를 쓰시오.

(1) Jake has two cousins, _____ live in Canada.

(2) My family had dinner at a Mexican restaurant, _____ is near the community center.

(3) My aunt, _____ lives next door, takes care of nine dogs.

(4) Mary accepted his idea of going out, _____ made him happy.

02 다음 우리말에 맞게 주어진 어구를 바르게 배열하시오. (2), (3)은 계속적 용법의 관계대명사를 쓰시오.

(1) 너는 비를 맞으면서 축구를 하지 말았어야 한다. (soccer, you, have, the rain, played, shouldn't, in)

➡ _____

(2) 그가 주연한 영화가 흥행에 성공했다. (the film, big hit, the leading role, he, which, is, plays, a, in)

➡ _____
_____

(3) 그 노부인을 내가 지하철에서 봤는데, 그녀는 유명한 배우였다. (the subway, I, the old lady, famous actress, was, saw, whom, a, on)

➡ _____
_____

03 다음 괄호 안의 단어를 활용하여 주어진 조건대로 빈칸을 알맞게 채우시오.

(1) There are no seats left at the restaurant. We _____ a reservation. (make, 후회하는 문장을 쓸 것.)

(2) Kimberly was absent from school yesterday. She _____ yesterday. (sick, 추측하는 문장을 쓸 것.)

(3) There were loud noises all night long. He _____ through all that noise. (sleep, 부정의 추측하는 문장을 쓸 것.)

04 다음 두 문장을 해석하고 그 차이를 설명하시오.

(1) Anne has two sons who are teachers.

(2) Anne has two sons, who are teachers.

➡ 해석 _____
_____

➡ 차이 _____
_____
_____
_____

05 다음 상황에 맞게 후회하는 문장을 10 단어로 쓰시오.

> I spent all my money buying clothes. I need to buy some pens today.

➡ _____
_____

06 다음 그림을 보고, 주어진 어휘를 이용하여 빈칸을 알맞게 채우시오.

Brian is my best friend, _____ _____ pass the exam. (encourage)

07 다음 우리말을 영작하시오.

(1) 그녀는 그 영화를 보지 말았어야 했다.
　➡ _____

(2) 그녀는 그 영화를 봤을 리가 없다.
　➡ _____

(3) 그녀는 그 영화를 봤을지도 모른다.
　➡ _____

(4) 그녀는 그 영화를 봤음에 틀림없다.
　➡ _____

08 다음 문장에서 <u>틀린</u> 것을 고쳐 다시 쓰시오.

I'm fond of the actor, who name is not known well.

➡ _____
_____

09 다음 관계대명사의 계속적 용법을 이용하여 주어진 두 문장을 하나의 문장으로 쓰시오.

(1) • Harry invited Lindsey to the party.
　• And it made her feel happy.
➡ _____
_____

(2) • Do you know Thomas Edison?
　• He invented the light bulb.
➡ _____
_____

(3) • The book contains very good contents.
　• The book is cheap.
➡ _____
_____

10 다음 문장에서 어법상 <u>어색한</u> 것을 바르게 고치시오.

(1) My mom is wearing a necklace, who my dad gave her for her birthday.
_____ ➡ _____

(2) Let me introduce Jane Goodall, which studied chimpanzees all her life.
_____ ➡ _____

(3) Spanish people are proud of Antoni Gaudi, that was a great architect.
_____ ➡ _____

(4) Emma got a terrible score on the test. She must have studied harder.
_____ ➡ _____

(5) Several people are coming out. The train cannot have already arrived.
_____ ➡ _____

(6) Lisa is very wise. She must have done such a foolish thing.
_____ ➡ _____

MY GRANDMOTHER'S BASEBALL DREAMS

My grandmother Helen used to be a cook in a restaurant in a small
town near South Bend, Indiana. She does not work anymore, but she
still enjoys making delicious food, which I love so much. Food is one
of the many things that connect us. What connects us most strongly,
however, is baseball.

When I visit her on weekends, my grandmother often tells me
exciting stories about playing baseball back in the 1940s. She must
have loved the sport very much. I listen to these stories over and over.
She always says, "Go after what you want, Sarah. Don't be afraid of
trying something new or challenging. Don't be ashamed of failing."
In 1943, the All-American Girls Professional Baseball League was
founded. This league was created for baseball fans because many of
America's young men were fighting in World War II.

Helen was told that there would be local tryouts right in South Bend.
She wondered, "What would it be like to be on a baseball team and to
make it to the finals for my hometown?" She imagined a large banner
hanging at the baseball field which included the name Helen Baker.

used to (과거에) ~이었다[했다]
not ~ anymore 더 이상 ~ 않다
connect 연결하다
over and over 반복해서
go after ~을 추구하다, ~을 얻기 위
해 노력하다
challenging 도전적인
be ashamed of ~을 부끄러워하다
league 리그, 연맹
found 설립하다
create 만들다, 창조하다
tryout 심사, 테스트
banner 현수막
include 포함하다

 확인문제

● 다음 문장이 본문의 내용과 일치하면 T, 일치하지 <u>않으면</u> F를 쓰시오.

1 Sarah's grandmother Helen was a cook in a restaurant in a small town near South
   Bend, Indiana, but she isn't a cook now. ☐

2 What connects Sarah and her grandmother most strongly is food. ☐

3 When Sarah visits her grandmother on weekends, her grandmother often tells her
   exciting stories about playing baseball back in the 1940s. ☐

4 A large banner hung at the baseball field which included the name Helen Baker. ☐

On the day of the tryouts, all the rules were explained by an old man in a suit, who sounded very serious and unkind. She thought that
앞의 an old man을 추가 설명하기 위해 쓰인 계속적 용법의 관계대명사
wearing a suit in the hot sun might have made him impatient. On that
동명사 주어   *과거에 대한 추측(~했을지도 모른다)*
day, Helen played baseball for hours with many other young women.

She was excited to go after her baseball dreams!
to부정사 부사적 용법(감정의 원인)

About a week later, Helen found a letter in the mailbox. It was from people who worked for the girls' baseball league in Chicago. It read that she had been invited to the league's main tryouts in Chicago!
본심사에 초청된 것은 편지를 읽은 것보다 앞선 시제이므로 과거완료(had p.p.)로 표현

As the days went by, however, Helen became worried that she might fail. She also became worried about traveling alone to Chicago, which
앞의 Chicago를 추가 설명하기 위해 쓰인 계속적 용법의 관계대명사
was far away from home. When the day of the main tryouts came, she was too afraid to go.
너무 ~해서 …하지 않다

My grandmother has spent the rest of her life regretting her decision.
spend+시간+-ing: ~하면서 시간을 보내다
When she watches a baseball game on TV, she often says, "I should have gone to Chicago. You know, all your dreams are worth chasing,
갔어야 한다   *be worth -ing: ~할 가치가 있다*
even if you catch only a few of them. Never miss an opportunity."
= your dreams

suit 정장	
serious 심각한, 진지한	
impatient 짜증 난, 참지 못하는	
read ~라고 적혀 있다	
go by 지나가다, 흐르다	
rest 나머지	
regret 후회하다	
decision 결정, 판단	
worth ~할 가치가 있는	
even if 비록 ~하더라도	
opportunity 기회	

 확인문제

● 다음 문장이 본문의 내용과 일치하면 T, 일치하지 <u>않으면</u> F를 쓰시오.

1 On the day of the tryouts, an old man in a suit explained all the rules. ☐

2 On the day of the tryouts, Helen played baseball alone for hours. ☐

3 Helen received an invitation letter from people who worked for the girls' baseball league in Chicago. ☐

4 When the day of the main tryouts came, Helen started for Chicago with many other young women. ☐

5 The writer's grandmother has spent the rest of her life regretting her decision. ☐

6 The writer's grandmother must have gone to Chicago. ☐

● 우리말을 참고하여 빈칸에 알맞은 말을 쓰시오.

1 MY GRANDMOTHER'S BASEBALL _____

2 My grandmother Helen _____ _____ _____ a cook in a restaurant in a small town near South Bend, Indiana.

3 She does not work _____, but she still enjoys making delicious food, _____ I love so much.

4 Food is one of the many things _____ _____ _____.

5 _____ connects us most strongly, however, _____ baseball.

6 When I visit her _____ _____, my grandmother often tells me exciting stories about playing baseball _____ in the 1940s.

7 She _____ _____ _____ the sport very much.

8 I listen to these stories _____ _____ _____.

9 She always says, "_____ _____ what you want, Sarah.

10 Don't be afraid of trying _____ _____ _____ _____.

11 _____ _____ _____ _____ failing."

12 In 1943, the All-American Girls Professional Baseball League _____ _____.

13 This league _____ _____ for baseball fans because many of America's young men _____ _____ in World War II.

14 Helen was told that _____ _____ _____ local tryouts right in South Bend.

15 She wondered, "_____ _____ _____ _____ _____ to be on a baseball team and to make it to the finals for my hometown?"

16 She imagined a large banner _____ at the baseball field _____ _____ the name Helen Baker.

1	할머니의 야구 꿈
2	우리 할머니 Helen은 Indiana주 South Bend 근처 작은 마을에 있는 식당의 요리사였다.
3	할머니는 더 이상 일을 하지 않지만 여전히 맛있는 음식을 즐겨 만드시고, 나는 그 음식들을 무척 좋아한다.
4	음식은 우리를 연결하는 많은 것 가운데 하나이다.
5	하지만 우리를 가장 강하게 연결하는 것은 바로 야구이다.
6	주말마다 할머니 댁에 가면, 할머니는 종종 과거 1940년대의 야구 경기에 관해 흥미로운 이야기를 내게 들려주신다.
7	그녀는 야구를 무척 좋아했던 게 분명하다.
8	나는 이 이야기들을 몇 번이고 듣는다.
9	그녀는 항상 "네가 원하는 것을 이루려고 노력하렴, Sarah.
10	새로운 것이나 도전적인 것을 시도해 보기를 두려워하지 말거라.
11	실패하는 것을 부끄러워하지 마라."라고 말씀하신다.
12	1943년, 전미 여자 프로야구 리그가 창립되었다.
13	미국의 청년 중 많은 사람들이 제2차 세계대전에 참전해 있었기 때문에 이 리그가 야구 팬들을 위해 만들어졌다.
14	Helen 할머니는 지역 심사가 바로 South Bend에서 있을 거라고 들었다.
15	그녀는 "야구 팀에 들어가서 고향을 위해 결승전까지 진출한다는 건 어떤 기분일까?"라며 궁금해했다.
16	그녀는 Helen Baker라는 이름이 포함된 큰 현수막이 야구장에 걸려 있는 것을 상상했다.

17 On the day of the tryouts, all the rules _____ _____ by an old man _____ _____ _____, who sounded very serious and unkind.

18 She thought that _____ _____ _____ in the hot sun might have made him _____.

19 On that day, Helen played baseball _____ _____ with many other young women.

20 She was excited _____ _____ _____ her baseball dreams!

21 About a week later, Helen _____ _____ _____ in the mailbox.

22 _____ _____ _____ people who worked for the girls' baseball league in Chicago.

23 _____ _____ that she _____ _____ _____ to the league's main tryouts in Chicago!

24 _____ the days went by, however, Helen became _____ that she might fail.

25 She also became worried about traveling alone to Chicago, _____ was _____ _____ _____ home.

26 When the day of the main tryouts came, she was _____ afraid _____ go.

27 My grandmother has spent the rest of her life _____ her decision.

28 When she watches a baseball game on TV, she often says, "I _____ _____ _____ to Chicago.

29 You know, all your dreams _____ _____ _____, even if you catch only a few of them.

30 _____ _____ an opportunity."

---

17 심사 당일 모든 규칙이 정장을 입은 나이 든 남자에 의해 설명 되었는데, 그는 무척 진지하고 불친절하게 들렸다.

18 뜨거운 태양 아래 정장을 입고 있는 것이 그를 짜증나게 만들 었을지도 모른다고 그녀는 생각 했다.

19 그날, Helen 할머니는 다른 젊은 여성들과 함께 몇 시간 동안 야구를 했다.

20 그녀는 자신의 야구 꿈을 좇아 가게 되어 신이 났다!

21 일주일쯤 지나, Helen 할머니는 우편함에서 편지 한 통을 발견 했다.

22 그것은 시카고에 있는 여자 야 구리그에서 일하는 사람들이 보 낸 것이었다.

23 그 편지에는 그녀가 시카고에서 열리는 리그의 본심사에 초청되 었다고 적혀 있었다!

24 하지만 하루하루 갈수록, Helen 할머니는 심사에 떨어질까봐 걱 정되었다.

25 그녀는 또한 시카고까지 혼자 여행하는 것이 걱정되었는데, 시카고는 집에서 멀리 떨어진 곳이었다.

26 본심사가 있는 날이 되었을 때, 그녀는 너무 두려워서 갈 수 없 었다.

27 할머니는 남은 인생을 자신의 결정을 후회하며 보내셨다.

28 텔레비전에서 야구 경기를 볼 때, 그녀는 종종 "난 시카고에 갔어야 해.

29 너도 알겠지만, 모든 꿈은 추구 할 가치가 있단다. 비록 일부만 이루게 되더라도 말이야.

30 절대 기회를 놓치지 마라."라고 말씀하신다.

● 우리말을 참고하여 본문을 영작하시오.

1 할머니의 야구 꿈

➡ _____

2 우리 할머니 Helen은 Indiana주 South Bend 근처 작은 마을에 있는 식당의 요리사였다.

➡ _____

_____

3 할머니는 더 이상 일을 하지 않지만 여전히 맛있는 음식을 즐겨 만드시고, 나는 그 음식들을 무척 좋아한다.

➡ _____

4 음식은 우리를 연결하는 많은 것 가운데 하나이다.

➡ _____

5 하지만 우리를 가장 강하게 연결하는 것은 바로 야구이다.

➡ _____

6 주말마다 할머니 댁에 가면, 할머니는 종종 과거 1940년대의 야구 경기에 관해 흥미로운 이야기를 내게 들려주신다.

➡ _____

_____

7 그녀는 야구를 무척 좋아했던 게 분명하다.

➡ _____

8 나는 이 이야기들을 몇 번이고 듣는다.

➡ _____

9 그녀는 항상 "네가 원하는 것을 이루려고 노력하렴, Sarah.

➡ _____

10 새로운 것이나 도전적인 것을 시도해 보기를 두려워하지 말거라.

➡ _____

11 실패하는 것을 부끄러워하지 마라."라고 말씀하신다.

➡ _____

12 1943년, 전미 여자 프로야구 리그가 창립되었다.

➡ _____

13 미국의 청년 중 많은 사람들이 제2차 세계대전에 참전해 있었기 때문에 이 리그가 야구 팬들을 위해 만들어졌다.

➡ _____

_____

14 Helen 할머니는 지역 심사가 바로 South Bend에서 있을 거라고 들었다.

➡ _____

15 그녀는 "야구 팀에 들어가서 고향을 위해 결승전까지 진출한다는 건 어떤 기분일까?"라며 궁금해했다.

➡ _____

_____

16 그녀는 Helen Baker라는 이름이 포함된 큰 현수막이 야구장에 걸려 있는 것을 상상했다.

➡ _____

_____

17 심사 당일 모든 규칙이 정장을 입은 나이 든 남자에 의해 설명되었는데, 그는 무척 진지하고 불친절하게 들렸다.

➡ _____

18 뜨거운 태양 아래 정장을 입고 있는 것이 그를 짜증나게 만들었을지도 모른다고 그녀는 생각했다.

➡ _____

19 그날, Helen 할머니는 다른 젊은 여성들과 함께 몇 시간 동안 야구를 했다.

➡ _____

20 그녀는 자신의 야구 꿈을 좇아가게 되어 신이 났다!

➡ _____

21 일주일쯤 지나, Helen 할머니는 우편함에서 편지 한 통을 발견했다.

➡ _____

22 그것은 시카고에 있는 여자 야구 리그에서 일하는 사람들이 보낸 것이었다.

➡ _____

23 그 편지에는 그녀가 시카고에서 열리는 리그의 본심사에 초청되었다고 적혀 있었다!

➡ _____

24 하지만 하루하루 갈수록, Helen 할머니는 심사에 떨어질까봐 걱정되었다.

➡ _____

25 그녀는 또한 시카고까지 혼자 여행하는 것이 걱정되었는데, 시카고는 집에서 멀리 떨어진 곳이었다.

➡ _____

26 본심사가 있는 날이 되었을 때, 그녀는 너무 두려워서 갈 수 없었다.

➡ _____

27 할머니는 남은 인생을 자신의 결정을 후회하며 보내셨다.

➡ _____

28 텔레비전에서 야구 경기를 볼 때, 그녀는 종종 "난 시카고에 갔어야 해.

➡ _____

29 너도 알겠지만, 모든 꿈은 추구할 가치가 있단다, 비록 일부만 이루게 되더라도 말이야.

➡ _____

30 절대 기회를 놓치지 마라."라고 말씀하신다.

➡ _____

[01~03] 다음 글을 읽고 물음에 답하시오.

My grandmother Helen (A)[used to / would] be a cook in a restaurant in a small town near South Bend, Indiana. She does not work anymore, but she still enjoys making delicious food, which I love so much. Food is one of the many things that connect us. (B)[That / What] connects us most strongly, however, is baseball.

When I visit her on weekends, my grandmother often tells me exciting stories about playing baseball back in the 1940s. She (C)[must / should] have loved the sport very much. I listen to these stories over and over. She always says, "Go after what you want, Sarah. ⓐDon't be afraid of trying something new or challenging. Don't be ashamed of failing."

서답형

01 위 글의 괄호 (A)~(C)에서 어법상 알맞은 낱말을 골라 쓰시오.

(A) _____ (B) _____ (C) _____

02 위 글의 밑줄 친 ⓐ에서 알 수 있는 Sarah의 할머니의 성격으로 가장 알맞은 것을 고르시오.

① stubborn ② indecisive
③ adventurous ④ conservative
⑤ timid

03 According to the passage, which is NOT true?

① Though Sarah's grandmother isn't a cook now, she was a cook in a restaurant.
② Sarah's grandmother still enjoys making delicious food.
③ Sarah and her grandmother have a common interest in baseball.
④ Sarah often tells her grandmother exciting stories about baseball.
⑤ It is certain that Sarah's grandmother loved baseball very much.

[04~06] 다음 글을 읽고 물음에 답하시오.

ⓐAs the days went by, however, Helen became worried that she might fail. She also became worried about traveling alone to Chicago, which was far away from home. When the day of the main tryouts came, she was too afraid to go.

My grandmother has spent the rest of her life regretting her decision. When she watches a baseball game on TV, she often says, "I should have gone to Chicago. You know, ⓑall your dreams are worth chasing, even if you catch only a few of them. Never miss an opportunity."

04 위 글의 밑줄 친 ⓐAs와 같은 의미로 쓰인 것을 고르시오.

① Leave the papers as they are.
② He is famous as a statesman.
③ As we go up, the air grows colder.
④ This is twice as large as that.
⑤ As I was tired, I soon fell asleep.

서답형

05 밑줄 친 ⓑ를 다음과 같이 바꿔 쓸 때 빈칸에 들어갈 알맞은 말을 쓰시오.

> it is worth while to chase _____
> _____ _____

06 위 글에 어울리는 속담으로 알맞은 것을 두 개 고르시오.

① Haste makes waste.

② Make hay while the sun shines.

③ It never rains but it pours.

④ Look before you leap.

⑤ Strike the iron while it is hot.

[07~09] 다음 글을 읽고 물음에 답하시오.

　In 1943, the All-American Girls Professional Baseball League was founded. This league was created for baseball fans because many of America's young men were fighting in ⓐWorld War Ⅱ.

　Helen was told that there would be local tryouts right in South Bend. She wondered, "What would it be like to be on a baseball team and ⓑto make it to the finals for my hometown?" She imagined a large banner hanging at the baseball field which included the name Helen Baker.

서답형

07 위 글의 밑줄 친 ⓐWorld War II를 영어로 읽는 법을 쓰시오.

➡ _____

08 아래 〈보기〉에서 위 글의 밑줄 친 ⓑto make와 to부정사의 용법이 다른 것의 개수를 고르시오.

> ┤ 보기 ├
> ① She went to the library to borrow books.
> ② It's important for me to practice English.
> ③ She has a special way to cook rice.
> ④ I am so happy to hear that.
> ⑤ It is about time to play basketball.

① 1개　② 2개　③ 3개　④ 4개　⑤ 5개

서답형

09 Why was the All-American Girls Professional Baseball League founded? Fill in the blanks (A) and (B) with suitable words.

> Many of America's (A)_____
> _____ were fighting in World War Ⅱ, so the All-American Girls Professional Baseball League was founded in 1943 for (B)_____ _____.

[10~12] 다음 글을 읽고 물음에 답하시오.

　About a week later, Helen found a letter in the mailbox. It was from people who worked for the girls' baseball league in Chicago. It read that she had been invited to the league's main tryouts in Chicago!

　As the days went by, ___ⓐ___, Helen became worried that she might fail. She also became worried about traveling alone to Chicago, which was far away from home. When the day of the main tryouts came, she was too afraid to go.

10 위 글의 빈칸 ⓐ에 들어갈 알맞은 말을 고르시오.

① for example   ② that is
③ in addition   ④ however
⑤ thus

11 위 글의 제목으로 가장 알맞은 것은?

① The Girls' Baseball League Held in Chicago
② Wow! I Was Invited to the League's Main Tryouts!
③ An Unfulfilled Dream out of Fear
④ What If I Fail?
⑤ Travel Alone to Chicago? No Way!

12 According to the passage, which is NOT true?

① Helen found a letter in the mailbox about a week later.
② People who worked for the girls' baseball league in Chicago sent an invitation letter to Helen.
③ Helen became worried that she might fail as the days went by.
④ Though Chicago wasn't far away from home, Helen became worried about traveling alone there.
⑤ When the day of the main tryouts came, Helen was so afraid that she couldn't go.

[13~14] 다음 글을 읽고 물음에 답하시오.

On the day of the tryouts, all the rules were explained by an old man ____ⓐ____ a suit, who sounded very serious and unkind. She thought that (A)뜨거운 태양 아래 정장을 입고 있는 것이 그를 짜증나게 만들었을지도 모른다. On that day, Helen played baseball for hours

with many other young women. She was excited to go ____ⓑ____ her baseball dreams!

13 위 글의 빈칸 ⓐ와 ⓑ에 들어갈 전치사가 바르게 짝지어진 것은?

    ⓐ   ⓑ   ⓐ   ⓑ   ⓐ   ⓑ
① for – on   ② in – after   ③ in – on
④ for – to   ⑤ on – after

서답형

14 밑줄 친 (A)의 우리말에 맞게 주어진 어휘를 이용하여 12 단어로 영작하시오.

> wearing, in, might, made, impatient

➡ _____

_____

15 주어진 글 다음에 이어질 글의 순서로 가장 적절한 것은?

My grandmother Helen used to be a cook in a restaurant in a small town near South Bend, Indiana. She does not work anymore, but she still enjoys making delicious food, which I love so much.

(A) I listen to these stories over and over. She always says, "Go after what you want, Sarah. Don't be afraid of trying something new or challenging. Don't be ashamed of failing."
(B) Food is one of the many things that connect us. What connects us most strongly, however, is baseball.
(C) When I visit her on weekends, my grandmother often tells me exciting stories about playing baseball back in the 1940s. She must have loved the sport very much.

① (A) – (C) – (B) ② (B) – (A) – (C)

③ (B) – (C) – (A) ④ (C) – (A) – (B)

⑤ (C) – (B) – (A)

[16~18] 다음 글을 읽고 물음에 답하시오.

My grandmother Helen ⓐ<u>used to</u> be a cook in a restaurant in a small town near South Bend, Indiana. She does not work anymore, but she still enjoys making delicious food, which I love so much. Food is one of the many things that connect us. ⓑ<u>What connect us most strongly, however, is baseball.</u>

When I visit her on weekends, my grandmother often tells me exciting stories about playing baseball back in the 1940s. She must have loved the sport very much. I listen to these stories over and over. She always says, "Go after what you want, Sarah. Don't be afraid of trying something new or challenging. Don't be ashamed of failing."

16 위 글의 밑줄 친 ⓐused to와 문법적 쓰임이 <u>다른</u> 것을 고르시오.

① Love <u>used to</u> be something more romantic than it is now.

② He isn't what he <u>used to</u> be three years ago.

③ There <u>used to</u> be many tall trees in front of the school buildings.

④ She <u>used to</u> live in Korea.

⑤ He <u>used to</u> call on me every Sunday.

서답형

17 위 글의 밑줄 친 ⓑ에서 어법상 틀린 부분을 찾아 고치시오.

_____ ➡ _____

18 위 글의 주제로 알맞은 것을 고르시오.

① Sarah's grandmother's love for cooking

② Sarah's grandmother's special dish

③ Sarah's grandmother's love for baseball

④ the exciting stories about playing baseball back in the 1940s

⑤ Sarah's grandmother's nursery story

[19~20] 다음 글을 읽고 물음에 답하시오.

On the day of the tryouts, all the rules were explained by an old man in a suit, who sounded very (A)[serious and unkind / seriously and unkindly]. She thought that wearing a suit in the hot sun might have made him (B)[impatient / impatiently]. On that day, Helen played baseball for hours with many other young women. She was excited to go after her baseball dreams!

About a week later, Helen found a letter in the mailbox. It was from people who worked for the girls' baseball league in Chicago. It (C)[read / was read] that she had been invited to the league's main tryouts in Chicago!

서답형

19 위 글의 괄호 (A)~(C)에서 문맥이나 어법상 알맞은 낱말을 골라 쓰시오.

(A) _____

(B) _____ (C) _____

20 위 글을 읽고 알 수 <u>없는</u> 것은?

① Who explained all the rules?

② With whom did Helen play baseball on the day of the tryouts?

③ Who sent the invitation letter to Helen?

④ Where would the league's main tryouts be held?

⑤ Did Helen participate in the league's main tryouts?

[01~03] 다음 글을 읽고 물음에 답하시오.

My grandmother Helen used to be a cook in a restaurant in a small town near South Bend, Indiana. ⓐShe does not work anymore, but she still enjoys making delicious food, that I love so much. Food is one of the many things that connect us. What connects us most strongly, however, is baseball.

When I visit her on weekends, my grandmother often tells me exciting stories about playing baseball back in the 1940s. ⓑ She must have loved the sport very much. I listen to these stories over and over. She always says, "Go after what you want, Sarah. Don't be afraid of trying something new or challenging. Don't be ashamed of failing."

01 위 글의 밑줄 친 ⓐ에서 어법상 틀린 부분을 찾아 고치시오.

_____ ➡ _____

02 위 글의 밑줄 친 ⓑ를 다음과 같이 바꿔 쓸 때 빈칸에 들어갈 알맞은 한 단어를 쓰시오.

It is certain that she _____ the sport very much.

03 다음 빈칸 (A)와 (B)에 알맞은 단어를 넣어 Sarah의 할머니에 대한 소개를 완성하시오.

Sarah's grandmother (A)_____ a cook in a restaurant, but now she isn't a cook anymore. Nevertheless, she still enjoys making delicious food, and (B)_____ loves it so much.

*nevertheless: 그렇기는 하지만, 그럼에도 불구하고

[04~07] 다음 글을 읽고 물음에 답하시오.

As the days went by, however, Helen became worried that she might fail. She also became worried about traveling alone to Chicago, which was far away from home. When the day of the main tryouts came, (A)she was too afraid to go.

My grandmother has spent the rest of her life ___ⓐ___ her decision. When she watches a baseball game on TV, she often says, "(B)I must have gone to Chicago. You know, all your dreams are worth chasing, even if you catch only a few of them. Never miss an opportunity."

04 위 글의 빈칸 ⓐ에 regret를 알맞은 형태로 쓰시오.

➡ _____

05 위 글의 밑줄 친 (A)를 다음과 같이 바꿔 쓸 때 빈칸에 들어갈 알맞은 말을 쓰시오.

she was _____ afraid _____ she _____ go

06 위 글의 밑줄 친 (B)에서 흐름상 어색한 부분을 찾아 고치시오.

_____ ➡ _____

07 Helen이 시카고에 가지 못한 이유 두 가지를 우리말로 쓰시오.

(1) _____
(2) _____
_____

[08~10] 다음 글을 읽고 물음에 답하시오.

My grandmother Helen used to be a cook in a restaurant in a small town near South Bend, Indiana. She does not work anymore, but she still enjoys making delicious food, which I love so much. Food is one of the many things that connect us. ⓐ우리를 가장 강하게 연결하는 것은, however, is baseball.

When I visit her ⓑon weekends, my grandmother often tells me exciting stories about playing baseball back in the 1940s. She must have loved the sport very much. I listen to ⓒthese stories over and over. She always says, "Go after what you want, Sarah. Don't be afraid of trying something new or challenging. Don't be ashamed of failing."

08 위 글의 밑줄 친 ⓐ의 우리말에 맞게 관계대명사를 사용하여 5 단어로 영작하시오.

➡ _____

09 위 글의 밑줄 친 ⓑon weekends와 바꿔 쓸 수 있는 말을 쓰시오.

➡ _____

10 위 글의 밑줄 친 ⓒthese stories가 가리키는 것을 본문에서 찾아 쓰시오.

➡ _____
_____

[11~13] 다음 글을 읽고 물음에 답하시오.

On the day of the tryouts, all the rules were explained by an old man in a suit, ⓐ who sounded very serious and unkind. She thought that wearing a suit in the hot sun might have made him impatient. On that day, Helen played baseball for hours with many other young women. She was excited to go after her baseball dreams!

About a week later, Helen found a letter in the mailbox. It was from people who worked for the girls' baseball league in Chicago. It read that she had been invited to the league's main tryouts in Chicago!

11 위 글의 밑줄 친 ⓐwho를 접속사를 포함한 두 단어로 바꿔 쓰시오.

➡ _____

12 What was written on the invitation letter? Fill in the blanks (A) and (B) with suitable words.

The fact that she _____ _____ _____ to the league's main tryouts in Chicago was written on the invitation letter.

13 본문의 내용과 일치하도록 다음 빈칸 (A)와 (B)에 알맞은 단어를 쓰시오.

Helen thought that (A)_____ _____ _____ in the hot sun might have caused an old man who explained all the rules to be impatient, and as a result, he sounded very (B)_____ _____ _____.

After You Read Graphic Organizer

Cause

The Second World War broke out.
발발했다

She loved baseball so much.

She was not sure of her success. Also, she was afraid of traveling alone.
~에 확신을 가졌다   동명사   = by herself

Effect

In 1943, the All-American Girls Professional Baseball League was founded.
found–founded–founded

She joined the local tryouts in South Bend.
= participated in

She didn't go to the main tryouts.

구문해설 • break out: 발발하다 • be sure of: ~에 확신을 가지다, ~을 믿다
• be afraid of: ~을 무서워하다 • league: 리그, 연맹 • found: 설립하다
• tryout: 심사, 테스트

My Writing Portfolio

JANE GOODALL, MOTHER OF CHIMPANZEES

Jane Goodall was born in London, England, in 1934. Her interest in
borne(✕)
chimpanzees began when she first read about Tarzan. She has been studying
현재완료진행형
wild chimpanzees in Africa since her twenties. She has also been working for
since+시간 명사, for+기간 명사   현재완료진행형
the protection of chimpanzees. In 1995, she received the Hubbard Medal for
protecting wild animals. Thanks to her lifelong study, we have come to know a
~하게 되다
lot about chimpanzees. Jane Goodall is one of the greatest scientists in history.
one of+복수 명사: ~ 중의 하나

구문해설 • protection: 보호 • wild animal: 야생 동물 • thanks to: ~ 덕분에 • lifelong: 일생[평생]의

Words in Action

The Cheetahs are winning the game, and their fans are singing a cheerful

song. If Jason stays calm and catches the ball, the game ends. Oh my! He
조건의 부사절을 이끄는 접속사
misses the ball! The Ducks make two runs, and the game continues. Jason

looks ashamed and nervous. The Ducks fans are going wild, while the
감정동사의 과거분사형(감정을 느낄 때 사용)   반면에(대조를 나타내는 접속사)
Cheetahs fans look scared and worried.
감정동사의 과거분사형(감정을 느낄 때 사용)

구문해설 • cheerful: 발랄한, 쾌활한, 즐거운 • stay calm: 침착함을 유지하다
• make two runs: 2루로 진루하다 • continue: 계속하다 • ashamed: 부끄러운, 창피한
• nervous: 불안해[초조해] 하는 • go wild: 미친 듯 열중하다
• scared: 무서워하는, 겁먹은 • worried: 걱정[우려]하는, 걱정스러워 하는

해석

원인
제2차 세계대전이 발발했다.
그녀는 야구를 무척 좋아했다.
그녀는 자신의 성공을 확신하지 못했다. 또한 그녀는 혼자 여행하는 것을 두려워했다.

결과
1943년, 전미 여자 프로야구 리그가 창립되었다.
그녀는 South Bend의 지역 심사에 참가했다.
그녀는 본심사에 가지 않았다.

Jane Goodall, 침팬지의 어머니
Jane Goodall은 1934년 영국 런던에서 태어났다. 침팬지에 대한 관심은 그녀가 타잔에 관해 읽었을 때 시작되었다. 그녀는 20대 때부터 아프리카에서 야생 침팬지를 연구해 오고 있다. 그녀는 침팬지 보호를 위해서도 노력해 오고 있다. 1995년에 그녀는 야생 동물 보호에 대한 공로를 인정받아 허버드상을 받았다. 일생을 바친 그녀의 연구 덕분에, 우리는 침팬지에 관해 많이 알게 되었다. Jane Goodall은 역사상 가장 위대한 과학자 중 한 명이다.

Cheetahs가 경기를 이기고 있고, 팬들이 신나는 노래를 부르고 있습니다. Jason이 침착함을 유지해서 공을 잡으면 경기가 끝납니다. 오, 이럴수가! 그가 공을 놓칩니다! Ducks는 2루로 진루하고, 경기는 계속됩니다. Jason은 창피하고 긴장한 것처럼 보입니다. Ducks 팬들은 열광하고 있는 반면, Cheetahs 팬들은 두렵고 걱정스러운 것처럼 보입니다.

---

01 다음 짝지어진 단어의 관계가 같도록 빈칸에 알맞은 말을 쓰시오.

> offer : proposal = determination : _____

02 다음 중 밑줄 친 부분의 뜻풀이가 바르지 <u>않은</u> 것은?

① As time <u>went by</u>, he got more and more wrinkles on his face. (지나갔다, 흘렀다)
② He spent the <u>rest</u> of his money on dinner. (나머지)
③ His speech is <u>worth</u> listening to over and over again. (~할 가치가 있는)
④ My sister was very nervous all night before the <u>tryouts</u>. (노력)
⑤ <u>Even if</u> you don't like it, you must do it. (비록 ~하더라도)

03 다음 주어진 문장의 밑줄 친 <u>apply</u>와 같은 의미로 쓰인 것은?

> You can <u>apply</u> for citizenship after five years' residency.

① <u>Apply</u> the paint with a fine brush.
② The rules don't <u>apply</u> here.
③ I should like to <u>apply</u> for the position of Sales Director.
④ He had to <u>apply</u> some force to open the door.
⑤ This rule doesn't <u>apply</u> to your case.

04 다음 우리말을 주어진 어구를 이용하여 영작하시오.

(1) 왜 이 선생님은 항상 야근을 하세요?
(come, Mr. Lee, work overtime)
➡ _____

(2) 네 꿈을 이루고 싶다면, 너는 그것을 추구해야만 한다. (accomplish, should, go, it)
➡ _____
_____

(3) 그 조리법은 달걀과 우유를 포함하나요?
(recipe, eggs, include)
➡ _____

05 다음 주어진 문장의 밑줄 친 rest와 같은 의미로 쓰인 것은?

> He spent the <u>rest</u> of his life in France.

① Jack divided up the <u>rest</u> of the cash.
② The doctor told me to <u>rest</u>.
③ I had a good night's <u>rest</u>.
④ <u>Rest</u> your head on my shoulder.
⑤ I don't want to <u>rest</u> on my past glory.

06 다음 영영풀이에 해당하는 단어로 알맞은 것은?

> to feel sorry about something that you did in the past

① practice   ② achieve
③ improve   ④ connect
⑤ regret

Conversation

[07~10] 다음 대화를 읽고 물음에 답하시오.

M: Nice to meet you, Sora. Did you do well on the drawing exam?

G: I'm not sure, but I did my best.

M: Okay. (①) What made you apply for Mana Animation High School?

G: Well, I've really loved drawing cartoons since I was a little child. (②)

M: (③) So, you want to be a cartoon artist?

G: (A)That's not quite right. I want to be a game designer. (④)

M: I see. (⑤) What do you think is the most important skill a game designer needs?

G: I'd say imagination. A good designer should create a completely new world in a game.

M: Sounds good.

07 위 대화의 (①)~(⑤) 중에서 주어진 문장이 들어가기에 가장 적절한 곳은?

> Let's start the interview.

① ② ③ ④ ⑤

08 위 대화의 밑줄 친 (A)와 의도가 같도록 2 단어로 쓰시오. (단어 wrong은 사용하지 말 것.)

➡ _____

09 위 대화의 내용과 일치하지 <u>않는</u> 것은?

① 남자는 소라에게 소묘 시험을 잘 봤는지 묻는다.
② 소라는 최선을 다했다고 답한다.

③ 소라는 어렸을 때부터 만화 그리는 것을 정말 좋아해서 마나 애니메이션 고등학교에 지원했다.
④ 소라는 만화가가 되고 싶다.
⑤ 소라는 게임 디자이너에게 필요한 가장 중요한 기량은 상상력이라고 생각한다.

10 Why does Sora think imagination is the most important skill a game designer needs? Answer in English beginning with "Because".

➡ _____
_____

[11~13] 다음 대화를 읽고 물음에 답하시오.

G: My computer has viruses.

B: (A)어쩌다가 그랬니?

G: I opened an e-mail from a stranger.
_____ (a) _____ (should, that)

B: (B)내가 너라면, 지금 바로 컴퓨터 서비스 센터에서 도움을 받겠어. (a computer service center, help, get, right, from)

11 빈칸 (a)에 알맞은 말을 주어진 단어를 이용해서 5 단어로 쓰시오.

➡ _____

12 위 대화의 밑줄 친 (A)의 우리말을 두 단어로 영작하시오.

➡ _____

13 위 대화의 밑줄 친 (B)의 우리말을 주어진 어휘를 이용하여 14 단어로 영작하시오.

➡ _____
_____

14 다음 중 짝지어진 대화가 <u>어색한</u> 것을 고르시오.

① A: The capital of Australia is Sydney, right?

B: I'm afraid you're wrong. The capital of Australia is Canberra.

② A: What's the matter?

B: My nose is getting longer. I should have told lies.

③ A: I should have sent her a thank-you letter.

B: I think texting might have been better.

④ A: Tom, I hear you're from Pittsburg.

B: That's not quite right. I'm from Gettysburg.

⑤ A: Tomatoes were first grown in Europe, weren't they?

B: I'm afraid you're mistaken. They were first grown in South America.

Grammar

15 다음 빈칸에 들어갈 말로 알맞은 것은?

> Tom showed me a picture, _____ he took yesterday.

① where   ② who   ③ what
④ that   ⑤ which

16 다음 중 어법상 <u>어색한</u> 문장을 <u>모두</u> 고르시오.

① You should have came to the meeting on time.

② She must have loved flowers.

③ He may be in Paris when Irene went to Finland.

④ I should have read more books because I want to be a writer.

⑤ She thought that wearing a suit in the hot sun might have made him impatient.

17 다음 그림을 참고하여 빈칸에 알맞게 쓰시오.

> This morning, I met Audrey, _____
> _____ I ran to school not to be late.

18 다음 두 문장의 의미가 비슷하도록 할 때, 빈칸에 알맞은 말을 쓰시오.

(1) I'm sorry you didn't go to the movies with her yesterday.

➡ You _____ to the movies with her yesterday.

(2) I'm sure you didn't go to the movies with her yesterday.

➡ You _____ to the movies with her yesterday.

(3) I'm sure you went to the movies with her yesterday.

➡ You _____ to the movies with her yesterday.

(4) It's a pity that you went to the movies with her yesterday.

➡ You _____ to the movies with her yesterday.

(5) It is probable that you went to the movies with her yesterday.

➡ You _____ to the movies with her yesterday.

19 다음 문장을 의미에 맞게 바르게 바꿔 쓴 문장을 고르시오.

> Maryanne, who was young, had to work every day.

① Maryanne, for she was young, had to work every day.
② Maryanne, though she was young, had to work every day.
③ Maryanne, and she was young, had to work every day.
④ Maryanne, so she was young, had to work every day.
⑤ Maryanne, unless she was young, had to work every day.

20 다음 빈칸에 알맞은 것은?

> He had a beautiful wife, _____ he loved greatly.

① that   ② what   ③ which
④ whom   ⑤ whose

21 다음 ⓐ~ⓖ 중 어법상 옳은 것을 모두 고르시오.

> ⓐ You may have left it in the classroom.
> ⓑ Minsu must have eat it. He was near the table a few minutes ago.
> ⓒ Thank you for helping me. I might have gotten lost without you.
> ⓓ My fish in the fish tank were dead. I should have forgotten to feed them.
> ⓔ Nick lost an umbrella, which he bought yesterday.
> ⓕ Dorothy Kamenshek, that was called "Dottie," was only 17 when she first played in the All-American Girls Professional Baseball League.

➡ _____

Reading

[22~24] 다음 글을 읽고 물음에 답하시오.

My grandmother Helen used to be a cook in a restaurant in a small town near South Bend, Indiana. (①) She does not work anymore, but she still enjoys making delicious food, which I love so much. (②) Food is one of the many things that connect us. (③)

When I visit her on weekends, my grandmother often tells me exciting stories about playing baseball back in the 1940s. (④) She must have loved the sport very much. (⑤) I listen to these stories over and over. She always says, "Go after what you want, Sarah. ⓐ새로운 것이나 도전적인 것을 시도해 보기를 두려워하지 말거라. Don't be ashamed of failing."

22 위 글의 흐름으로 보아, 주어진 문장이 들어가기에 가장 적절한 곳은?

> What connects us most strongly, however, is baseball.

①   ②   ③   ④   ⑤

23 위 글의 제목으로 알맞은 것을 고르시오.

① My Grandma, the Greatest Cook Ever
② Grandma Still Enjoys Making Delicious Food!
③ Baseball, What Connects Us Most Strongly
④ Playing Baseball Back in the 1940s
⑤ How to Go after What You Want

24 위 글의 밑줄 친 ⓐ의 우리말에 맞게 주어진 어휘를 알맞게 배열하시오.

> trying / don't / be / new / afraid / challenging / of / or / something

➡ _____

_____

[25~26] 다음 글을 읽고 물음에 답하시오.

In 1943, the All-American Girls Professional Baseball League was (A)[found / founded]. This league was created for baseball fans because many of America's young men were fighting in World War Ⅱ.

Helen was told that there would be local tryouts right in South Bend. She (B)[wandered / wondered], "(C)[How / What] would it be like to be on a baseball team and to make it to the finals for my hometown?" She imagined a large banner hanging at the baseball field which included the name Helen Baker.

25 위 글의 괄호 (A)~(C)에서 문맥이나 어법상 알맞은 낱말을 골라 쓰시오.

(A) _____ (B) _____ (C) _____

26 According to the passage, which is NOT true?

① The All-American Girls Professional Baseball League was created for baseball fans.

② In 1943, many of America's young men were fighting in World War Ⅱ.

③ Someone told Helen that there would be local tryouts right in South Bend.

④ Helen was on a baseball team and made it to the finals for her hometown.

⑤ Helen imagined a large banner hanging at the baseball field which included her name.

[27~28] 다음 글을 읽고 물음에 답하시오.

On the day of the tryouts, all the rules were explained by an old man in a suit, who sounded very serious and unkind. She thought that ⓐwearing a suit in the hot sun might have made him impatient. On that day, Helen played baseball for hours with many other young women. She was excited to go after her baseball dreams!

About a week later, Helen found a letter in the mailbox. ⓑIt was from people who worked for the girls' baseball league in Chicago. It read that she had been invited to the league's main tryouts in Chicago!

27 위 글의 밑줄 친 ⓐwearing과 문법적 쓰임이 같은 것을 모두 고르시오.

① He was thinking about wearing a suit.

② Do you know the man wearing a suit?

③ He is wearing a suit.

④ I saw him wearing a suit.

⑤ He didn't mind wearing a suit in the hot sun.

28 위 글의 밑줄 친 ⓑIt이 가리키는 것을 본문에서 찾아 쓰시오.

➡ _____

01 다음 영영풀이가 가리키는 것을 고르시오.

출제율90%

> to have something as part of a group or total

① improve　　② include　　③ create
④ chase　　　⑤ found

02 다음 〈보기〉에서 알맞은 단어를 골라 문장을 완성하시오.

출제율95%

보기
> gloomy regretful curious jealous
> relieved

(1) I am _____ about your opinion on the new employee.
(2) If you don't study hard now, you will be _____ later.
(3) They are very _____ of my good reputation.
(4) You'll be _____ to know your jobs are safe.
(5) Cloudy days like this make me feel _____.

[03~05] 다음 대화를 읽고 물음에 답하시오.

W: Nice to meet you, Seongho.
B: Nice to meet you, (A)[either / too].
W: Are you nervous?
B: A bit, but I'm fine.
W: Okay, let's start the interview. (a)왜 우리 학교에 지원했나요?
B: I like the curriculum of this school (B)[because / because of] it has various subjects. I'm certain (C)[that / if] (b)they'll help me in many ways.
W: I see. Good luck to you.
B: Thank you.

03 위 대화의 (A)~(C)에 들어갈 말로 바르게 짝지어진 것은?

출제율100%

	(A)	(B)	(C)
①	either	because	if
②	either	because of	if
③	too	because	that
④	too	because of	that
⑤	too	because	if

04 위 대화의 밑줄 친 (a)의 우리말을 make를 이용하여 영작하시오.

출제율90%

➡ _____

05 위 대화의 밑줄 친 (b)they가 가리키는 것을 찾아 쓰시오.

출제율95%

➡ _____

[06~07] 다음 대화를 읽고 물음에 답하시오.

B: Hi, Sora. What are you doing?
G: I'm drawing cartoons. I'm preparing for the exam for Mana Animation High School.
B: Oh, do you? When is the exam?
G: On Friday, so I only have two days left.
B: How's it going?
G: It's not easy to draw what I want to express. I should have practiced more.
B: Don't worry! You can make it!
G: Thanks.

06 위 대화에서 어법상 어색한 것을 하나 찾아 바르게 고치시오.

출제율95%

_____ ➡ _____

위 대화에 나타난 소라의 심경으로 적절한 것을 고르시오.

① delighted ② nervous ③ peaceful
④ regretful ⑤ relieved

[08~09] 다음 대화를 읽고 물음에 답하시오.

M: Nice to meet you, Sora. Did you do well on the drawing exam?

G: I'm not sure, but I did my best.

M: Okay. Let's start the interview. What made you apply for Mana Animation High School?

G: Well, I've really loved drawing cartoons since I was a little child.

M: So, you want to be a cartoon artist?

G: (A)꼭 그렇지는 않습니다. I want to be a game designer.

M: I see. What do you think is the most important skill a game designer needs?

G: I'd say imagination. A good designer should create a completely new world in a game.

M: Sounds good.

08 위 대화를 읽고 답할 수 없는 질문을 고르시오.

① Did Sora do her best on the drawing exam?
② Why did Sora apply for Mana Animation High School?
③ Does Sora want to be a cartoon artist?
④ Since when has Sora wanted to be a game designer?
⑤ Why does Sora think imagination is the most important skill a game designer needs?

09 위 대화의 밑줄 친 (A)의 우리말을 right를 이용하여 4 단어로 영작하시오.

➡ _____

10 다음 중 짝지어진 대화가 어색한 것을 고르시오.

① A: Pad thai is a famous Vietnamese dish.
   B: I'm afraid you're mistaken. Pad thai is a famous Thai dish.
② A: A volcano called Paricutin appeared in three days.
   B: I'm afraid you're wrong. A volcano called Paricutin appeared overnight.
③ A: Are you nervous?
   B: A bit, but I'm fine.
④ A: You're late again. You're always late.
   B: I'm so sorry. I should have made you wait.
⑤ A: My house has blown away. I should have built it with stronger material.
   B: Don't worry. I'll help you to build your house again.

11 다음 빈칸에 들어갈 수 있는 말이 다른 하나는?

① Einstein, _____ was born in Germany, is famous for the theory of relativity.
② I visited my friend in Mokpo, _____ welcomed me.
③ Our homeroom teacher is Mr. Hong, _____ teaches us history.
④ Uncle Ben went on a trip to Africa, _____ was his lifelong dream.
⑤ The writer, _____ was taking a walk in the park, sat down on the bench.

12 다음 중 어법상 적절한 문장을 <u>모두</u> 고르시오.

① I should have practice more to improve my speaking skills.

② I think sending text messages might have be better.

③ You shouldn't have made the same mistake again.

④ It must rain last night.

⑤ Mike may have been sick last weekend.

13 다음 두 문장이 같은 뜻이 되도록 빈칸에 알맞은 말을 두 단어로 쓰시오.

This painting is *Sunflowers*, which was painted by Vincent van Gogh.

= This painting is *Sunflowers*, _____ _____ was painted by Vincent van Gogh.

14 'should'와 괄호 안의 단어를 이용하여 다음 상황에 알맞은 충고의 말을 완성하시오.

(1) I spent all the money on snacks. I need some money to buy the book.

➡ You _____ money more carefully. (spend)

(2) I wasted my time playing computer games. I need more time to finish the project.

➡ You _____ your time. (waste)

(3) It's very dark. I need a light to find the way.

➡ You _____ a lantern. (bring)

15 다음 빈칸에 들어갈 알맞은 말을 순서대로 묶은 것은?

• It's very hot here. You _____ have worn a T-shirt and shorts.

• My favorite city is Sydney, _____ is located on the east coast of Australia.

① should – who
② should – which
③ must – who
④ must – which
⑤ may – that

[16~18] 다음 글을 읽고 물음에 답하시오.

My grandmother Helen used to be a cook in a restaurant in a small town near South Bend, Indiana. She does not work anymore, but she still enjoys ____ⓐ____ delicious food, which I love so much. Food is one of the many things that connect us. ⓑWhat connects us most strongly, however, is baseball.

When I visit her on weekends, my grandmother often tells me exciting stories about playing baseball back in the 1940s. She must have loved the sport very much. I listen to these stories ⓒover and over. She always says, "Go after what you want, Sarah. Don't be afraid of trying something new or challenging. Don't be ashamed of failing."

16 위 글의 빈칸 ⓐ에 make를 알맞은 형태로 쓰시오.

➡ _____

17 위 글의 밑줄 친 ⓑWhat과 문법적 쓰임이 같은 것을 고르시오.

① What is your name?

② He always does what he believes is right.

③ What kind of music do you like?

④ What do you think this is?

⑤ What day of the week is it today?

18 위 글의 밑줄 친 ⓒover and over와 바꿔 쓸 수 없는 말을 고르시오.

① time and again ② repeatedly

③ step by step ④ many times

⑤ time after time

[19~21] 다음 글을 읽고 물음에 답하시오.

> On the day of the tryouts, all the rules were explained by an old man in a suit, who sounded very serious and unkind. (①) She thought that wearing a suit in the hot sun might have made him impatient. (②) On that day, Helen played baseball for hours with many other young women. (③) She was excited to go after her baseball dreams!
>
> (④) It was from people who worked for the girls' baseball league in Chicago. (⑤) It read that she had been invited to the league's main tryouts in Chicago!

19 위 글의 흐름으로 보아, 주어진 문장이 들어가기에 가장 적절한 곳은?

> About a week later, Helen found a letter in the mailbox.

① ② ③ ④ ⑤

20 위 글의 주제로 알맞은 것을 고르시오.

① the hot weather on the day of the tryouts

② the important of wearing a suit

③ to play baseball with other women

④ Helen's excitement from going after her baseball dreams

⑤ the girls' baseball league in Chicago

21 위 글에서 알 수 있는 Helen의 심경으로 가장 알맞은 것을 고르시오.

① regretful ② afraid

③ puzzled ④ disappointed

⑤ excited

[22~23] 다음 글을 읽고 물음에 답하시오.

> My grandmother has spent the rest of her life regretting her decision. When she watches a baseball game on TV, she often says, "ⓐI should have gone to Chicago. You know, all your dreams are worth chasing, even if you catch only a few of ⓑthem. Never miss an opportunity."

22 위 글의 밑줄 친 ⓐ를 다음과 같이 바꿔 쓸 때 빈칸에 들어갈 알맞은 말을 두 단어로 쓰시오.

> I am sorry that I _____ _____ to Chicago.

23 위 글의 밑줄 친 ⓑ가 가리키는 것을 본문에서 찾아 쓰시오.

➡ _____

[01~03] 다음 대화를 읽고 물음에 답하시오.

G: Hi, Jiho.

B: Hi, Amber. It's nice to see you on the bus.

G: Yeah, but I'm afraid we're going to be late.

B: Yeah. I hate to be late for the school festival.

G: Me, too. I should have set my alarm. I forgot.

B: I understand. That happens a lot to me when I'm tired, too.

G: How about you? What made you late?

B: Well, I got up early. But it took me some time to do my hair.

G: Oh, I see. We're stuck in a heavy traffic jam. We should get off and run.

B: No, you're mistaken. The traffic is starting to move again. Let's stay on.

G: Okay. I just hope we're not terribly late.

01 Where are Jiho and Amber going now? Answer with 7 words.

➡ _____

02 Why is Jiho late? Answer in English beginning with "Because".

➡ _____

_____

03 Why did Amber suggest that they get off the bus and run? Answer in English beginning with "Because".

➡ _____

_____

04 계속적 용법의 관계대명사를 사용하여 주어진 두 문장을 한 문장으로 바꾸시오.

(1) • This book is about Abraham Lincoln.
 • Abraham Lincoln was the 16th President of the U.S.

➡ _____

_____

(2) • My grandmother's house is still nice to live in.
 • My grandmother's house was built 100 years ago.

➡ _____

_____

(3) • She enjoys making delicious food.
 • She finds satisfaction from making delicious food.

➡ _____

_____

05 다음 문장에서 틀린 것을 고쳐 다시 쓰시오.

(1) Fallen leaves are on the ground. It should have been windy.

➡ _____

_____

(2) Sam looks very tired this morning. He should have stayed up late last night.

➡ _____

_____

(3) His favorite place is his house, that is next to mine.

➡ _____

_____

(4) My brother, who major was history, is a professor of the university.

➡ _____

06 다음 우리말을 주어진 어휘를 이용하여 영작하시오.

(1) 기차가 역에 도착했을지도 모른다.
(arrive, the station)

➡ _____

_____

(2) 그가 이것을 혼자 했을 리가 없다.
(do, this, by himself)

➡ _____

(3) 이 스마트폰은 내가 지난달에 샀는데, 디자인이 매우 좋다. (have a great design)

➡ _____

_____

[07~09] 다음 글을 읽고 물음에 답하시오.

My grandmother Helen used to be a cook in a restaurant in a small town near South Bend, Indiana. She does not work anymore, but she still enjoys making delicious food, ⓐwhich I love so much. Food is one of the many things that connect us. What connects us most strongly, however, is baseball.

When I visit her on weekends, my grandmother often tells me exciting stories about playing baseball back in the ⓑ1940s. She must have loved the sport very much. I listen to these stories over and over. She always says, "Go after what you want, Sarah. Don't be afraid of trying something new or challenging. Don't be ashamed of failing."

07 위 글의 밑줄 친 ⓐ를 접속사를 사용하여 바꿔 쓰시오.

➡ _____

08 위 글의 밑줄 친 ⓑ1940s를 영어로 읽는 법을 쓰시오.

➡ _____

09 본문의 내용과 일치하도록 다음 빈칸에 알맞은 단어를 쓰시오.

Sarah's grandmother always tells Sarah to go after _____ _____ _____.

[10~12] 다음 글을 읽고 물음에 답하시오.

On the day of the tryouts, (A)all the rules were explained by an old man in a suit, who sounded very serious and unkind. She thought that wearing a suit in the hot sun might have made him impatient. On that day, Helen played baseball for hours with many other young women. She was excited to go after her baseball dreams!

About a week later, Helen found a letter in the mailbox. It was from people who worked for the girls' baseball league in Chicago. It read that she ____ⓐ____ to the league's main tryouts in Chicago!

10 위 글의 빈칸 ⓐ에 invite를 알맞은 형태로 쓰시오.

➡ _____

11 위 글의 밑줄 친 (A)를 능동태로 고치시오.

➡ _____

12 본문의 내용과 일치하도록 다음 빈칸 (A)와 (B)에 알맞은 단어를 쓰시오.

Helen received an invitation (A)_____ from people who worked for the girls' baseball league in Chicago where the league's (B)_____ _____ would be held.

01 다음 내용에서 필자가 후회하고 있는 것을 찾아 우리말로 쓰시오.

> My school life was mostly fun, but there are some things that I regret. First of all, I should have read more books because I want to be a writer. Second, I shouldn't have played online games so much. Thirdly, I should have been nicer to my teachers and classmates. Lastly, I shouldn't have eaten so much fast food. In high school, I'll try my best so that there won't be anything that I'll regret.

(1) _____

(2) _____

(3) _____

(4) _____

02 '조동사+have p.p.'를 사용하여 빈칸에 본인만의 문장을 쓰시오.

(1) In the morning the road is muddy. _____

(2) Emma doesn't answer my call. _____

(3) I didn't get a good grade in the math test. _____

03 다음 내용을 바탕으로 전기문을 쓰시오.

> • What is the person's name?
>   - Jane Goodall
> • Where and when was the person born?
>   - London, England / 1934
> • What did the person do?
>   - studied wild chimpanzees in Africa, worked for the protection of chimpanzees
> • What are other facts about the person?
>   - received the Hubbard Medal

> ### JANE GOODALL, MOTHER OF CHIMPANZEES
> Jane Goodall was born (A)_____, in 1934. Her interest in chimpanzees began when she first read about Tarzan. She has been studying (B)_____ in Africa since her twenties. She has also been working for (C)_____. In 1995, she received (D)_____ for protecting wild animals. Thanks to her lifelong study, we have come to know a lot about chimpanzees. Jane Goodall is one of the greatest scientists in history.

단원별 모의고사

01 다음의 영영풀이가 가리키는 것은?

> good or important enough for something

① calm　　② worth　　③ lifelong
④ serious　　⑤ challenging

02 다음 빈칸에 알맞은 것을 고르시오.

> _____ you do not like it, you must do it.

① As　　② Despite　　③ Even if
④ If　　⑤ When

03 다음 우리말에 맞게 빈칸에 알맞은 말을 쓰시오.

(1) 약간의 상상력을 이용하면 너는 정답을 알 수 있을 것이다.
　➡ You can get the answer if you use a little _____.

(2) 나는 내 대답이 맞다고 자신한다.
　➡ I'm _____ that my answer is correct.

(3) 팬들은 그들의 팀이 또 다른 경기에서 지자 실망했다.
　➡ The fans were _____ that their team lost another game.

[04~05] 다음 대화를 읽고 물음에 답하시오.

B: Hi, Sora. What are you doing?
G: I'm drawing cartoons. I'm preparing for the exam for Mana Animation High School.
B: Oh, are you? When is the exam?
G: On Friday, so I only have two days left.
B: How's it going?
G: It's not easy to draw what I want to express. I should have practiced more.
B: Don't worry! (A)넌 해낼 수 있어! (make)
G: Thanks.

04 위 대화의 밑줄 친 (A)의 우리말을 주어진 단어를 사용하여 영작하시오.

➡ _____

05 When will Sora have the exam for Mana Animation High School?

➡ _____
_____

[06~08] 다음 대화를 읽고 물음에 답하시오.

G: Hi, Jiho.
B: Hi, Amber. It's nice to see you on the bus.
G: Yeah, but I'm afraid we're going to be late.
B: Yeah. I hate to be late for the school festival.
G: Me, too. I should have set my alarm. I forgot.
B: (①) I understand. That happens a lot to me when I'm tired, too.
G: How about you? What made you late?
B: (②) Well, I got up early. But it took me some time to do my hair.
G: (③) Oh, I see. We're stuck in a heavy traffic jam. We should get off and run.
B: (④) The traffic is starting to move again. Let's stay on.
G: (⑤) Okay. I just hope we're not terribly late.

06 위 대화의 (①)~(⑤) 중에서 주어진 문장이 들어가기에 가장 적절한 곳은?

> No, you're mistaken.

①　　②　　③　　④　　⑤

07 What did Amber forget to do last night?

➡ _____

08 Why did Amber suggest they get off the bus and run?

➡ _____

_____

09 주어진 두 문장 사이에 대화가 자연스럽게 이어지도록 순서 대로 배열하시오.

> W: Are you nervous?

> (A) Okay, let's start the interview. What made you apply for our school?
> (B) A bit, but I'm fine.
> (C) I see. Good luck to you.
> (D) I like the curriculum of this school because it has various subjects. I'm certain that they'll help me in many ways.

> B: Thank you.

➡ _____

[10~11] 다음 대화를 읽고 물음에 답하시오.

> B: What do you want to do when you grow up?
> G: I want to work with robots.
> B: Are you interested in making robots?
> G: No, (A)that's not quite right. I want to repair robots.
> B: I see. But why?
> G: Because I think it'll be a good job in the future.

10 위 대화의 밑줄 친 (A)와 바꾸어 쓰기 어색한 것은?

① That's not true.
② I don't think that's right.
③ That's wrong.
④ You're quite correct.
⑤ You're mistaken.

11 Write the reason why G wants to repair robots. Answer in English beginning with "It's because".

➡ _____

_____

12 다음 그림을 보고 우리말에 맞게 괄호 안에 주어진 단어를 활용하여 주어진 조건대로 영작하시오. (두 문장으로 쓰고 필요시 1 단어를 추가할 것.)

> Mina는 커피를 타다가 손가락을 데었는데 커피는 그녀가 가장 좋아하는 음료이다. 그녀는 더 조심했어야 했다.
> (coffee, got her finger, her favorite drink, making, ought, while, burned)

(1) 조건: 콤마와 관계대명사를 이용할 것.

➡ _____

_____

(2) 조건: 접속사 and와 조동사 should를 이용할 것.

➡ _____

_____

13 다음 중 어법상 옳은 문장을 모두 고르시오.

① He is my son, which works at the amusement park.

② I got up late. I may have set my alarm.

③ I must have left my wallet in the movie theater.

④ One of my friends, that wants to be a teacher, is Abigail.

⑤ On the day of the tryouts, all the rules were explained by an old man in a suit, who sounded very serious and unkind.

⑥ You should not have wasted your pocket money on useless things.

⑦ She also became worried about traveling alone to Chicago, who was far away from home.

14 다음 그림을 보고 우리말에 맞게 괄호 안에 주어진 단어를 활용하여 주어진 조건대로 영작하시오. (두 문장으로 쓰고 필요시 1 단어를 추가할 것.)

Uncle Ben went on a trip to Turkey. He _____ _____ _____ very happy to make his lifelong dream come true. (be)

15 다음 빈칸에 알맞은 말로 짝지어진 것을 고르시오.

- You _____ up earlier.
- You _____ too much fast food.

① should have get – should have not eaten

② should have get – should not have eaten

③ should have got – should not have ate

④ should have got – should not have eaten

⑤ should got – should have not eaten

16 다음 밑줄 친 부분과 바꿔 쓸 수 있는 것은?

Mike didn't keep his promise, and it made Kay really upset.

① which   ② that   ③ what

④ who   ⑤ where

17 다음 문장에서 어법상 어색한 것을 바르게 고쳐 다시 쓰시오.

(1) She does not work anymore, but she still enjoys making delicious food, that I love it so much.

   ➡ _____

   _____

(2) She is my friend, Nida, which I met in Germany.

   ➡ _____

   _____

(3) Gogh met Gauguin in Arles, that changed his life.

   ➡ _____

   _____

(4) The rabbit should have slept during the race to beat the turtle.

➡ _____

_____

(5) Hanju ought to have lost his umbrella in the subway. He doesn't have it now.

➡ _____

_____

19 위 글의 밑줄 친 ⓑthese stories가 가리키는 것을 본문에서 찾아 쓰시오.

➡ _____

_____

[20~21] 다음 글을 읽고 물음에 답하시오.

In 1943, the All-American Girls Professional Baseball League was founded. This league was created ___ⓐ___ baseball fans because many of America's young men were fighting in World War Ⅱ.

Helen was told that there would be local tryouts (A)right in South Bend. She wondered, "What would it be like to be ___ⓑ___ a baseball team and to make it to the finals for my hometown?" She imagined a large banner hanging at the baseball field which included the name Helen Baker.

[18~19] 다음 글을 읽고 물음에 답하시오.

My grandmother Helen used to be a cook in a restaurant in a small town near South Bend, Indiana. She does not work anymore, but she still enjoys making delicious food, which I love so much. Food is one of the many things that connect us. What connects us most strongly, ___ⓐ___, is baseball.

When I visit her on weekends, my grandmother often tells me exciting stories about playing baseball back in the 1940s. She must have loved the sport very much. I listen to ⓑthese stories over and over. She always says, "Go after what you want, Sarah. Don't be afraid of trying something new or challenging. Don't be ashamed of failing."

20 위 글의 빈칸 ⓐ와 ⓑ에 들어갈 전치사가 바르게 짝지어진 것은?

	ⓐ	ⓑ		ⓐ	ⓑ		ⓐ	ⓑ
①	by	at	②	for	to	③	for	on
④	to	at	⑤	by	on			

18 위 글의 빈칸 ⓐ에 들어갈 알맞은 말을 고르시오.

① therefore ② moreover

③ in other words ④ as a result

⑤ however

21 위 글의 밑줄 친 (A)right와 같은 의미로 쓰인 것을 고르시오.

① She gave the right answer.

② Lee was standing right behind her.

③ What gives you the right to do that?

④ Keep on the right side of the road.

⑤ I hope we're doing the right thing.

[22~23] 다음 글을 읽고 물음에 답하시오.

On the day of the tryouts, all the rules were explained by an old man in a suit, who sounded very serious and unkind. She thought that wearing a suit in the hot sun might have made him impatient. On that day, Helen played baseball for hours with many other young women. She was excited to go after her baseball dreams!

About a week later, Helen found a letter in the mailbox. It was from people who worked for the girls' baseball league in Chicago. It ⓐ read that she had been invited to the league's main tryouts in Chicago!

22 위 글의 밑줄 친 ⓐread와 같은 의미로 쓰인 것을 고르시오.

① The sign read 'No admittance'.
② He liked to read to his grandchildren.
③ She's still learning to read.
④ She read us a story.
⑤ I can't read your writing.

23 According to the passage, which is NOT true?

① An old man in a suit explained all the rules on the day of the tryouts.
② The old man sounded very serious and unkind.
③ Helen played baseball for hours with many other young women on the day of the tryouts.
④ The old man who explained all the rules on the day of the tryouts sent an invitation letter to Helen.
⑤ Helen had been invited to the league's main tryouts in Chicago.

[24~25] 다음 글을 읽고 물음에 답하시오.

As the days went by, however, Helen became worried that she might fail. (①) When the day of the main tryouts came, she was too afraid to go. (②)

My grandmother has spent the rest of her life regretting her decision. (③) When she watches a baseball game on TV, she often says, "ⓐI should have gone to Chicago. (④) You know, all your dreams are worth chasing, even if you catch only a few of them. (⑤) Never miss an opportunity."

24 위 글의 흐름으로 보아, 주어진 문장이 들어가기에 가장 적절한 곳은?

> She also became worried about traveling alone to Chicago, which was far away from home.

①   ②   ③   ④   ⑤

25 위 글의 밑줄 친 ⓐ에서 알 수 있는 필자의 할머니 심경으로 가장 알맞은 것을 고르시오.

① confused   ② regretful
③ ashamed   ④ nervous
⑤ depressed

MEMO

Reading for Fun 4

Keep Out

교과서

Words & Expressions

Key Words

- **actually** [ǽktʃuəli] ⊕ 실제(로)는, 사실은
- **breathe** [briːð] ⊛ 숨 쉬다
- **cast** [kæst] ⊜ 석고붕대, 깁스
- **cycle** [sáikl] ⊛ 자전거를 타다
- **dirt** [dəːrt] ⊜ 흙, 먼지
- **entrance** [éntrəns] ⊜ 입구, 입장
- **gateway** [géitwei] ⊜ 입구, 관문
- **hurt** [həːrt] ⊛ 고통을 주다, 아프다
- **lesson** [lésn] ⊜ 교훈
- **manager** [mǽnidʒər] ⊜ 경영자, 관리자
- **opening** [óupəniŋ] ⊜ 열린 구멍, 창(窓), 구멍, 틈, 입구
- **particular** [pərtíkjulər] ⊚ 특별한

- **record** [rékərd] ⊜ 기록
- **relief** [rilíːf] ⊜ 안도, 안심
- **safety product** 안전 제품
- **scream** [skriːm] ⊜ 비명
- **shout** [ʃaut] ⊛ 외치다, 소리[고함]치다
- **thick** [θik] ⊚ 두터운, 빽빽한
- **though** [ðou] ⊕ 그러나, 그래도
- **throughout** [θruːáut] ㉠ ~ 내내, ~ 동안 쭉
- **thumping** [θʌ́mpiŋ] ⊚ 쿵쾅거리는
- **whisper** [hwíspər] ⊛ 속삭이다
- **wooden** [wúdn] ⊚ 나무로 된, 목재의
- **would** [wəd] ㉣ ~하곤 했다(과거의 불규칙적 습관)

Key Expressions

- **after a while** 얼마 후에
- **all of a sudden** 갑자기
- **as ~ as one can** 최대한[가능한 한] ~한[하게]
- **as soon as** ~하자마자
- **as usual** 여느 때처럼
- **at first** 처음에는
- **day in and day out** 매일
- **in other words** 다시 말해서, 즉
- **in reply** 대답으로
- **inch by inch** 조금씩

- **keep out** 들어가지 않다
- **manage to** 간신히 ~하다
- **one behind the other** 한 사람 뒤에 다른 한 사람
- **reach out** (손·팔·다리 등을) 뻗다
- **set off** 출발하다
- **side by side** 나란히
- **stop ~ from -ing** ~가 …하는 것을 막다
- **thanks to** ~ 덕분에
- **used to** ~하곤 했다(과거의 규칙적이고 반복적인 동작이나 상태)

Word Power

※ 서로 비슷한 뜻을 가진 어휘

□ **acatually** 실제(로)는, 사실은 - **really** 사실, 참으로

□ **all of a sudden** 갑자기 - **suddenly** 갑자기

□ **at first** 처음에는 - **in the beginning** 처음에는

□ **day in and day out** 매일 - **day after day** 매일

□ **entrance** 입구 - **gateway** 입구

□ **hurt** 고통을 주다, 아프다 - **ache** 아프다, 쑤시다

□ **lesson** 교훈 - **instruction** 교훈, 가르침

□ **particular** 특별한 - **special** 특별한

□ **shout** 외치다, 소리[고함]치다 - **cry** 소리치다, 외치다

□ **stop ~ from -ing** ~가 …하는 것을 막다
　keep ~ from -ing ~가 …하는 것을 막다

※ 서로 반대의 뜻을 가진 어휘

□ **at first** 처음에는 ↔ **at last** 마침내, 드디어

□ **hurt** 고통을 주다, 아프다 ↔ **heal** 고치다, 낫게 하다

□ **entrance** 입구 ↔ **exit** 출구

□ **thick** 두터운, 빽빽한 ↔ **thin** 얇은, 드문드문한

English Dictionary

□ **breathe** 숨 쉬다
　→ to take a breath
　　숨을 쉬다

□ **cycle** 자전거를 타다
　→ to ride a bicycle
　　자전거를 타다

□ **dirt** 흙, 먼지
　→ loose or packed soil or sand
　　흐트러지거나 뭉친 흙이나 모래

□ **entrance** 입구
　→ the way you go in
　　안으로 들어가는 길

□ **gateway** 입구
　→ an opening for a gate
　　문으로 향하는 열린 구멍

□ **manager** 경영자, 관리자
　→ a person who is responsible for running part of a business organization
　　사업 조직의 일부를 운영하는 책임을 지는 사람

□ **particular** 특별한
　→ worthy of notice; special; unusual
　　주목할 가치가 있는; 특별한; 평범하지 않은

□ **relief** 안도, 안심
　→ removal of something painful
　　고통스러운 어떤 것의 제거

□ **scream** 비명
　→ a loud sharp cry or noise
　　크고 날카로운 울음이나 소음

□ **thick** 두터운, 빽빽한
　→ close-packed with units or individuals
　　단일체나 개체로 밀집한

□ **throughout** ~ 내내, ~ 동안 쭉
　→ during the whole period of
　　전체 기간 동안

□ **thumping** 쿵쾅거리는
　→ hitting something in a heavy, continuous way
　　심하게, 그리고 계속해서 무엇인가를 때리는

□ **wooden** 나무로 된, 목재의
　→ made of wood
　　나무로 만들어진

Reading

교과서

Keep Out

Every summer, my family used to go on holiday to the coast.
'~하곤 했다'라는 뜻으로 과거의 규칙적이고 반복적인 동작이나 상태를 나타냄.

We always went to the same place and stayed at the same small

guesthouse. We would stay for two weeks, swimming in the sea and
과거의 불규칙적인 습관을 나타내는 조동사(~하곤 했다)   분사구문(~하면서)

walking around the little town. In other words, we never did anything
분사 구문(~하면서)

special, and nothing ever really happened on these vacations.

At the time of this story I was twelve years old. Most people can

remember this particular summer, as it was the hottest summer England
이유를 나타내는 접속사(~ 때문에)

had had since records began. It did not rain throughout June and July,
관계대명사 that이 생략된 형용사절, 주절보다 먼저 있었던 일을 언급하므로 과거완료 (had had)

and the sun shone day in and day out.

But Ron and I loved the heat and the sun. Every day, we would ride

our bicycles further and further away from the guesthouse.
far의 비교급

One day Ron decided that we should ride our bikes along the old
~을 따라

train tracks to see where they would take us. I was happy to follow
to부정사의 부사적 용법(목적)   동사 see의 목적어 역할을 하는 간접의문문

Ron, as usual, and we set off after breakfast.

in other words 다시 말해서, 즉 (= namely)

particular 특별한

throughout ~ 내내, ~ 동안 쭉

day in and day out 매일 (= day after day)

as usual 여느 때처럼

set off 출발하다

📎 **확인문제**

● 다음 문장이 본문의 내용과 일치하면 T, 일치하지 <u>않으면</u> F를 쓰시오.

1 Every summer, the writer's family used to go on holiday to the coast. ☐

2 Every summer, the writer's family did something special. ☐

3 Ron and the writer loved the heat and the sun. ☐

4 Ron and the writer would ride their bicycles near the guesthouse every day. ☐

5 One day Ron decided that they should ride their bikes along the old train tracks to
   see where they would take them. ☐

6 Ron and the writer set off before breakfast. ☐

At first, the tracks were easy to follow, and we cycled along side
by side. After a while, the grass grew thicker, and we had to ride one
behind the other. Ron was ahead. The tracks went toward the woods
and it grew darker as the trees stood tall and formed a roof over the
tracks.

Ron stopped suddenly. "Look ahead!" he shouted. I stopped next to
him and saw a white, wooden gateway across a black opening.

"It's a tunnel," I said.

"Yes, and it says, 'Keep Out' on the gate," replied Ron. "Do you want
to have a look inside?"

Actually, I did not want to go inside. I felt a little cold all of a sudden,
and I wanted to go back into the sunlight. But I answered, "Sure," and
moved ahead.

We left our bikes at the gate and climbed over. We entered the cool
tunnel. The air inside was heavy. Above our heads there was a sound
that grew louder and louder.

"What's that?" I called out.

"Bats," said Ron, "Keep your head down." Then he moved on.

"Don't go so fast." I called after him. I meant, "Don't leave me
behind" but I didn't say so.

cycle 자전거를 타다

side by side 나란히

after a while 얼마 후에

thick 두터운, 빽빽한

wooden 나무로 된, 목재의

gateway 입구

all of a sudden 갑자기

🔖 **확인문제**

● 다음 문장이 본문의 내용과 일치하면 T, 일치하지 <u>않으면</u> F를 쓰시오.

1   At first, the tracks were easy to follow, and Ron and the writer cycled along side by side. ☐

2   Ron and the writer saw a white, wooden gateway next to a black opening. ☐

3   Ron asked, "Do you want to have a look inside?" ☐

4   The writer wanted to go inside. ☐

5   Ron and the writer left their bikes at the gate and climbed over. ☐

6   Above their heads there was a sound that faded away. ☐

The next thing I heard was a loud noise right above us, a thumping
_{The next thing과 I heard 사이에는 관계대명사 that이 생략되었다.} _{a loud noise와 a thumping sound는 동격}
sound like an express train and then a scream.

"Ron!" I shouted. "Ron, what's up? Can you hear me?" No reply.

"Speak to me, Ron. Tell me what's happened."
_{= what has}

I slowly walked toward where Ron had been and found only dirt and
_{관계부사 where 앞에 선행사 the place가 생략되어 있음.}
small rocks. As I reached out my hands, I felt something wet—Ron's

face! His eyes were closed, and he was breathing weakly. "It's okay,

Ron," I whispered. "I'll get you out."

"I think I've broken my leg. It really hurts. Just go and get help, Ben."

"No," I replied. "I'll get you out of here to safety first." I started
_{= a safe place}
moving away the dirt and rocks with my hands.

I felt calm, and I felt in control. It took a long time to clear away the
_{It takes+시간+to부정사: ∼하는 데 …의 시간이 걸리다}
earth covering Ron. Finally, I managed to free his body. Holding him
_{현재분사 covering은 앞의 명사 the earth를 수식} _{부대상황을 나타내는 분사 구문. = As I held}
under the arms, I pulled him backward, inch by inch, toward the tunnel

entrance.

thumping 쿵쾅거리는
scream 비명
dirt 흙, 먼지
breathe 숨 쉬다
safety 안전, 안전한 곳
manage to 간신히 ∼하다
entrance 입구

 확인문제

● 다음 문장이 본문의 내용과 일치하면 T, 일치하지 않으면 F를 쓰시오.

1 There was a thumping sound like an express train. ☐

2 Ron said to me, "Speak to me. Tell me what's happened." ☐

3 Ron's eyes were closed, and he was breathing weakly. ☐

4 Ben started moving away the dirt and rocks with his hands. ☐

5 Ron and the writer walked toward the tunnel entrance. ☐

It <u>seemed to</u> take ages, but finally I was able to get Ron out of the
~인 것처럼 보였다
tunnel. He didn't look too well, though. His face was white, and he
was trying hard to <u>stop himself from crying</u> out. I found our bikes and
stop ~ from -ing: ~가 …하는 것을 막다, 이때 stop은 prevent의 뜻
brought the two water bottles to Ron.

"Here, drink these," I said. "I'll go and get help. I'll be as quick as I
can." In reply, Ron simply pressed my hands.
= possible

I got on my bicycle and raced back along the tracks until I got to the
nearest farmhouse. I ran past the gate and found a woman <u>washing</u>
현재분사
some dishes in the kitchen.

Thanks to her, Ron was taken to the hospital, <u>where</u> his leg was put
계속적 용법의 관계부사 where = and there(and in the hospital)
in a cast. As soon as our parents arrived at the hospital and saw us,
my mother cried with relief. But all <u>my father said</u> was, "Let that <u>be</u> a
선행사 all을 수식하며, 앞에 관계대명사 that이 생략되어 있음   사역동사 let 뒤에는 목적보어로
동사원형을 씀.
lesson to you."

And what was the lesson? It was "*Keep out* means *Stay out of*
stay out of trouble: 재난(곤란, 어려움, 문젯거리 등)으로부터 벗어나다
trouble." Ron is now the manager of a big company which produces
helmets and other safety products. And me? I am a fire fighter.

thanks to ~ 덕분에

relief 안도, 안심

manager 경영자, 관리자

 확인문제

● 다음 문장이 본문의 내용과 일치하면 T, 일치하지 <u>않으면</u> F를 쓰시오.

1 Finally the writer was able to get Ron out of the tunnel. ☐

2 Ron couldn't stop himself from crying out. ☐

3 The writer found their bikes and brought the two water bottles to Ron. ☐

4 Ron said, "Come back as soon as you can." ☐

5 The writer got on his bicycle and raced back along the tracks until he got to the

   nearest farmhouse. ☐

6 As soon as their parents arrived at the hospital and saw them, their father cried with

   relief. ☐

● 우리말을 참고하여 빈칸에 알맞은 말을 쓰시오.

1 _____ _____

2 Every summer, my family _____ _____ _____ on holiday to the coast.

3 We always went to the same place and _____ _____ the same small guesthouse.

4 We would stay for two weeks, _____ in the sea and _____ around the little town.

5 _____ _____ _____, we never did _____ _____, and nothing ever really happened on these vacations.

6 _____ _____ _____ _____ this story I was twelve years old.

7 Most people can remember this particular summer, as it was the hottest summer England _____ _____ since records began.

8 It did not rain throughout June and July, and the sun shone _____ _____ _____ _____ _____.

9 But Ron and I loved _____ _____ and the sun.

10 Every day, we would ride our bicycles _____ _____ _____ away from the guesthouse.

11 One day Ron decided that we should ride our bikes along the old train tracks to see where they would _____ _____.

12 I was happy to follow Ron, _____ _____, and we _____ _____ after breakfast.

13 At first, the tracks were easy to follow, and we cycled along _____ _____ _____.

1	들어가지 마시오
2	여름마다 나의 가족은 해안으로 휴가를 가곤 했다.
3	우리는 항상 같은 곳에 가서 똑같은 작은 게스트하우스에 묵었다.
4	우리는 2주 가량 머물며 바다에서 수영하고 작은 마을 주위를 돌아다니곤 했다.
5	다시 말해서, 그런 휴가에서 우리는 특별한 일을 하지 않았고 정말 아무 일도 일어나지 않았다.
6	이 이야기는 내가 12살 때 일이다.
7	관측 이래 영국이 겪은 가장 더운 여름이었기 때문에, 대부분의 사람들은 이 특별한 여름을 기억할 수 있다.
8	6월과 7월 내내 비가 오지 않았고 태양은 연일 쨍쨍했다.
9	하지만 Ron과 나는 그 더위와 태양을 사랑했다.
10	매일 우리는 게스트하우스에서 조금씩 먼 곳으로 자전거를 타고 가곤 했다.
11	어느 날, Ron은 낡은 철로가 우리를 어디로 데려다줄지 알아보려고 그 철로를 따라 자전거를 타기로 결정했다.
12	난 늘 그랬듯 Ron을 따르는 게 즐거웠고, 아침 식사 후에 우리는 출발했다.
13	처음에는 철길을 따라가는 게 어렵지 않아 우리는 나란히 자전거를 타고 갔다.

14 After a while, the grass grew thicker, and we had to ride _____ _____ _____ _____.

15 Ron was _____.

16 The tracks went toward the woods and it _____ _____ as the trees stood tall and _____ _____ _____ over the tracks.

17 Ron stopped suddenly. "_____ _____!" he shouted.

18 I stopped _____ _____ _____ and saw a white, wooden gateway across a black opening.

19 "It's _____ _____," I said.

20 "Yes, and it says, '_____ _____' on the gate," replied Ron.

21 "Do you want to _____ _____ inside?"

22 _____, I did not want to go inside.

23 I felt a little cold _____ _____ _____ _____, and I wanted to go back into the sunlight.

24 But I answered, "Sure," and _____ _____.

25 We _____ our bikes at the gate and climbed over.

26 We _____ the cool tunnel.

27 The air inside was _____.

28 Above our heads there was a sound that _____ _____ _____ _____.

29 "What's that?" I _____ _____.

30 "Bats," said Ron, "_____ your head _____." Then he moved on.

31 "Don't go so fast." I _____ _____ him.

---

14 한참 후, 풀이 점점 우거져서 우리는 한 사람이 앞서가고 다른 사람이 뒤에서 가야 했다.

15 Ron이 앞서가고 있었다.

16 철길은 숲으로 이어졌고 나무가 높이 자라 철길 위로 지붕을 형성하며 점점 더 어두워졌다.

17 Ron이 갑자기 멈췄다. "앞을 봐!"라고 그가 외쳤다.

18 나는 그의 옆에 멈춰서 캄캄한 입구를 가로지르는 흰색 나무문을 보았다.

19 "터널이네." 내가 말했다.

20 "맞아. 그리고 문에 '들어가지 마시오'라고 적혀 있어." Ron이 대답했다.

21 "안을 보고 싶니?"

22 사실, 난 안으로 들어가고 싶지 않았다.

23 갑자기 나는 한기를 살짝 느꼈고 햇빛 속으로 되돌아가고 싶었다.

24 그렇지만 나는 "물론이지."라고 답하며 앞으로 움직였다.

25 우리는 문 앞에 자전거를 남겨두고 넘어갔다.

26 우리는 서늘한 터널로 들어갔다.

27 안의 공기는 묵직했다.

28 우리 머리 위로 점점 더 커지는 소리가 났다.

29 "저게 뭐야?"라고 내가 소리쳤다.

30 "박쥐야." Ron이 말했다. "머리를 숙여." 그러고 나서 그는 계속 움직였다.

31 "너무 빨리 가지 마." 나는 그를 부르며 뒤쫓았다.

32 I meant, "Don't _____ me _____" but I didn't say so.

33 The next thing I heard was a loud noise right above us, a _____ sound _____ _____ _____ _____ and then a scream.

34 "Ron!" I shouted. "Ron, _____ _____? Can you hear me?" No reply.

35 "Speak to me, Ron. Tell me _____ _____."

36 I slowly walked toward _____ _____ _____ _____ and found only dirt and small rocks.

37 As I reached out my hands, I felt _____ _____ — Ron's face!

38 His eyes _____ _____, and he was breathing weakly.

39 "It's okay, Ron," I whispered. "I'll _____ _____ _____."

40 "I think I'_____ _____ my leg. It really hurts. Just _____ _____ _____ _____, Ben."

41 "No," I replied. "I'll _____ to safety first."

42 I started _____ _____ the dirt and rocks with my hands.

43 I felt calm, and I felt _____ _____.

44 It took a long time to clear away the earth _____ Ron.

45 Finally, I _____ _____ _____ his body.

46 _____ him under the arms, I pulled him backward, _____ _____ _____, toward the tunnel entrance.

47 It seemed _____ _____ _____, but finally I was able to get Ron out of the tunnel.

48 He didn't _____ _____ _____, though.

32 '나를 두고 가지 마'라고 말하고 싶었지만, 나는 그렇게 말하지 않았다.

33 그다음 내가 들은 것은 바로 앞에서 나는 큰 소음이었는데, 그것은 마치 고속열차 같은 쿵쾅거리는 소리였다. 이어서 비명이 들렸다.

34 "Ron!" 나는 외쳤다. "Ron, 무슨 일이야? 내 말 들려?" 아무 응답이 없었다.

35 "Ron, 나에게 말해 봐. 무슨 일이 생겼는지 말해 줘."

36 나는 천천히 Ron이 있던 곳으로 걸어갔고 흙과 작은 자갈만을 발견했다.

37 손을 뻗었을 때 나는 축축한 무언가를 느꼈다. Ron의 얼굴이었다!

38 그의 눈은 감겨 있었고 약하게 숨을 쉬고 있었다.

39 "괜찮아, Ron." 나는 속삭였다. "내가 꺼내 줄게."

40 "다리가 부러진 것 같아. 정말 아파. 그냥 가서 도움을 요청해, Ben."

41 "안 돼." 나는 대답했다. "우선 안전한 곳까지 여기에서 형을 꺼낼 거야."

42 나는 손으로 흙과 자갈을 치우기 시작했다.

43 나는 침착했고 내가 잘할 수 있다고 느꼈다.

44 Ron을 뒤덮은 흙을 치우는 데에 오랜 시간이 걸렸다.

45 드디어 나는 그의 몸을 자유롭게 할 수 있었다.

46 팔 밑으로 그를 안고서 그를 터널 입구 쪽으로 조금씩 뒤로 끌어당겼다.

47 오랜 시간이 걸린 듯했지만 결국 나는 Ron을 터널 밖으로 데리고 나올 수 있었다.

48 그는 별로 좋아 보이지 않았다.

49 His face was white, and he was trying hard to _____ himself _____ _____ _____ from crying out.

50 I found our bikes and brought the _____ _____ _____ to Ron.

51 "Here, drink these," I said. "I'll _____ _____ _____. I'll be as quick as I can."

52 _____ _____, Ron simply _____ _____ _____.

53 I got on my bicycle and _____ _____ along the tracks until I got to the nearest farmhouse.

54 I ran past the gate and found a woman _____ _____ _____ in the kitchen.

55 _____ _____ _____, Ron was taken to the hospital, _____ his leg was put in a cast.

56 As soon as our parents arrived at the hospital and saw us, my mother cried _____ _____.

57 But all my father said was, "_____ _____ to you."

58 And what was the lesson? It was "*Keep out* means _____ _____ _____ _____."

59 Ron is now the manager of a big company which produces helmets and other _____ _____.

60 And me? I am a _____ _____.

49 그의 얼굴은 창백했고 울음을 터뜨리지 않으려고 몹시 애쓰고 있었다.

50 나는 우리 자전거를 찾아서 Ron 에게 물병 두 개를 가져다주었다.

51 "여기, 이거 마셔." 나는 말했다. "내가 가서 도움을 구할게. 최대한 빨리 올게."

52 대답으로 Ron은 그저 내 손을 꽉 잡았다.

53 나는 자전거를 타고 왔던 철길을 따라 달려, 마침내 가장 가까운 농가에 도착했다.

54 대문을 지나 달려가 나는 부엌에서 설거지를 하고 있는 부인을 발견했다.

55 그 부인 덕분에 Ron은 병원으로 이송되었고, 병원에서 다리에 석고붕대를 했다.

56 부모님이 병원에 도착해서 우리를 보자마자, 어머니는 안도감에 울음을 터뜨리셨다.

57 하지만 아버지가 하신 말씀은 "이 일이 너희에게 교훈이 되기를 바란다."가 전부였다.

58 그래서 교훈이 무엇이었을까? 그것은 '들어가지 마시오'라는 말은 '곤경을 멀리하라'는 뜻이라는 것이다.

59 Ron은 지금 안전모와 여러 안전 제품을 생산하는 큰 회사의 관리자이다.

60 그럼 나는? 나는 소방관이다.

● 우리말을 참고하여 본문을 영작하시오.

1 들어가지 마시오

➡ _____

2 여름마다 나의 가족은 해안으로 휴가를 가곤 했다.

➡ _____

3 우리는 항상 같은 곳에 가서 똑같은 작은 게스트하우스에 묵었다.

➡ _____

4 우리는 2주 가량 머물며 바다에서 수영하고 작은 마을 주위를 돌아다니곤 했다.

➡ _____

5 다시 말해서, 그런 휴가에서 우리는 특별한 일을 하지 않았고 정말 아무 일도 일어나지 않았다.

➡ _____
_____

6 이 이야기는 내가 12살 때 일이다.

➡ _____

7 관측 이래 영국이 겪은 가장 더운 여름이었기 때문에, 대부분의 사람들은 이 특별한 여름을 기억할 수 있다.

➡ _____

8 6월과 7월 내내 비가 오지 않았고 태양은 연일 쨍쨍했다.

➡ _____

9 하지만 Ron과 나는 그 더위와 태양을 사랑했다.

➡ _____

10 매일 우리는 게스트하우스에서 조금씩 먼 곳으로 자전거를 타고 가곤 했다.

➡ _____

11 어느 날, Ron은 낡은 철로가 우리를 어디로 데려다줄지 알아보려고 그 철로를 따라 자전거를 타기로 결정했다.

➡ _____
_____

12 난 늘 그랬듯 Ron을 따르는 게 즐거웠고, 아침 식사 후에 우리는 출발했다.

➡ _____

13 처음에는 철길을 따라가는 게 어렵지 않아 우리는 나란히 자전거를 타고 갔다.

➡ _____

14 한참 후, 풀이 점점 우거져서 우리는 한 사람이 앞서가고 다른 사람이 뒤에서 가야 했다.

➡ _____

15 Ron이 앞서가고 있었다.

➡ _____

16 철길은 숲으로 이어졌고 나무가 높이 자라 철길 위로 지붕을 형성하며 점점 더 어두워졌다.

➡ _____

_____

17 Ron이 갑자기 멈췄다. "앞을 봐!"라고 그가 외쳤다.

➡ _____

18 나는 그의 옆에 멈춰서 캄캄한 입구를 가로지르는 흰색 나무문을 보았다.

➡ _____

19 "터널이네." 내가 말했다.

➡ _____

20 "맞아. 그리고 문에 '들어가지 마시오'라고 적혀 있어." Ron이 대답했다.

➡ _____

21 "안을 보고 싶니?"

➡ _____

22 사실, 난 안으로 들어가고 싶지 않았다.

➡ _____

23 갑자기 나는 한기를 살짝 느꼈고 햇빛 속으로 되돌아가고 싶었다.

➡ _____

24 그렇지만 나는 "물론이지."라고 답하며 앞으로 움직였다.

➡ _____

25 우리는 문 앞에 자전거를 남겨 두고 넘어갔다.

➡ _____

26 우리는 서늘한 터널로 들어갔다.

➡ _____

27 안의 공기는 묵직했다.

➡ _____

28 우리 머리 위로 점점 더 커지는 소리가 났다.

➡ _____

29 "저게 뭐야?"라고 내가 소리쳤다.

➡ _____

30 "박쥐야." Ron이 말했다. "머리를 숙여." 그러고 나서 그는 계속 움직였다.

➡ _____

31 "너무 빨리 가지 마." 나는 그를 부르며 뒤쫓았다.

➡ _____

32 '나를 두고 가지 마.'라고 말하고 싶었지만, 나는 그렇게 말하지 않았다.

➡ _____

33 그다음 내가 들은 것은 바로 앞에서 나는 큰 소음이었는데, 그것은 마치 고속열차 같은 쿵쾅거리는 소리였다. 이어서 비명이 들렸다.

➡ _____

_____

34 "Ron!" 나는 외쳤다. "Ron, 무슨 일이야? 내 말 들려?" 아무 응답이 없었다.

➡ _____

35 "Ron, 나에게 말해 봐. 무슨 일이 생겼는지 말해 줘."

➡ _____

36 나는 천천히 Ron이 있던 곳으로 걸어갔고 흙과 작은 자갈만을 발견했다.

➡ _____

37 손을 뻗었을 때 나는 축축한 무언가를 느꼈다. Ron의 얼굴이었다!

➡ _____

38 그의 눈은 감겨 있었고 약하게 숨을 쉬고 있었다.

➡ _____

39 "괜찮아, Ron." 나는 속삭였다. "내가 꺼내 줄게."

➡ _____

40 "다리가 부러진 것 같아. 정말 아파. 그냥 가서 도움을 요청해, Ben."

➡ _____

41 "안 돼." 나는 대답했다. "우선 안전한 곳까지 여기에서 형을 꺼낼 거야."

➡ _____

42 나는 손으로 흙과 자갈을 치우기 시작했다.

➡ _____

43 나는 침착했고 내가 잘할 수 있다고 느꼈다.

➡ _____

44 Ron을 뒤덮은 흙을 치우는 데에 오랜 시간이 걸렸다.

➡ _____

45 드디어 나는 그의 몸을 자유롭게 할 수 있었다.

➡ _____

46 팔 밑으로 그를 안고서 그를 터널 입구 쪽으로 조금씩 뒤로 끌어당겼다.

➡ _____

47 오랜 시간이 걸린 듯했지만 결국 나는 Ron을 터널 밖으로 데리고 나올 수 있었다.

➡ _____

48 그는 별로 좋아 보이지 않았다.

➡ _____

49 그의 얼굴은 창백했고 울음을 터뜨리지 않으려고 몹시 애쓰고 있었다.

➡ _____

50 나는 우리 자전거를 찾아서 Ron에게 물병 두 개를 가져다주었다.

➡ _____

51 "여기, 이거 마셔." 나는 말했다. "내가 가서 도움을 구할게. 최대한 빨리 올게."

➡ _____

52 대답으로 Ron은 그저 내 손을 꽉 잡았다.

➡ _____

53 나는 자전거를 타고 왔던 철길을 따라 달려, 마침내 가장 가까운 농가에 도착했다.

➡ _____

54 대문을 지나 달려가 나는 부엌에서 설거지를 하고 있는 부인을 발견했다.

➡ _____

55 그 부인 덕분에 Ron은 병원으로 이송되었고, 병원에서 다리에 석고붕대를 했다.

➡ _____

56 부모님이 병원에 도착해서 우리를 보자마자, 어머니는 안도감에 울음을 터뜨리셨다.

➡ _____

57 하지만 아버지가 하신 말씀은 "이 일이 너희에게 교훈이 되기를 바란다."가 전부였다.

➡ _____

58 그래서 교훈이 무엇이었을까? 그것은 '들어가지 마시오'라는 말은 '곤경을 멀리하라'는 뜻이라는 것이다.

➡ _____

59 Ron은 지금 안전모와 여러 안전 제품을 생산하는 큰 회사의 관리자이다.

➡ _____

60 그럼 나는? 나는 소방관이다.

➡ _____

01 다음 짝지어진 단어의 관계가 같도록 빈칸에 알맞은 단어를 주어진 철자로 시작하여 쓰시오.

> entrance : exit = thick : t_____

02 다음 문장의 빈칸에 들어갈 말을 〈보기〉에서 골라 쓰시오.

> ┤ 보기 ├
>
> all of a sudden / thumping / managed to / in other words

(1) The washing machine made a _____ sound.

(2) He was broke. _____ _____ _____, he had no money.

(3) He _____ _____ fix the computer by himself.

(4) _____ _____ _____ _____, there was a scream behind us.

03 다음 우리말에 맞게 빈칸에 알맞은 말을 쓰시오.

(1) 그녀는 자신의 문제들에도 불구하고 평상시처럼 일을 계속했다.
  ➡ Despite her problems, she carried on working _____ _____.

(2) 내가 처음에는 그 일이 힘들었지만 곧 익숙해졌다.
  ➡ I found the job tiring _____ _____ but I soon got used to it.

(3) 나는 그 방에 들어서는 순간 뭔가가 잘못되었다는 것을 알았다.
  ➡ _____ _____ _____ I walked in the room, I knew that something was wrong.

04 다음 중 어법상 어색한 것을 골라 바르게 고쳐 쓰시오.

① The next thing I heard was a loud noise right above us, a thumping sound like an express train and then a scream.

② I slowly walked toward where Ron had been and found only dirt and small rocks.

③ Ron decided that we ride our bikes along the old train tracks.

④ We must stop him from seeing her somehow.

⑤ Being no objection, the meeting was put off.

➡ _____
_____

05 다음 문장에서 어법상 틀린 곳을 찾아 바르게 고쳐 쓰시오.

(1) He would be a pilot, but now he has a desk job.
  _____ ➡ _____

(2) We had many difficulties, while covered this case.
  _____ ➡ _____

(3) Is this the building which it happened?
  _____ ➡ _____

(4) Tell me that has happened.
  _____ ➡ _____

(A)Every summer, my family used to go on holiday to the coast. We always went to the same place and stayed at the same small guesthouse. We would stay for two weeks, swimming in the sea and walking around the little town. In other words, we never did anything special, and nothing ever really happened on these vacations.

At the time of this story I was twelve years old. Most people can remember this particular summer, as it was the hottest summer England ___ⓐ___ since records began. It did not rain throughout June and July, and the sun shone day in and day out.

But Ron and I loved the heat and the sun. Every day, we would ride our bicycles further and further away from the guesthouse.

06 위 글의 빈칸 ⓐ에 have를 알맞은 형태로 쓰시오.

➡ _____

07 위 글의 밑줄 친 (A)를 다음과 같이 바꿔 쓸 때 빈칸에 들어 갈 알맞은 단어를 쓰시오.

(1) Every summer, my family was in the habit of _____ on holiday to the coast.

(2) Every summer, my family made it a rule _____ _____ on holiday to the coast.

08 Why does the writer say that most people can remember this particular summer? Answer in English beginning with "Because".

➡ _____

_____

I slowly walked toward (A)[which / where] Ron had been and found only dirt and small rocks. As I reached out my hands, I felt something wet—Ron's face! His eyes were closed, and he was breathing weakly. "It's okay, Ron," I whispered. "I'll get you out."

"I think I've broken my leg. It really hurts. Just go and get help, Ben."

"No," I replied. "I'll get you out of here to safety first." I started moving away the dirt and rocks with my hands.

I felt (B)[calm / calmly], and I felt in control. ⓐRon을 뒤덮은 흙을 치우는 데에 오랜 시간이 걸렸다. Finally, I managed (C)[to free / freeing] his body. Holding him under the arms, I pulled him backward, inch by inch, toward the tunnel entrance.

09 위 글의 괄호 (A)~(C)에서 문맥이나 어법상 알맞은 낱말을 골라 쓰시오.

(A) _____ (B) _____ (C) _____

10 위 글의 밑줄 친 ⓐ의 우리말에 맞게 주어진 어휘를 이용하여 12 단어로 영작하시오.

took, time, clear away, earth, covering

➡ _____

_____

11 다음 문장에서 위 글의 내용과 <u>다른</u> 부분을 찾아서 고치시오.

Ben started moving away the dirt and rocks with a shovel.

_____ ➡ _____

01 다음 문장의 빈칸에 들어갈 말을 〈보기〉에서 골라 쓰시오.

> ─── 보기 ───
>
> thanks to / wooden / relief /
> after a while / cast

(1) There is a _____ table in the living room.

(2) My _____ is finally off and there's serious muscle loss.

(3) I met a lot of nice people, _____ _____ you.

(4) _____ _____ _____, we naturally started talking about the children.

(5) My mother breathed a sigh of _____.

[02~03] 다음 영영풀이가 가리키는 것을 고르시오.

02

> a loud sharp cry or noise

① scream ② treat ③ dirt
④ lesson ⑤ breath

03

> removal of something painful

① thick ② entrance ③ hurt
④ relief ⑤ whisper

04 다음 중 밑줄 친 부분의 뜻풀이가 바르지 <u>않은</u> 것은?

① Where is the <u>entrance</u> of the museum? (입구)

② You should keep a <u>record</u> of your expenses. (기록)

③ We <u>set off</u> for the station after lunch. (출발하다)

④ She would try to <u>stop</u> him <u>from</u> going fishing. (~가 …하는 것을 막다)

⑤ Three girls were walking along the bank <u>side by side</u>. (한 줄로)

05 다음 문장에 공통으로 들어갈 말을 쓰시오.

> • I was thankful that he hadn't been _____.
>
> • None of the passengers were badly _____.
>
> • There was _____ and real anger in her voice.

06 다음 우리말과 일치하도록 주어진 어구를 배열하여 영작하시오.

(1) 그녀가 몸을 기울여 그의 귀에 대고 뭔가를 속삭였다. (she / his / something / ear / whispered / leaned / and / over / in)

➡ _____

_____

(2) 나는 빈 녹음실에서 종종 각본을 읽는 연습을 하곤 했다. (I / the scripts / the / recording room / reading / practice / would / empty / often / in)

➡ _____

_____

(3) 제 연기가 조금씩 향상되고 있다는 걸 보여주고 싶었어요. (I / I / inch / inch / show / wanted / improve / could / acting / that / my / by / to)

➡ _____

_____

출제율 95%

07 다음 우리말을 주어진 어구를 이용하여 영작하시오.

(1) 매일 같은 식당에서 밥 먹는 것도 이젠 신물이나. (day, so tired, eating, in, out)

➡ _____

_____

(2) 저 방에는 들어가지 마세요. (that, please, keep, of)

➡ _____

(3) 손을 뻗었을 때 나는 축축한 무언가를 느꼈다. (my hand, reach, wct, as)

➡ _____

출제율 90%

08 다음 중 어법상 올바른 것을 고르시오.

① It took a long time to clear away the earth covering Ron.

② Most people can remember this particular summer, as it was the hottest summer England has had since records began.

③ It makes my heart to ache seeing her suffer.

④ He was trying hard to stop himself to cry out.

⑤ After a while, the grass grew thicker, and the two boys had to ride one behind other.

출제율 95%

09 다음 괄호 안에 주어진 조건대로 바꿔 쓰시오.

(1) It did not rain throughout June and July, and the sun shone day in and day out. (분사구문으로)

➡ _____

_____

(2) As it was the hottest summer England had had since records began, most people can remember this particular summer. (분사구문으로)

➡ _____

_____

(3) Ron decided that we should ride our bikes along the old train tracks so that we could see where they would take us. (to부정사를 이용하여)

➡ _____

_____

(4) I'd like to see. Can she give me a hand? (if를 이용하여 한 문장으로)

➡ _____

_____

출제율 95%

10 다음 문장에서 어법상 어색한 것을 바르게 고쳐 다시 쓰시오.

(1) The book is a detailed piece of work covered all aspects of the subject.

➡ _____

_____

(2) The two men were walking quickly, one behind other.

➡ _____

_____

(3) Ron was taken to the hospital, in where his leg was put in a cast.

➡ _____

_____

(4) It took her some time realizing the dangers of her situation.

➡ _____

_____

11 다음 중 어법상 어색한 것을 고르시오.

① Holding him under the arms, I pulled him backward, inch by inch, toward the tunnel entrance.

② It seemed that it took ages, but finally I was able to get Ron out of the tunnel.

③ Mike was trying hard to stop himself from crying out.

④ I'll be as quickly as I can.

⑤ It was easy to follow the tracks.

[12~13] 다음 글을 읽고 물음에 답하시오.

At the time of this story I was twelve years old. Most people can remember this particular summer, ⓐas it was the hottest summer England had had since records began. It did not rain throughout June and July, and the sun shone day in and day out.

But Ron and I loved the heat and the sun. Every day, we would ride our bicycles further and further away from the guesthouse.

12 위 글의 밑줄 친 문장 ⓐ의 had had와 과거완료 용법이 같은 것을 모두 고르시오.

① I had never seen such a strange animal before.

② He had lived there for ten years when his father died.

③ When I reached the station, the train had already started.

④ I bought an umbrella yesterday, for I had lost my old one.

⑤ When we called on her, she had been ill in bed for a week.

13 According to the passage, which is NOT true?

① At the time of this story the writer was twelve years old.

② It was the hottest summer England had had since records began.

③ It did not rain throughout June and July.

④ Ron and the writer loved the heat and the sun.

⑤ Every day, Ron and the writer would ride their bicycles near the guesthouse.

[14~16] 다음 글을 읽고 물음에 답하시오.

One day Ron decided that we should ride our bikes along the old train tracks to see where ⓐthey would take us. (①) I was happy to follow Ron, as usual, and we set off after breakfast. (②)

At first, the tracks were easy ⓑto follow, and we cycled along side by side. (③) Ron was ahead. (④) The tracks went toward the woods and it grew darker as the trees stood tall and formed a roof over the tracks. (⑤)

14 위 글의 밑줄 친 ⓐthey가 가리키는 것을 본문에서 찾아 쓰시오.

➡ _____

15 위 글의 흐름으로 보아, 주어진 문장이 들어가기에 가장 적절한 곳은?

After a while, the grass grew thicker, and we had to ride one behind the other.

①   ②   ③   ④   ⑤

16 아래 〈보기〉에서 위 글의 밑줄 친 ⓑto follow와 to부정사의 용법이 같은 것의 개수를 고르시오.

> ┌─ 보기 ─┐
> ① There is no one to do it.
> ② He can't be rich to ask me for some money.
> ③ My hobby is to collect stamps.
> ④ They came here to ask me a question.
> ⑤ It is important to use your time well.

① 1개　② 2개　③ 3개　④ 4개　⑤ 5개

[17~19] 다음 글을 읽고 물음에 답하시오.

Ron stopped ⓐsuddenly. "Look ahead!" he shouted. I stopped next to him and ⓑ캄캄한 입구를 가로지르는 흰색 나무 문을 보았다.

"It's a tunnel," I said.

"Yes, and it says, 'Keep Out' on the gate," replied Ron. "Do you want to have a look inside?"

Actually, I did not want to go inside. I felt a little cold all of a sudden, and I wanted to go back into the sunlight. But I answered, "Sure," and moved ahead.

17 위 글의 밑줄 친 ⓐsuddenly와 바꿔 쓸 수 있는 말을 본문에서 찾아 쓰시오.

➡ _____

18 위 글의 밑줄 친 ⓑ의 우리말에 맞게 주어진 어휘를 알맞게 배열하시오.

> across / opening / saw / gateway / a /
> wooden / black / a / white / , /

➡ _____
_____

19 What words were written on the gate? Fill in the blanks with suitable words.

> The warning words, _____ _____,
> were written on the gate.

[20~22] 다음 글을 읽고 물음에 답하시오.

We left our bikes at the gate and climbed over. We entered the cool tunnel. The air inside was heavy. Above our heads there was a sound that grew louder and louder.

"What's that?" I called out.

"Bats," said Ron, "Keep ⓐyour head down." Then he moved on.

"Don't go so fast." I called after ⓑhim. I meant, "Don't leave ⓒme behind" but I didn't say so.

The next thing ⓓI heard was a loud noise right above us, a thumping sound like an express train and then a scream.

"Ron!" I shouted. "Ron, what's up? Can ⓔyou hear me?" No reply. "Speak to me, Ron. Tell me what's happened."

20 밑줄 친 ⓐ~ⓔ 중에서 가리키는 대상이 서로 같은 것은?

① ⓐ－ⓑ　　　　② ⓑ－ⓒ
③ ⓑ－ⓓ　　　　④ ⓑ－ⓔ
⑤ ⓓ－ⓔ

✏️ 출제율 100%

21 위 글의 분위기로 가장 알맞은 것을 고르시오.

① exciting ② urgent

③ festive ④ gloomy

⑤ monotonous

✏️ 출제율 95%

22 Which question CANNOT be answered after reading the passage?

① Where did they leave their bikes?

② Where did they enter?

③ What were there above their heads?

④ Who said "Keep your head down"?

⑤ What's happened to Ron?

✏️ 출제율 95%

23 위 글의 밑줄 친 ⓐ를 다음과 같이 바꿔 쓸 때 빈칸에 들어갈 알맞은 말을 한 칸에 한 단어씩 쓰시오.

| and _____ his leg was put in a cast |
| = and _____ _____ _____ his leg was put in a cast |

✏️ 출제율 90%

24 위 글의 밑줄 친 ⓑ에서 어법상 틀린 부분을 찾아 고치시오.

_____ ➡ _____

[23~25] 다음 글을 읽고 물음에 답하시오.

Thanks to her, Ron was taken to the hospital, ⓐwhere his leg was put in a cast. As soon as our parents arrived at the hospital and saw us, my mother cried with relief. But all my father said was, "ⓑLet that being a lesson to you."

And what was the lesson? It was "Keep out means Stay out of trouble." Ron is now the manager of a big company which produces helmets and other safety products. And me? I am a fire fighter.

✏️ 출제율 85%

25 What did they learn from the accident? Fill in the blanks with suitable words.

| They learned "*Keep out* means _____ _____ _____ _____." |

MEMO

MEMO

INSIGHT
on the textbook

교과서 파헤치기

※ 다음 영어를 우리말로 쓰시오.

01 dust _____

02 disturb _____

03 earthquake _____

04 relieve _____

05 sandstorm _____

06 drought _____

07 effect _____

08 erupt _____

09 crop _____

10 resource _____

11 eruption _____

12 destroy _____

13 issue _____

14 flood _____

15 typhoon _____

16 volume _____

17 scenery _____

18 wildfire _____

19 prevent _____

20 yellow dust _____

21 warning _____

22 volcano _____

23 tsunami _____

24 entire _____

25 sudden _____

26 threaten _____

27 landslide _____

28 rainfall _____

29 locate _____

30 nearby _____

31 occur _____

32 ash _____

33 chance _____

34 circle _____

35 put A in danger _____

36 make use of _____

37 get hurt _____

38 name after _____

39 keep ~ in mind _____

40 have an effect on _____

41 prevent A from -ing _____

42 shoot ~ into … _____

43 in harmony with _____

※ 다음 영어를 우리말로 쓰시오.

※ 다음 우리말을 영어로 쓰시오.

01	강우, 강우량	22	황사
02	가뭄	23	전체의, 온
03	활동 중인	24	자원
04	농작물	25	모래 폭풍
05	파괴하다	26	태풍
06	지진	27	화산
07	방해하다	28	갑작스러운
08	분출	29	분출하다
09	완화하다, 줄이다	30	막다, 예방하다
10	위협하다	31	발표하다, 발행하다
11	해일	32	토양
12	범람하다; 홍수	33	둘러싸다
13	일어나다, 발생하다	34	하룻밤 사이에
14	먼지	35	수백만의
15	부피, 용적	36	~을 …으로 내뿜다
16	경치, 풍경	37	갇히다
17	주의, 경고	38	~을 따라 이름 짓다
18	산사태	39	~에 영향을 미치다
19	영향, 효과, 결과	40	~을 이용하다
20	재	41	A를 위험하게 하다
21	산불	42	~와 조화를 이루어
		43	~으로 돌아오는 길에

※ 다음 영영풀이에 알맞은 단어를 <보기>에서 골라 쓴 후, 우리말 뜻을 쓰시오.

1 _____ : a sudden outbreak of something: _____

2 _____ : involved in a particular activity: _____

3 _____ : to make a line in the shape of a ring: _____

4 _____ : the movement of cars, ships or aircraft: _____

5 _____ : a sudden shaking of Earth's surface: _____

6 _____ : even and smooth without curved or high parts: _____

7 _____ : to keep something from happening: _____

8 _____ : the grey powder that remains after something has burnt: _____

9 _____ : a large amount of water covering an area that is usually dry: _____

10 _____ : the amount of rain that falls on a particular area: _____

11 _____ : a plant such as a grain or fruit grown in large amounts: _____

12 _____ : dry powder that consists of very small bits of earth or sand: _____

13 _____ : a large round object in space that moves around a star: _____

14 _____ : to interrupt someone when they are trying to work, sleep, etc.: _____

15 _____ : a mountain with a big hole at the top, through which lava is pushed up: _____

16 _____ : a mass of earth, rock, etc. that falls down the slope of a mountain or a cliff: _____

보기			
disturb	earthquake	landslide	flat
crop	active	dust	eruption
volcano	ash	planet	prevent
rainfall	traffic	flood	circle

※ 다음 우리말과 일치하도록 빈칸에 알맞은 말을 쓰시오.

Listen - Listen & Answer Talk 1

M: Hi, this is Cha Gisang from the Weather Station. Here is today's weather. Typhoon Doni is moving north and is going to _____ Jejudo tonight. A typhoon _____ has been _____. There will be lots of _____ with a high chance of _____ in some areas. Please stay _____ because Typhoon Doni will come with strong winds. Also, please _____ _____ you _____ _____ _____ our reports. Thank you.

남: 안녕하세요, 기상대에서 차기상입니다. 오늘 날씨를 말씀드리겠습니다. 태풍 도니가 북상 중이며 오늘 밤에 제주도를 강타할 예정입니다. 태풍 주의보가 발효되었습니다. 많은 양의 비가 내릴 예정이고 일부 지역에서는 홍수의 가능성이 높습니다. 태풍 도니는 강한 바람을 동반하므로 실내에 머무십시오. 또, 보도를 계속 청취해 주시기를 당부 드립니다. 감사합니다.

Listen - Listen & Answer Dialog 2

M: Sora, can you _____ me _____ _____?
G: What is it, Dad?
M: A _____ is coming tonight. Can you _____ _____ the clothes from _____?
G: _____ problem. What about your _____?
M: I'll _____ _____ _____ it after I finish the _____.
G: Okay. Do you want me to call Grandma and tell her about the _____?
M: Yes. Please _____ her _____ _____ _____.
G: Okay, Dad.

남: 소라야, 부탁 좀 들어줄래?
여: 뭔데요, 아빠?
남: 오늘 밤 태풍이 온다는구나. 바깥에서 옷가지들을 들여와 주겠니?
여: 그럴게요. 아빠의 자전거는 어떻게 할까요?
남: 자전거는 설거지를 끝낸 후에 내가 처리하마.
여: 알겠어요. 할머니께 전화해서 태풍에 관해 말씀드릴까요?
남: 그래. 할머니께 집안에 계시라고 말씀드리렴.
여: 네, 아빠.

Listen - Listen More

B: Jimin, are you _____ _____?
G: Yeah. I'm going to buy some _____ at Choi's.
B: Are you walking there?
G: No. I'll _____ _____ _____.
B: That's _____. Can you do me _____ _____?
G: Sure. What is it?
B: Can you buy chocolate ice cream for me _____ _____ _____?
G: No _____.
B: Thanks. Please _____ _____ you _____ a helmet and _____ ear phones!
G: _____ _____ about that.

남: 지민아, 외출하니?
여: 응. '최가네'에서 샌드위치 좀 사려고.
남: 그곳에 걸어서 갈 거니?
여: 아니. 자전거를 타고 갈 거야.
남: 잘됐다. 부탁 좀 들어줄래?
여: 그럼. 뭔데?
남: 돌아오는 길에 초콜릿 아이스크림 좀 사다 줄 수 있어?
여: 물론이야.
남: 고마워. 헬멧 꼭 쓰고, 이어폰은 안 돼!
여: 걱정하지 마.

Speak - Talk in pairs.

A: Can I start now?

B: _____ _____ _____ before you start.

A: Okay. No _____.

B: One _____ thing. Make sure _____ _____ _____ _____

_____ _____.

A: I'll _____ that in _____.

A: 이제 시작할까요?

B: 시작하기 전에 손을 씻어라.

A: 네. 알겠어요.

B: 하나 더. 칼을 갖고 놀면 안 된다는 것을 명심해라.

A: 명심할게요.

Wrap Up 5

(The phone rings.)

B: Hi, Mom.

W: Hi, Junho. Are you _____ _____ _____ _____ with Dad?

B: Yeah. Today we visited Dokdo.

W: That sounds _____. What are you _____ to do tomorrow?

B: We're _____ _____ on a boat.

W: Great. Please _____ _____ you _____ _____ _____

_____.

B: Okay, Mom. I'll _____ that _____ _____.

(전화벨이 울린다.)

남: 여보세요, 엄마.

여: 그래, 준호야. 아빠랑 좋은 시간 보내고 있니?

남: 네. 오늘 우리는 독도에 다녀왔어요.

여: 굉장하구나. 내일은 뭘 할 거니?

남: 우리는 보트를 타고 낚시하러 갈 거예요.

여: 좋겠구나. 구명조끼를 꼭 입도록 해라.

남: 네, 엄마. 명심할게요.

Wrap Up 6

W: Can you _____ _____ _____ _____?

B: _____, Grandma. What is it?

W: I want to go to the Tom Dylan concert _____ _____. Can you

_____ some _____ for me?

B: No _____. How many _____ _____ _____ _____?

W: Two tickets, please.

여: 부탁 좀 들어줄 수 있니?

남: 물론이죠, 할머니. 뭔데요?

여: 크리스마스에 Tom Dylan 콘서트에 가고 싶구나. 나를 위해 표를 좀 구매해 주겠니?

남: 문제없어요. 표가 몇 장 필요하세요?

여: 두 장을 부탁한다.

※ 다음 우리말에 맞도록 대화를 영어로 쓰시오.

해석

Listen - Listen & Answer Talk 1

M: _____

_____

_____

_____

_____

_____

남: 안녕하세요, 기상대에서 차기상입니다. 오늘 날씨를 말씀드리겠습니다. 태풍 도니가 북상 중이며 오늘 밤에 제주도를 강타할 예정입니다. 태풍 주의보가 발효되었습니다. 많은 양의 비가 내릴 예정이고 일부 지역에서는 홍수의 가능성이 높습니다. 태풍 도니는 강한 바람을 동반하므로 실내에 머무십시오. 또, 보도를 계속 청취해 주시기를 당부 드립니다. 감사합니다.

Listen - Listen & Answer Dialog 2

M: _____

G: _____

M: _____

G: _____

M: _____

G: _____

M: _____

G: _____

남: 소라야, 부탁 좀 들어줄래?
여: 뭔데요, 아빠?
남: 오늘 밤 태풍이 온다는구나. 바깥에서 옷가지들을 들여와 주겠니?
여: 그럴게요. 아빠의 자전거는 어떻게 할까요?
남: 자전거는 설거지를 끝낸 후에 내가 처리하마.
여: 알겠어요. 할머니께 전화해서 태풍에 관해 말씀드릴까요?
남: 그래. 할머니께 집안에 계시라고 말씀드리렴.
여: 네, 아빠.

Listen - Listen More

B: _____

G: _____

B: _____

G: _____

B: _____

G: _____

B: _____

G: _____

B: _____

G: _____

남: 지민아, 외출하니?
여: 응. '최가네'에서 샌드위치 좀 사려고.
남: 그곳에 걸어서 갈 거니?
여: 아니. 자전거를 타고 갈 거야.
남: 잘됐다. 부탁 좀 들어줄래?
여: 그럼. 뭔데?
남: 돌아오는 길에 초콜릿 아이스크림 좀 사다 줄 수 있어?
여: 물론이야.
남: 고마워. 헬멧 꼭 쓰고, 이어폰은 안 돼!
여: 걱정하지 마.

Speak - Talk in pairs.

A: _____

B: _____

A: _____

B: _____

A: _____

A: 이제 시작할까요?
B: 시작하기 전에 손을 씻어라.
A: 네. 알겠어요.
B: 하나 더. 칼을 갖고 놀면 안 된다는 것을 명심해라.
A: 명심할게요.

Wrap Up 5

(The phone rings.)

B: _____

W: _____

B: _____

W: _____

B: _____

W: _____

B: _____

(전화벨이 울린다.)
남: 여보세요, 엄마.
여: 그래, 준호야. 아빠랑 좋은 시간 보내고 있니?
남: 네. 오늘 우리는 독도에 다녀왔어요.
여: 굉장하구나. 내일은 뭘 할 거니?
남: 우리는 보트를 타고 낚시하러 갈 거예요.
여: 좋겠구나. 구명조끼를 꼭 입도록 해라.
남: 네, 엄마. 명심할게요.

Wrap Up 6

W: _____

B: _____

W: _____

_____

B: _____

W: _____

여: 부탁 좀 들어줄 수 있니?
남: 물론이죠, 할머니. 뭔데요?
여: 크리스마스에 Tom Dylan 콘서트에 가고 싶구나. 나를 위해 표를 좀 구매해 주겠니?
남: 문제없어요. 표가 몇 장 필요하세요?
여: 두 장을 부탁한다.

※ 다음 우리말과 일치하도록 빈칸에 알맞은 것을 골라 쓰시오.

1 The _____ of _____
   A. Volcanoes   B. Power

2 What do Jejudo, Sicily, and Hawaii _____ _____ _____?
   A. common   B. have   C. in

3 They are _____, _____ _____.
   A. of   B. islands   C. course

4 In _____, they are all _____ made from _____ _____.
   A. volcanic   B. fact   C. eruptions   D. islands

5 Volcanoes are very _____, _____ they are _____ _____ Vulcan, the Roman god of fire.
   A. named   B. so   C. after   D. powerful

6 They can _____ big islands _____ or _____ cities like Pompeii.
   A. appear   B. entire   C. make   D. destroy

7 _____, they _____ be _____ and _____.
   A. studied   B. therefore   C. understood   D. should

8 Nobody knows _____ _____ how many _____ are in the world.
   A. volcanoes   B. sure   C. there   D. for

9 _____ to scientists, there are about 1,500 _____ volcanoes _____ sca _____.
   A. above   B. according   C. active   D. level

10 Many more are _____, and they are _____ _____ _____.
   A. underwater   B. hard   C. locate   D. to

11 _____, scientists have _____ a large _____ of them so _____.
   A. far   B. discovered   C. number   D. still

12 Many of the _____ on Earth are _____ _____ the Ring of Fire that _____ the Pacific Ocean.
   A. located   B. volcanoes   C. along   D. circles

13 The ring is _____ 40,000 kilometers _____, and it is _____ to _____ 75% of the world's active volcanoes.
   A. home   B. long   C. about   D. around

---

1 화산의 힘

2 제주도, 시칠리아, 하와이의 공통점은 무엇일까?

3 물론, 그것들은 섬이다.

4 사실, 그것들은 모두 화산 분출에 의해 형성된 섬이다.

5 화산은 매우 강력한 힘을 가지고 있어서 로마의 불의 신, 불카누스에게서 이름을 따왔다.

6 화산은 큰 섬이 생겨나게 하거나 폼페이 같은 도시 전체를 파멸시킬 수도 있다.

7 그러므로 화산은 연구되고, 이해되어야 한다.

8 세계에 얼마나 많은 화산이 있는지 누구도 정확히 알지 못한다.

9 과학자들에 따르면, 해수면 위에 대략 1,500개의 활화산이 있다.

10 더 많은 화산이 해저에 존재하는데, 그것들은 정확한 위치를 파악하기가 어렵다.

11 그럼에도 불구하고, 과학자들은 지금까지 그중 많은 수를 발견했다.

12 지구상에 있는 많은 화산들은 태평양을 둘러싸는 '불의 고리(환태평양조산대)'를 따라 위치한다.

13 그 고리는 길이가 약 40,000km에 달하며, 전 세계 활화산의 약 75%가 여기에 있다.

14 Indiesia _____ has over 120 active volcanoes _____ the country _____ _____ the Ring of Fire.

   A. since   B. lies   C. alone   D. on

15 This ring is also the _____ where _____ of the world's _____ _____.

   A. occur   B. most   C. area   D. earthquakes

16 A _____ _____

   A. Volcano   B. Sudden

17 _____ on a _____ one day in 1943, farmers in Mexico found _____ _____.

   A. something   B. cornfield   C. working   D. surprising

18 A volcano _____ _____ on a _____ _____.

   A. flat   B. appeared   C. cornfield   D. overnight

19 _____ watched the volcano _____ _____ 100 meters tall _____ a week.

   A. grow   B. within   C. residents   D. over

20 The volcano, _____ Paricutin, _____ growing, and it finally _____ _____ at 424 meters in 1952.

   A. stopped   B. kept   C. called   D. growing

21 You _____ think volcanoes _____ _____ _____ only on Earth.

   A. be   B. may   C. found   D. can

22 However, they have _____ _____ on other planets, too, _____ _____ Mars and Jupiter.

   A. such   B. been   C. discovered   D. as

23 In _____, "Olympus Mons" on Mars is the _____ _____ volcano in the _____ system.

   A. solar   B. fact   C. known   D. largest

24 Its volume is about 100 _____ _____ than that of Mauna Loa, the _____ _____ on Earth.

   A. greater   B. volcano   C. times   D. largest

14 인도네시아에만 120개가 넘는 활화산이 있는데, 이 나라가 '불의 고리'에 위치하고 있기 때문이다.

15 이 고리는 또한 전 세계 지진의 대부분이 발생하는 곳이다.

16 갑작스럽게 생겨난 화산

17 1943년 어느 날 옥수수 밭에서 일을 하다가 멕시코의 농부들이 놀라운 것을 발견했다.

18 밤사이에 평평한 옥수수 밭 위로 화산이 생겨난 것이다.

19 주민들은 그 화산이 일주일이 못 되는 사이 100m 넘게 자라는 것을 지켜보았다.

20 'Paricutin(파리쿠틴)'이라고 불리는 이 화산은 계속 자라났고, 1952년에 424m로 드디어 성장을 멈추었다.

21 화산이 지구에만 존재한다고 생각할지 모른다.

22 그러나 화산은 화성이나 목성 같은 다른 행성에서도 발견되어 왔다.

23 사실 화성에 있는 Olympus Mons(올림푸스 몬스)가 태양계에서 가장 크다고 알려진 화산이다.

24 그것의 부피는 지구에서 가장 큰 화산 Mauna Loa(마우나로아)의 부피보다 약 100배 더 크다.

25 _____ very powerful and _____, volcanoes do _____ to people in many _____.

    A. harm   B. dangerous   C. ways   D. being

26 Sometimes people _____ _____, or they _____ _____ their houses.

    A. hurt   B. lose   C. get   D. may

27 Crops _____ be _____, and air traffic can _____ _____.

    A. destroyed   B. may   C. threatened   D. be

28 Volcanoes can also _____ _____ _____ _____ world weather.

    A. effects   B. have   C. serious   D. on

29 A volcanic eruption _____ lots of ash and dust into the air, _____ some of the sunlight from _____ Earth and thus _____ usual weather patterns.

    A. preventing   B. disturbing   C. shoots   D. reaching

30 A _____ _____

    A. Volcano   B. Deadly

31 Mt. Tambora, an _____ _____ on the _____ of Sumbawa, Indonesia, _____ in 1815.

    A. erupted   B. island   C. volcano   D. active

32 The _____ killed _____ _____ 10,000 _____.

    A. residents   B. eruption   C. than   D. more

33 It also _____ an _____ cold summer _____ the world the _____ year.

    A. around   B. unusually   C. caused   D. following

34 _____ _____ do is not always bad for _____, _____.

    A. humans   B. volcanoes   C. what   D. however

35 The _____ near a _____ is _____ for _____.

    A. farming   B. soil   C. good   D. volcano

36 _____ are also a _____ _____ _____.

    A. tourist   B. volcanoes   C. attraction   D. great

37 _____ for fantastic _____, _____ of _____ visit Mt. Halla in Jejudo, Mt. Etna in Sicily, or Diamond Head in Hawaii every year.

    A. millions   B. scenery   C. tourists   D. looking

38 Volcanoes can _____ _____ to _____ _____, too.

    A. produce   B. be   C. electricity   D. used

39 Iceland, _____ example, actively _____ its _____ heat energy _____ electricity.

    A. turns   B. for   C. volcanoes'   D. into

40 Today people around the world are studying _____ to live in greater _____ with volcanoes, and they are _____ that more ways will be _____ soon.

    A. ways   B. harmony   C. hopeful   D. found

---

25 매우 강력하고 위험하기 때문에, 화산은 여러 면에서 사람들에게 해를 끼친다.

26 때로는 사람들이 다치기도 하고, 집을 잃기도 한다.

27 작물이 파괴되거나, 항공 교통이 위협받을 수도 있다.

28 화산은 또한 세계 날씨에 심각한 영향을 미치기도 한다.

29 화산 분출은 다량의 화산재와 먼지를 공중으로 내뿜어, 태양 광선의 일부가 지구에 도달하는 것을 방해하고 그리하여 정상적인 기상 패턴을 깨뜨린다.

30 목숨을 앗아 가는 화산

31 인도네시아 Sumbawa(숨바와) 섬에 위치한 활화산, Tambora(탐보라) 산이 1815년에 분출했다.

32 분출은 주민 1만 명 이상을 죽음에 이르게 했다.

33 또한 이듬해 전 세계에 비정상적으로 추운 여름을 초래했다.

34 그러나 화산이 인류에게 항상 나쁜 것만은 아니다.

35 화산 인근의 토양은 농사에 좋다.

36 화산은 또한 매우 훌륭한 관광 명소이다.

37 환상적인 경관을 찾아 매년 수백만 명의 여행객들이 제주도의 한라산, 시칠리아의 Etna(에트나) 산, 하와이의 Diamond Head(다이아몬드헤드)를 방문한다.

38 화산은 또한 전기를 생산하는 데에도 이용될 수 있다.

39 예를 들어, 아이슬란드는 적극적으로 화산의 열에너지를 전기로 바꾼다.

40 오늘날 전 세계에서 사람들이 화산과 더 조화롭게 살 방법을 연구하고 있으며, 더 많은 방법이 곧 발견될 것으로 기대하고 있다.

※ 다음 우리말과 일치하도록 빈칸에 알맞은 말을 쓰시오.

1 The _____ of _____

2 What do Jejudo, Sicily, and Hawaii _____ ?

3 They are _____, _____ _____.

4 In _____, they are all islands made from _____.

5 Volcanoes are very powerful, so they _____ _____ _____ Vulcan, the Roman god of fire.

6 They can _____ _____ or _____ entire cities like Pompeii.

7 Therefore, they _____.

8 Nobody knows for sure _____ _____ in the world.

9 _____ _____ scientists, there are _____ 1,500 active volcanoes _____ _____ _____.

10 Many more are _____, and they are _____ _____ _____.

11 Still, scientists have discovered _____ _____ them _____ _____.

12 Many of the volcanoes on Earth _____ _____ _____ the Ring of Fire that circles the Pacific Ocean.

13 The ring is about 40,000 kilometers long, and it is _____ _____ around 75% of the world's _____ _____.

14 Indonesia _____ has over 120 active volcanoes _____ the country _____ _____ the Ring of Fire.

15 This ring is also the area _____ most of the world's earthquakes _____.

16 A _____ Volcano

17 _____ on a cornfield one day in 1943, farmers in Mexico found _____ _____.

18 A volcano _____ _____ on a _____ _____.

19 Residents watched the volcano _____ over 100 meters tall _____ a week.

20 The volcano, called Paricutin, _____, and it finally _____ _____ at 424 meters in 1952.

21 You may think volcanoes _____ _____ _____ only on Earth.

22 However, they _____ _____ _____ on other planets, too, _____ _____ Mars and Jupiter.

23 In fact, "Olympus Mons" on Mars is _____ _____ volcano in the _____ _____ .

24 Its volume is about _____ _____ _____ Mauna Loa, the largest volcano on Earth.

25 Being very powerful and dangerous, volcanoes _____ _____ __ _____ people _____ _____ _____ .

26 Sometimes people _____ _____ , or they may lose their houses.

27 Crops _____ _____ _____ , and air traffic _____ _____ _____ .

28 Volcanoes can also _____ _____ _____ _____ world weather.

29 A volcanic eruption _____ lots of ash and dust _____ the air, _____ some of the sunlight _____ _____ Earth and thus _____ usual weather patterns.

30 A _____ _____

31 Mt. Tambora, an _____ _____ on the island of Sumbawa, Indonesia, _____ in 1815.

32 The _____ killed _____ _____ 10,000 residents.

33 It also caused an _____ cold summer around the world the _____ _____ .

34 _____ _____ _____ is _____ _____ bad for humans, however.

35 The soil near a volcano _____ _____ _____ farming.

36 Volcanoes are also a great _____ _____ .

37 _____ _____ fantastic scenery, _____ _____ tourists visit Mt. Halla in Jejudo, Mt. Etna in Sicily, or Diamond Head in Hawaii every year.

38 Volcanoes _____ _____ _____ to produce electricity, too.

39 Iceland, for example, actively _____ its volcanoes' heat energy _____ _____ .

40 Today people around the world are studying ways to live in _____ _____ _____ volcanoes, and they are hopeful that more ways _____ _____ _____ soon.

21 화산이 지구에만 존재한다고 생각할지 모른다.

22 그러나 화산은 화성이나 목성 같은 다른 행성에서도 발견되어 왔다.

23 사실 화성에 있는 Olympus Mons(올림푸스 몬스)가 태양계에서 가장 크다고 알려진 화산이다.

24 그것의 부피는 지구에서 가장 큰 화산 Mauna Loa(마우나로아)의 부피보다 약 100배 더 크다.

25 매우 강력하고 위험하기 때문에, 화산은 여러 면에서 사람들에게 해를 끼친다.

26 때로는 사람들이 다치기도 하고, 집을 잃기도 한다.

27 작물이 파괴되거나, 항공 교통이 위협받을 수도 있다.

28 화산은 또한 세계 날씨에 심각한 영향을 미치기도 한다.

29 화산 분출은 다량의 화산재와 먼지를 공중으로 내뿜어, 태양 광선의 일부가 지구에 도달하는 것을 방해하고 그리하여 정상적인 기상 패턴을 깨뜨린다.

30 목숨을 앗아 가는 화산

31 인도네시아 Sumbawa(숨바와) 섬에 위치한 활화산, Tambora(탐보라) 산이 1815년에 분출했다.

32 분출은 주민 1만 명 이상을 죽음에 이르게 했다.

33 또한 이듬해 전 세계에 비정상적으로 추운 여름을 초래했다.

34 그러나 화산이 인류에게 항상 나쁜 것만은 아니다.

35 화산 인근의 토양은 농사에 좋다.

36 화산은 또한 매우 훌륭한 관광 명소이다.

37 환상적인 경관을 찾아 매년 수백만 명의 여행객들이 제주도의 한라산, 시칠리아의 Etna(에트나) 산, 하와이의 Diamond Head(다이아몬드헤드)를 방문한다.

38 화산은 또한 전기를 생산하는 데에도 이용될 수 있다.

39 예를 들어, 아이슬란드는 적극적으로 화산의 열에너지를 전기로 바꾼다.

40 오늘날 전 세계에서 사람들이 화산과 더 조화롭게 살 방법을 연구하고 있으며, 더 많은 방법이 곧 발견될 것으로 기대하고 있다.

※ 다음 문장을 우리말로 쓰시오.

1 The Power of Volcanoes

➡ _____

2 What do Jejudo, Sicily, and Hawaii have in common?

➡ _____

3 They are islands, of course.

➡ _____

4 In fact, they are all islands made from volcanic eruptions.

➡ _____

5 Volcanoes are very powerful, so they are named after Vulcan, the Roman god of fire.

➡ _____

6 They can make big islands appear or destroy entire cities like Pompeii.

➡ _____

7 Therefore, they should be studied and understood.

➡ _____

8 Nobody knows for sure how many volcanoes there are in the world.

➡ _____

9 According to scientists, there are about 1,500 active volcanoes above sea level.

➡ _____

10 Many more are underwater, and they are hard to locate.

➡ _____

11 Still, scientists have discovered a large number of them so far.

➡ _____

12 Many of the volcanoes on Earth are located along the Ring of Fire that circles the Pacific Ocean.

➡ _____

13 The ring is about 40,000 kilometers long, and it is home to around 75% of the world's active volcanoes.

➡ _____

14 Indonesia alone has over 120 active volcanoes since the country lies on the Ring of Fire.

➡ _____

15 This ring is also the area where most of the world's earthquakes occur.

➡ _____

16 A Sudden Volcano

➡ _____

17 Working on a cornfield one day in 1943, farmers in Mexico found something surprising.

➡ _____

18 A volcano appeared overnight on a flat cornfield.

➡ _____

19 Residents watched the volcano grow over 100 meters tall within a week.

➡ _____

20 The volcano, called Paricutin, kept growing, and it finally stopped growing at 424 meters in 1952.

➡ _____

※ 다음 문장을 우리말로 쓰시오.

21 You may think volcanoes can be found only on Earth.
➡ _____

22 However, they have been discovered on other planets, too, such as Mars and Jupiter.
➡ _____

23 In fact, "Olympus Mons" on Mars is the largest known volcano in the solar system.
➡ _____

24 Its volume is about 100 times greater than that of Mauna Loa, the largest volcano on Earth.
➡ _____

25 Being very powerful and dangerous, volcanoes do harm to people in many ways.
➡ _____

26 Sometimes people get hurt, or they may lose their houses.
➡ _____

27 Crops may be destroyed, and air traffic can be threatened.
➡ _____

28 Volcanoes can also have serious effects on world weather.
➡ _____

29 A volcanic eruption shoots lots of ash and dust into the air, preventing some of the sunlight from reaching Earth and thus disturbing usual weather patterns.
➡ _____

30 A Deadly Volcano
➡ _____

31 Mt. Tambora, an active volcano on the island of Sumbawa, Indonesia, erupted in 1815.
➡ _____

32 The eruption killed more than 10,000 residents.
➡ _____

33 It also caused an unusually cold summer around the world the following year.
➡ _____

34 What volcanoes do is not always bad for humans, however.
➡ _____

35 The soil near a volcano is good for farming.
➡ _____

36 Volcanoes are also a great tourist attraction.
➡ _____

37 Looking for fantastic scenery, millions of tourists visit Mt. Halla in Jejudo, Mt. Etna in Sicily, or Diamond Head in Hawaii every year.
➡ _____

38 Volcanoes can be used to produce electricity, too.
➡ _____

39 Iceland, for example, actively turns its volcanoes' heat energy into electricity.
➡ _____

40 Today people around the world are studying ways to live in greater harmony with volcanoes, and they are hopeful that more ways will be found soon.
➡ _____

※ 다음 괄호 안의 단어들을 우리말에 맞도록 바르게 배열하시오.

1 (Power / The / Volcanoes / of)
➡ _____

2 (do / what / Sicily, / Jejudo, / and / have / Hawaii / common? / in)
➡ _____

3 (are / they / of / islands, / course.)
➡ _____

4 (fact, / in / are / they / islands / all / from / made / eruptions. / volcanic)
➡ _____

5 (are / volcanoes / powerful, / very / they / so / named / are / Vulcan, / after / Roman / the / of / god / fire.)
➡ _____
_____

6 (can / they / big / make / appear / islands / or / entire / destroy / like / cities / Pompeii.)
➡ _____

7 (they / therefore, / be / should / studied / understood. / and)
➡ _____

8 (knows / nobody / sure / for / many / how / volacnoes / are / there / the / in / world.)
➡ _____

9 (to / according / scientists, / are / there / 1,500 / about / volcanoes / active / sea / above / level.)
➡ _____
_____

10 (more / many / underwater, / are / they / and / hard / are / locate. / to)
➡ _____

11 (scientists / still, / discovered / have / large / a / number / them / of / far. / so)
➡ _____

12 (of / many / volcanoes / the / Earth / on / located / are / the / along / of / Ring / Fire / circles / that / the / Ocean. / Pacific)
➡ _____

13 (ring / the / about / is / kilometers / 40,000 / long, / it / and / is / to / home / around / of / 75% / active / world's / the / volcanoes.)
➡ _____
_____

---

1 화산의 힘

2 제주도, 시칠리아, 하와이의 공통점은 무엇일까?

3 물론, 그것들은 섬이다.

4 사실, 그것들은 모두 화산 분출에 의해 형성된 섬이다.

5 화산은 매우 강력한 힘을 가지고 있어서 로마의 불의 신, 불카누스에게서 이름을 따왔다.

6 화산은 큰 섬이 생겨나게 하거나 폼페이 같은 도시 전체를 파멸시킬 수도 있다.

7 그러므로 화산은 연구되고, 이해되어야 한다.

8 세계에 얼마나 많은 화산이 있는지 누구도 정확히 알지 못한다.

9 과학자들에 따르면, 해수면 위에 대략 1,500개의 활화산이 있다.

10 더 많은 화산이 해저에 존재하는데, 그것들은 정확한 위치를 파악하기가 어렵다.

11 그럼에도 불구하고, 과학자들은 지금까지 그중 많은 수를 발견했다.

12 지구상에 있는 많은 화산들은 태평양을 둘러싸는 '불의 고리(환태평양조산대)'를 따라 위치한다.

13 그 고리는 길이가 약 40,000km에 달하며, 전 세계 활화산의 약 75%가 여기에 있다.

14 (alone / Indonesia / over / has / active / 120 / volcanoes / the / since / country / on / lies / Ring / the / Fire. / of)

➡ _____

15 (ring / this / also / is / area / the / most / where / the / of / earthquakes / world's / occur.)

➡ _____

16 (Sudden / A / Volcano)

➡ _____

17 (on / working / cornfield / a / day / one / 1943, / in / in / farmers / found / Mexico / surprising. / something)

➡ _____

_____

18 (volcano / a / overnight / appeared / a / on / cornfield. / flat)

➡ _____

19 (watched / residents / volcano / the / over / grow / meters / 100 / tall / a / within / week.)

➡ _____

20 (volcano, / the / Paricutin, / called / growing, / kept / it / and / stopped / finally / at / growing / 424 / in / meters / 1952.)

➡ _____

_____

21 (may / you / volcanoes / think / be / can / only / found / Earth. / on)

➡ _____

22 (they / however, / been / have / on / discovered / planets, / other / too, / as / such / Jupiter. / and / Mars)

➡ _____

_____

23 (fact, / in / Mons" / "Olympus / on / is / Mars / largest / the / volcano / known / the / in / system. / solar)

➡ _____

_____

24 (volume / its / about / is / times / 100 / greater / that / than / Mauna / of / Loa, / largest / the / on / volcano / Earth.)

➡ _____

_____

14 인도네시아에만 120개가 넘는 활화산이 있는데, 이 나라가 '불의 고리'에 위치하고 있기 때문이다.

15 이 고리는 또한 전 세계 지진의 대부분이 발생하는 곳이다.

16 갑작스럽게 생겨난 화산

17 1943년 어느 날 옥수수 밭에서 일을 하다가 멕시코의 농부들이 놀라운 것을 발견했다.

18 밤사이에 평평한 옥수수 밭 위로 화산이 생겨난 것이다.

19 주민들은 그 화산이 일주일이 못 되는 사이 100m 넘게 자라는 것을 지켜보았다.

20 'Paricutin(파리쿠틴)'이라고 불리는 이 화산은 계속 자랐고, 1952년에 424m로 드디어 성장을 멈추었다.

21 화산이 지구에만 존재한다고 생각할지 모른다.

22 그러나 화산은 화성이나 목성 같은 다른 행성에서도 발견되어 왔다.

23 사실 화성에 있는 Olympus Mons(올림푸스 몬스)가 태양계에서 가장 크다고 알려진 화산이다.

24 그것의 부피는 지구에서 가장 큰 화산 Mauna Loa(마우나로아)의 부피보다 약 100배 더 크다.

25 (very / being / and / powerful / dangerous, / do / volcanoes / harm / people / to / many / in / ways.)
➡ _____

26 (people / sometimes / hurt, / get / they / or / lose / may / houses. / their)
➡ _____

27 (may / crops / destroyed, / be / air / and / can / traffic / threatened. / be)
➡ _____

28 (can / volanoes / have / also / effects / serious / world / on / weather.)
➡ _____

29 (volcanic / a / shoots / eruption / of / lots / ash / dust / and / into / air, / the / some / preventing / the / of / from / sunlight / reaching / and / Earth / disturbing / thus / weather / usual / patterns.)
➡ _____
_____
_____

30 (Deadly / A / Volcano)
➡ _____

31 (Tambora, / Mt. / active / an / on / volcano / the / of / island / Sumbawa / erupted / Indonesia, / 1815. / in)
➡ _____
_____

32 (eruption / the / more / killed / 10,000 / than / residents.)
➡ _____

33 (also / it / an / caused / cold / unusually / around / summer / the / world / following / the / year.)
➡ _____
_____

34 (volcanoes / what / is / do / always / not / for / bad / however. / humans,)
➡ _____

35 (soil / the / a / near / is / volcano / for / good / farming.)
➡ _____

36 (are / volcanoes / a / also / tourist / great / attraction.)
➡ _____

37 (for / lookiing / scenery, / fantastic / of / millions / visit / tourists / Halla / Mt. / Jejudo, / in / Etna / Mt. / Sicily, / in / Diamond / or / in / Head / every / Hawaii / year.)
➡ _____
_____

38 (can / volcanoes / be / used / produce / to / too. / electricity,)
➡ _____

39 (for / Iceland, / example, / turns / actively / volcanoes' / its / energy / heat / electricity. / into)
➡ _____
_____

40 (people / today / the / around / world / studying / are / to / ways / in / live / harmony / greater / volcanoes, / with / they / and / hopeful / are / more / that / will / ways / found / be / soon.)
➡ _____
_____
_____

25 매우 강력하고 위험하기 때문에, 화산은 여러 면에서 사람들에게 해를 끼친다.

26 때로는 사람들이 다치기도 하고, 집을 잃기도 한다.

27 작물이 파괴되거나, 항공 교통이 위협받을 수도 있다.

28 화산은 또한 세계 날씨에 심각한 영향을 미치기도 한다.

29 화산 분출은 다량의 화산재와 먼지를 공중으로 내뿜어, 태양 광선의 일부가 지구에 도달하는 것을 방해하고 그리하여 정상적인 기상 패턴을 깨뜨린다.

30 목숨을 앗아 가는 화산

31 인도네시아 Sumbawa(숨바와) 섬에 위치한 활화산, Tambora(탐보라) 산이 1815년에 분출했다.

32 분출은 주민 1만 명 이상을 죽음에 이르게 했다.

33 또한 이듬해 전 세계에 비정상적으로 추운 여름을 초래했다.

34 그러나 화산이 인류에게 항상 나쁜 것만은 아니다.

35 화산 인근의 토양은 농사에 좋다.

36 화산은 또한 매우 훌륭한 관광 명소이다.

37 환상적인 경관을 찾아 매년 수백만 명의 여행객들이 제주도의 한라산, 시칠리아의 Etna(에트나) 산, 하와이의 Diamond Head(다이아몬드헤드)를 방문한다.

38 화산은 또한 전기를 생산하는 데에도 이용될 수 있다.

39 예를 들어, 아이슬란드는 적극적으로 화산의 열에너지를 전기로 바꾼다.

40 오늘날 전 세계에서 사람들이 화산과 더 조화롭게 살 방법을 연구하고 있으며, 더 많은 방법이 곧 발견될 것으로 기대하고 있다.

※ 다음 우리말을 영어로 쓰시오.

1 화산의 힘
➡

2 제주도, 시칠리아, 하와이의 공통점은 무엇일까?
➡

3 물론, 그것들은 섬이다.
➡

4 사실, 그것들은 모두 화산 분출에 의해 형성된 섬이다.
➡

5 화산은 매우 강력한 힘을 가지고 있어서 로마의 불의 신, 불카누스에게서 이름을 따왔다.

6 화산은 큰 섬이 생겨나게 하거나 폼페이 같은 도시 전체를 파멸시킬 수도 있다.
➡

7 그러므로 화산은 연구되고, 이해되어야 한다.
➡

8 세계에 얼마나 많은 화산이 있는지 누구도 정확히 알지 못한다.
➡

9 과학자들에 따르면, 해수면 위에 대략 1,500개의 활화산이 있다.
➡

10 더 많은 화산이 해저에 존재하는데, 그것들은 정확한 위치를 파악하기가 어렵다.
➡

11 그럼에도 불구하고, 과학자들은 지금까지 그중 많은 수를 발견했다.
➡

12 지구상에 있는 많은 화산들은 태평양을 둘러싸는 '불의 고리(환태평양조산대)'를 따라 위치한다.
➡

13 그 고리는 길이가 약 40,000km에 달하며, 전 세계 활화산의 약 75%가 여기에 있다.

14 인도네시아에만 120개가 넘는 활화산이 있는데, 이 나라가 '불의 고리'에 위치하고 있기 때문이다.
➡

15 이 고리는 또한 전 세계 지진의 대부분이 발생하는 곳이다.
➡

16 갑작스럽게 생겨난 화산
➡

17 1943년 어느 날 옥수수 밭에서 일을 하다가 멕시코의 농부들이 놀라운 것을 발견했다.
➡

18 밤사이에 평평한 옥수수 밭 위로 화산이 생겨난 것이다.
➡

19 주민들은 그 화산이 일주일이 못 되는 사이 100m 넘게 자라는 것을 지켜보았다.
➡

20 'Paricutin(파리쿠틴)'이라 불리는 이 화산은 계속 자라났고, 1952년에 424m로 드디어 성장을 멈추었다.
➡

21 화산이 지구에만 존재한다고 생각할지 모른다.
➡ _____

22 그러나 화산은 화성이나 목성 같은 다른 행성에서도 발견되어 왔다.
➡ _____

23 사실 화성에 있는 Olympus Mons(올림푸스 몬스)가 태양계에서 가장 크다고 알려진 화산이다.
➡ _____

24 그것의 부피는 지구에서 가장 큰 화산 Mauna Loa(마우나 로아)의 부피보다 약 100배 더 크다.
➡ _____

25 매우 강력하고 위험하기 때문에, 화산은 여러 면에서 사람들에게 해를 끼친다.
➡ _____

26 때로는 사람들이 다치기도 하고, 집을 잃기도 한다.
➡ _____

27 작물이 파괴되거나, 항공 교통이 위협받을 수도 있다.
➡ _____

28 화산은 또한 세계 날씨에 심각한 영향을 미치기도 한다.
➡ _____

29 화산 분출은 다량의 화산재와 먼지를 공중으로 내뿜어, 태양 광선의 일부가 지구에 도달하는 것을 방해하고 그리하여 정상적인 기상 패턴을 깨트린다.
➡ _____
_____

30 목숨을 앗아 가는 화산
➡ _____

31 인도네시아 Sumbawa(숨바와) 섬에 위치한 활화산, Tambora(탐보라) 산이 1815년에 분출했다.
➡ _____

32 분출은 주민 1만 명 이상을 죽음에 이르게 했다.
➡ _____

33 또한 이듬해 전 세계에 비정상적으로 추운 여름을 초래했다.
➡ _____

34 그러나 화산이 인류에게 항상 나쁜 것만은 아니다.
➡ _____

35 화산 인근의 토양은 농사에 좋다.
➡ _____

36 화산은 또한 매우 훌륭한 관광 명소이다.
➡ _____

37 환상적인 경관을 찾아 매년 수백만 명의 여행객들이 제주도의 한라산, 시칠리아의 Etna(에트나) 산, 하와이의 Diamond Head(다이아몬드헤드)를 방문한다.
➡ _____

38 화산은 또한 전기를 생산하는 데에도 이용될 수 있다.
➡ _____

39 예를 들어, 아이슬란드는 적극적으로 화산의 열에너지를 전기로 바꾼다.
➡ _____

40 오늘날 전 세계에서 사람들이 화산과 더 조화롭게 살 방법을 연구하고 있으며, 더 많은 방법이 곧 발견될 것으로 기대하고 있다.
➡ _____
_____

※ 다음 우리말과 일치하도록 빈칸에 알맞은 말을 쓰시오.

My Speaking Portfolio Step 1

1. The _____ is _____.

2. The pan _____ _____ _____.

3. I _____ _____ in the elevator.

4. I _____ _____ _____ in hot water.

5. I _____ _____ the steps and _____ my arm.

1. 정전됐어요.
2. 프라이팬에 불이 붙었어요.
3. 나는 엘리베이터에 갇혔어요.
4. 나는 뜨거운 물에 손을 데었어요.
5. 나는 계단에서 넘어져서 팔이 부러졌어요.

After You Read Details

1. The name "_____" _____ _____ the Roman god of fire. - Mila

2. 75% of _____ _____ _____ _____ _____ _____ the Ring of Fire. - James

3. The volcano Paricutin in Mexico _____ _____. - Lucy

4. _____ _____ of Mt. Tambora _____ _____ _____ _____ _____ _____ in 1816. - David

1. "화산"이라는 이름은 로마의 불의 신에게서 이름을 따왔다. – Mila
2. 전 세계 화산의 75%는 '불의 고리(환태평양조산대)'를 따라 위치한다. – James
3. 멕시코의 Paricutin 화산은 성장을 멈추었다. – Lucy
4. Tambora산의 분출은 1816년에 비정상적으로 추운 여름을 초래했다. – David

My Writing Portfolio

1. The _____ _____

2. I _____ the movie *The Perfect Storm* _____ _____.

3. The movie _____ _____ in 2000, and it _____ _____ _____ the German director Wolfgang Petersen.

4. It is _____ a big storm _____ _____ _____ _____ _____ that put a fishing boat _____ _____.

5. I liked the movie _____ _____ _____ and very _____.

6. Also, I liked the _____ _____ _____ _____ _____ George Clooney.

7. From the movie, I _____ that _____ _____ _____ _____ can be very _____.

1. 퍼펙트 스톰
2. 나는 지난 주말에 영화 '퍼펙트 스톰'을 봤다.
3. 그 영화는 2000년에 개봉했고, 독일 감독 Wolfgang Petersen이 연출했다.
4. 그것은 어선을 위험에 빠뜨린 대서양의 거대한 폭풍에 관한 것이다.
5. 나는 장면들이 흥미진진하고 매우 사실적이었기 때문에 이 영화가 좋았다.
6. 또한, 나는 주연 배우 George Clooney의 훌륭한 연기도 마음에 들었다.
7. 이 영화를 통해 나는 폭풍과 같은 자연재해가 매우 위험할 수 있다는 것을 배웠다.

※ 다음 우리말을 영어로 쓰시오.

My Speaking Portfolio Step 1

1. A: 정전됐어요.
   ➡ _____

2. 프라이팬에 불이 붙었어요.
   ➡ _____

3. 나는 엘리베이터에 갇혔어요.
   ➡ _____

4. 나는 뜨거운 물에 손을 데었어요.
   ➡ _____

5. 나는 계단에서 넘어져서 팔이 부러졌어요.
   ➡ _____

After You Read Details

1. "화산"이라는 이름은 로마의 불의 신에게서 이름을 따왔다. – Mila
   ➡ _____

2. 전 세계 활화산의 75%는 '불의 고리(환태평양조산대)'를 따라 위치한다. – James
   ➡ _____

3. 멕시코의 Paricutin 화산은 성장을 멈추었다. – Lucy
   ➡ _____

4. Tambora산의 분출은 1816년에 비정상적으로 추운 여름을 초래했다. – David
   ➡ _____

My Writing Portfolio

1. 퍼펙트 스톰
   ➡ _____

2. 나는 지난 주말에 영화 '퍼펙트 스톰'을 봤다.
   ➡ _____

3. 그 영화는 2000년에 개봉했고, 독일 감독 Wolfgang Petersen이 연출했다.
   ➡ _____

4. 그것은 어선을 위험에 빠뜨린 대서양의 거대한 폭풍에 관한 것이다.
   ➡ _____

5. 나는 장면들이 흥미진진하고 매우 사실적이었기 때문에 이 영화가 좋았다.
   ➡ _____

6. 또한, 나는 주연 배우 George Clooney의 훌륭한 연기도 마음에 들었다.
   ➡ _____

7. 이 영화를 통해 나는 폭풍과 같은 자연재해가 매우 위험할 수 있다는 것을 배웠다.
   ➡ _____

※ 다음 영어를 우리말로 쓰시오.

01	achieve	_____
02	confident	_____
03	banner	_____
04	tryout	_____
05	worried	_____
06	calm	_____
07	capital	_____
08	offer	_____
09	opportunity	_____
10	lifelong	_____
11	chase	_____
12	protection	_____
13	worth	_____
14	completely	_____
15	impatient	_____
16	connect	_____
17	delighted	_____
18	rule	_____
19	save	_____
20	serious	_____
21	express	_____

22	scared	_____
23	cheerful	_____
24	regret	_____
25	challenging	_____
26	found	_____
27	imagination	_____
28	improve	_____
29	repair	_____
30	include	_____
31	mistaken	_____
32	decision	_____
33	rest	_____
34	skill	_____
35	break down	_____
36	may[might] have p.p.	_____
37	deal with	_____
38	break out	_____
39	used to	_____
40	be ashamed of	_____
41	apply for	_____
42	hang out with	_____
43	over and over	_____

※ 다음 우리말을 영어로 쓰시오.

01 확신하는, 자신만만한		
02 향상시키다, 개선하다		
03 현수막		
04 완전히, 전적으로		
05 포함하다		
06 일생[평생]의		
07 이루다, 달성[성취]하다		
08 침착한, 냉정한		
09 표현하다		
10 연결하다		
11 설립하다		
12 기분 좋은, 즐거운		
13 아주 기뻐하는		
14 쫓다, 추적하다		
15 연습하다, 훈련하다		
16 후회하다		
17 수도		
18 심사, 테스트		
19 보호		
20 도전적인		
21 짜증 난, 참지 못하는		

22 기회		
23 ～할 가치가 있는		
24 상상, 상상력		
25 수리하다		
26 기량, 기술		
27 결정, 판단		
28 구하다, 절약하다		
29 무서워하는, 겁먹은		
30 심각한, 진지한		
31 잘못 알고 있는		
32 나머지, 휴식		
33 뽑다, 고르다		
34 꽤, 상당히		
35 지나가다, 흐르다		
36 반복해서		
37 고장 나다		
38 ～했음에 틀림없다		
39 ～을 부끄러워하다		
40 발발[발생]하다		
41 ～와 시간을 보내다		
42 ～을 다루다		
43 ～에 지원하다, ～을 신청하다		

※ 다음 영영풀이에 알맞은 단어를 <보기>에서 골라 쓴 후, 우리말 뜻을 쓰시오.

1 _____ : to establish: _____

2 _____ : to join together: _____

3 _____ : the part that is left: _____

4 _____ : to make something new: _____

5 _____ : to have or give information: _____

6 _____ : chance for doing something: _____

7 _____ : showing a lack of patience: _____

8 _____ : the act of making up one's mind: _____

9 _____ : difficult in a way that is usually enjoyable: _____

10 _____ : a test of the potential of someone: _____

11 _____ : a long piece of cloth with words written on it: _____

12 _____ : to have something as part of a group or total: _____

13 _____ : acting or speaking sincerely and without joking: _____

14 _____ : a group of sports teams that play against each other: _____

15 _____ : to feel sorry about something that you did in the past: _____

16 _____ : good or important enough for something: _____

보기			
regret	decision	league	opportunity
banner	found	challenging	rest
worth	read	serious	impatient
tryout	connect	include	create

※ 다음 우리말과 일치하도록 빈칸에 알맞은 말을 쓰시오.

Listen - Listen & Answer Dialog 1

B: Hi, Sora. _____ are you doing?

G: I'm _____ _____. I'm _____ _____ the exam for Mana Animation High School.

B: Oh, _____ you? _____ is the exam?

G: _____ Friday, so I only have two days _____.

B: _____ it _____?

G: _____'s not easy _____ _____ _____ I want _____ _____. I _____ _____ _____ more.

B: Don't _____! You can _____ _____!

G: Thanks.

Listen - Listen & Answer Dialog 2

M: Nice _____ _____ you, Sora. Did you _____ _____ _____ the _____ _____?

G: I'm not _____, but I _____ _____ _____.

M: Okay. Let's start the interview. _____ _____ you _____ _____ Mana Animation High School?

G: Well, I'_____ really _____ drawing cartoons _____ I was a _____ _____.

M: So, you want to be a _____ _____?

G: That's not _____ _____. I want to be a game designer.

M: I see. _____ do you _____ is the _____ _____ _____ a game designer needs?

G: _____ _____ imagination. A good designer should create a _____ new world in a game.

M: Sounds good.

Speak - Talk in pairs.

A: What's the _____?

B: I feel _____. I should have _____ food for the winter.

A: _____ worry. I'll _____ my food _____ you.

B: Thanks.

남: 안녕, 소라야. 뭘 하고 있니?
여: 만화를 그리고 있어. 마나 애니메이션 고등학교 입학시험을 준비하고 있어.
남: 아, 그래? 시험이 언제야?
여: 금요일, 그래서 이틀밖에 안 남았어.
남: 어떻게 되고 있니?
여: 내가 표현하고 싶은 것을 그리기가 쉽지 않아. 나는 더 연습했어야 해.
남: 걱정하지 마! 넌 해낼 수 있어!
여: 고마워.

남: 소라 학생, 만나서 반가워요. 소묘 시험은 잘 봤나요?
여: 잘 모르겠지만 최선을 다했습니다.
남: 알겠어요. 면접을 시작합시다. 왜 마나 애니메이션 고등학교에 지원했나요?
여: 음, 저는 어렸을 때부터 만화 그리는 것을 정말 좋아했습니다.
남: 그렇다면, 만화가가 되고 싶나요?
여: 꼭 그렇지는 않습니다. 저는 게임 디자이너가 되고 싶습니다.
남: 그렇군요. 게임 디자이너에게 필요한 가장 중요한 기량이 무엇이라고 생각하나요?
여: 상상력이라고 말씀드리겠습니다. 훌륭한 게임 디자이너는 게임 속에서 완전히 새로운 세계를 창조해야 하거든요.
남: 좋습니다.

A: 무슨 일이야?
B: 배가 고파. 나는 겨울용 식량을 저장해 놨어야 해.
A: 걱정하지 마. 내가 내 식량을 나눠 줄게.
B: 고마워.

Listen - Listen More

G: Hi, Jiho.

B: Hi, Amber. It's nice _____ _____ you on the bus.

G: Yeah, but _____ _____ we're going to _____ _____.

B: Yeah. I _____ _____ _____ _____ _____ the school festival.

G: Me, too. I _____ _____ _____ my alarm. I forgot.

B: I understand. That _____ _____ to me when I'm _____, too.

G: How about you? _____ _____ you _____?

B: Well, I _____ _____ early. But _____ _____ me some time to _____ _____ _____.

G: Oh, I see. _____ _____ _____ a heavy _____ _____. We should _____ _____ and run.

B: No, _____ _____. The traffic is starting to move again. Let's _____ _____.

G: Okay. I just hope we're not _____ late.

여: 지호야, 안녕.
남: Amber, 안녕. 버스에서 너를 보다니 반갑다.
여: 맞아, 그런데 걱정스럽게도 우리가 늦을 것 같아.
남: 그러게. 학교 축제에 늦고 싶지 않은데.
여: 나도 그래. 알람을 맞출걸. 내가 깜빡했어.
남: 이해해. 나도 피곤할 때 그런 일이 많이 일어나.
여: 너는? 무슨 일로 늦었어?
남: 음, 난 일찍 일어났어. 그런데 머리를 손질하느라 시간이 좀 걸렸어.
여: 아, 그렇구나. 우리 교통 체증에 갇혔어. 버스에서 내려서 뛰어가지.
남: 아니, 네가 잘못 생각하는 거야. 차들이 다시 움직이기 시작해. 내리지 말자.
여: 알았어. 너무 늦지 않기를 바랄 뿐이야.

Wrap Up 6

B: What do you want to do _____ you _____ _____?

G: I want to work _____ robots.

B: Are you _____ _____ _____ robots?

G: No, _____ not _____ _____. I want to _____ robots.

B: I see. But _____?

G: _____ I _____ it'll be a good job in the future.

남: 너는 커서 무엇을 하고 싶니?
여: 나는 로봇과 관련된 일을 하고 싶어.
남: 로봇 제작하는 것에 관심 있니?
여: 아니, 꼭 그렇지는 않아. 나는 로봇을 수리하고 싶어.
남: 그렇구나. 그런데 왜?
여: 그것이 미래에 좋은 직업이 될 거라고 생각하기 때문이야.

Wrap Up 7

G: My computer _____ _____.

B: _____ come?

G: I opened an e-mail from a stranger. I _____ _____ _____ that.

B: If I _____ _____, _____ _____ help from a computer service center _____ _____.

여: 내 컴퓨터가 바이러스에 걸렸어.
남: 어쩌다가 그랬니?
여: 모르는 사람에게서 온 이메일을 열었지. 그러지 말았어야 해.
남: 내가 너라면, 지금 바로 컴퓨터 서비스 센터에서 도움을 받겠어.

대화문 Test

※ 다음 우리말에 맞도록 대화를 영어로 쓰시오.

Listen - Listen & Answer Dialog 1

B: _____

G: _____
_____

B: _____

G: _____

B: _____

G: _____

B: _____

G: _____

남: 안녕, 소라야. 뭘 하고 있니?
여: 만화를 그리고 있어. 마나 애니메이션 고등학교 입학시험을 준비하고 있어.
남: 아, 그래? 시험이 언제야?
여: 금요일, 그래서 이틀밖에 안 남았어.
남: 어떻게 되고 있니?
여: 내가 표현하고 싶은 것을 그리기가 쉽지 않아. 나는 더 연습했어야 해.
남: 걱정하지 마! 넌 해낼 수 있어!
여: 고마워.

Listen - Listen & Answer Dialog 2

M: _____

G: _____

M: _____
_____

G: _____

M: _____

G: _____

M: _____

G: _____
_____

M: _____

남: 소라 학생, 만나서 반가워요. 소묘 시험은 잘 봤나요?
여: 잘 모르겠지만 최선을 다했습니다.
남: 알겠어요. 면접을 시작합시다. 왜 마나 애니메이션 고등학교에 지원했나요?
여: 음, 저는 어렸을 때부터 만화 그리는 것을 정말 좋아했습니다.
남: 그렇다면, 만화가가 되고 싶나요?
여: 꼭 그렇지는 않습니다. 저는 게임 디자이너가 되고 싶습니다.
남: 그렇군요. 게임 디자이너에게 필요한 가장 중요한 기량이 무엇이라고 생각하나요?
여: 상상력이라고 말씀드리겠습니다. 훌륭한 게임 디자이너는 게임 속에서 완전히 새로운 세계를 창조해야 하거든요.
남: 좋습니다.

Speak - Talk in pairs.

A: _____

B: _____

A: _____

B: _____

A: 무슨 일이야?
B: 배가 고파. 나는 겨울용 식량을 저장해 놨어야 해.
A: 걱정하지 마. 내가 내 식량을 나눠 줄게.
B: 고마워.

Listen - Listen More

G: _____

B: _____

G: _____

B: _____

G: _____

B: _____

G: _____

B: _____

G: _____

B: _____

G: _____

Wrap Up 6

B: _____

G: _____

B: _____

G: _____

B: _____

G: _____

Wrap Up 7

G: _____

B: _____

G: _____

B: _____

여: 지호야, 안녕.

남: Amber, 안녕. 버스에서 너를 보다니 반갑다.

여: 맞아. 그런데 걱정스럽게도 우리가 늦을 것 같아.

남: 그러게. 학교 축제에 늦고 싶지 않은데.

여: 나도 그래. 알람을 맞출걸. 내가 깜빡했어.

남: 이해해. 나도 피곤할 때 그런 일이 많이 일어나.

여: 너는? 무슨 일로 늦었어?

남: 음, 난 일찍 일어났어. 그런데 머리를 손질하느라 시간이 좀 걸렸어.

여: 아, 그렇구나. 우리 교통 체증에 갇혔어. 버스에서 내려서 뛰어가자.

남: 아니, 네가 잘못 생각하는 거야. 자들이 다시 움직이기 시작해. 내리지 말자.

여: 알았어. 너무 늦지 않기를 바랄 뿐이야.

남: 너는 커서 무엇을 하고 싶니?

여: 나는 로봇과 관련된 일을 하고 싶어.

남: 로봇 제작하는 것에 관심 있니?

여: 아니, 꼭 그렇지는 않아. 나는 로봇을 수리하고 싶어.

남: 그렇구나. 그런데 왜?

여: 그것이 미래에 좋은 직업이 될 거라고 생각하기 때문이야.

여: 내 컴퓨터가 바이러스에 걸렸어.

남: 어쩌다가 그랬니?

여: 모르는 사람에게서 온 이메일을 열었지. 그러지 말았어야 해.

남: 내가 너라면, 지금 바로 컴퓨터 서비스 센터에서 도움을 받겠어.

※ 다음 우리말과 일치하도록 빈칸에 알맞은 것을 골라 쓰시오.

1 MY _____ _____ _____

    A. DREAMS   B. BASEBALL   C. GRANDMOTHER'S

2 My grandmother Helen _____ _____ be a _____ in a restaurant in a small town _____ South Bend, Indiana.

    A. near   B. to   C. cook   D. used

3 She does not _____ _____, but she still enjoys making _____ food, _____ I love so much.

    A. which   B. anymore   C. delicious   D. work

4 Food is _____ of the many things _____ _____ _____.

    A. connect   B. one   C. us   D. that

5 _____ _____ us most _____, _____, is baseball.

    A. however   B. what   C. strongly   D. connects

6 _____ I visit her on _____, my grandmother often tells me _____ stories about playing baseball _____ in the 1940s.

    A. back   B. weekends   C. exciting   D. when

7 She _____ _____ _____ the sport very much.

    A. have   B. must   C. loved

8 I _____ _____ these stories _____ _____ over.

    A. over   B. to   C. and   D. listen

9 She always _____, "_____ _____ _____ you want, Sarah.

    A. after   B. go   C. says   D. what

10 Don't be _____ of trying _____ _____ or _____.

    A. challenging   B. afraid   C. something   D. new

11 _____ be _____ _____ _____."

    A. ashamed   B. don't   C. of   D. failing

12 _____ 1943, the All-American Girls _____ Baseball League _____ _____.

    A. founded   B. in   C. was   D. Professional

13 This league was _____ for baseball fans _____ many of America's young men _____ _____ in World War II.

    A. fighting   B. created   C. because   D. were

14 Helen was told that _____ _____ be _____ _____ right in South Bend.

    A. would   B. tryouts   C. there   D. local

15 She wondered, "_____ _____ it be _____ to be on a baseball team and to make it to the _____ for my hometown?"

    A. like   B. what   C. finals   D. would

16 She _____ a large banner _____ at the baseball field _____ the name Helen Baker.

    A. included   B. imagined   C. which   D. hanging

1 할머니의 야구 꿈

2 우리 할머니 Helen은 Indiana주 South Bend 근처 작은 마을에 있는 식당의 요리사였다.

3 할머니는 더 이상 일을 하지 않지만 여전히 맛있는 음식을 즐겨 만드시고, 나는 그 음식들을 무척 좋아한다.

4 음식은 우리를 연결하는 많은 것 가운데 하나이다.

5 하지만 우리를 가장 강하게 연결하는 것은 바로 야구이다.

6 주말마다 할머니 댁에 가면, 할머니는 종종 과거 1940년대의 야구 경기에 관해 흥미로운 이야기를 내게 들려주신다.

7 그녀는 야구를 무척 좋아했던 게 분명하다.

8 나는 이 이야기들을 몇 번이고 듣는다.

9 그녀는 항상 "네가 원하는 것을 이루려고 노력하렴, Sarah.

10 새로운 것이나 도전적인 것을 시도해 보기를 두려워하지 말거라.

11 실패하는 것을 부끄러워하지 마라."라고 말씀하신다.

12 1943년, 전미 여자 프로야구 리그가 창립되었다.

13 미국의 청년 중 많은 사람들이 제2차 세계대전에 참전해 있었기 때문에 이 리그가 야구 팬들을 위해 만들어졌다.

14 Helen 할머니는 지역 심사가 바로 South Bend에서 있을 거라고 들었다.

15 그녀는 "야구 팀에 들어가서 고향을 위해 결승전까지 진출한다는 건 어떤 기분일까?"라며 궁금해했다.

16 그녀는 Helen Baker라는 이름이 포함된 큰 현수막이 야구장에 걸려 있는 것을 상상했다.

17 On the day of the tryouts, all the rules were _____ by an old man in a _____, who sounded very _____ and _____.

  A. suit   B. unkind   C. explained   D. serious

18 She _____ that _____ a suit in the hot sun might have _____ him _____.

  A. impatient   B. wearing   C. made   D. thought

19 _____ that day, Helen played baseball _____ _____ with many _____ young women.

  A. hours   B. on   C. other   D. for

20 She was _____ _____ _____ _____ her baseball dreams!

  A. after   B. excited   C. go   D. to

21 _____ a week _____, Helen _____ a letter in the _____.

  A. mailbox   B. about   C. found   D. later

22 _____ was _____ people who _____ _____ the girls' baseball league in Chicago.

  A. worked   B. from   C. for   D. it

23 It _____ that she _____ been invited to the league's _____ _____ in Chicago!

  A. main   B. had   C. tryouts   D. read

24 _____ the days _____ _____, however, Helen became _____ that she might fail.

  A. worried   B. as   C. went   D. by

25 She also became worried about _____ alone to Chicago, _____ was _____ _____ from home.

  A. which   B. away   C. traveling   D. far

26 When the day of the main _____ came, she was _____ _____ _____ go.

  A. too   B. tryouts   C. to   D. afraid

27 My grandmother has _____ the _____ of her life _____ her _____.

  A. regretting   B. spent   C. decision   D. rest

28 When she _____ a baseball game on TV, she often says, "I _____ _____ to Chicago.

  A. have   B. watches   C. should   D. gone

29 You know, all your dreams are _____ _____, _____ if you catch only a _____ of them.

  A. chasing   B. few   C. worth   D. even

30 _____ _____ an _____."

  A. miss   B. never   C. opportunity

17 심사 당일 모든 규칙이 정장을 입은 나이 든 남자에 의해 설명되었는데, 그는 무척 진지하고 불친절하게 들렸다.

18 뜨거운 태양 아래 정장을 입고 있는 것이 그를 짜증나게 만들었을지도 모른다고 그녀는 생각했다.

19 그날, Helen 할머니는 다른 젊은 여성들과 함께 몇 시간 동안 야구를 했다.

20 그녀는 자신의 야구 꿈을 좇아가게 되어 신이 났다!

21 일주일쯤 지나, Helen 할머니는 우편함에서 편지 한 통을 발견했다.

22 그것은 시카고에 있는 여자 야구 리그에서 일하는 사람들이 보낸 것이었다.

23 그 편지에는 그녀가 시카고에서 열리는 리그의 본심사에 초청되었다고 적혀 있었다!

24 하지만 하루하루 갈수록, Helen 할머니는 심사에 떨어질까봐 걱정되었다.

25 그녀는 또한 시카고까지 혼자 여행하는 것이 걱정되었는데, 시카고는 집에서 멀리 떨어진 곳이었다.

26 본심사가 있는 날이 되었을 때, 그녀는 너무 두려워서 갈 수 없었다.

27 할머니는 남은 인생을 자신의 결정을 후회하며 보내셨다.

28 텔레비전에서 야구 경기를 볼 때, 그녀는 종종 "난 시카고에 갔어야 해.

29 너도 알겠지만, 모든 꿈은 추구할 가치가 있단다. 비록 일부만 이루게 되더라도 말이야.

30 절대 기회를 놓치지 마라."라고 말씀하신다.

※ 다음 우리말과 일치하도록 빈칸에 알맞은 것을 골라 쓰시오.

1 MY _____ BASEBALL _____

2 My grandmother Helen _____ _____ _____ _____ in a restaurant in a small town _____ South Bend, Indiana.

3 She does not work _____, but she still _____ _____ delicious food, _____ I love so much.

4 Food is _____ of the many things _____ _____ _____ .

5 _____ _____ us most _____, however, _____ baseball.

6 When I visit her _____ _____, my grandmother often tells me _____ _____ about playing baseball _____ in the 1940s.

7 She _____ _____ _____ the sport very much.

8 I _____ _____ these stories _____ _____ _____ .

9 She always says, "_____ _____ _____ you want, Sarah.

10 Don't be _____ _____ trying _____ _____ _____ _____ .

11 _____ _____ _____ _____ failing."

12 In 1943, the All-American Girls Professional Baseball League _____ _____ .

13 This league _____ _____ for baseball fans because many of America's young men _____ _____ in World War II.

14 Helen was told that _____ _____ _____ _____ _____ right in South Bend.

15 She wondered, "_____ _____ _____ _____ to be on a baseball team and to make it to _____ _____ for my hometown?"

16 She _____ a large banner _____ at the baseball field _____ _____ the name Helen Baker.

---

1 할머니의 야구 꿈

2 우리 할머니 Helen은 Indiana주 South Bend 근처 작은 마을에 있는 식당의 요리사였다.

3 할머니는 더 이상 일을 하지 않지만 여전히 맛있는 음식을 즐겨 만드시고, 나는 그 음식들을 무척 좋아한다.

4 음식은 우리를 연결하는 많은 것 가운데 하나이다.

5 하지만 우리를 가장 강하게 연결하는 것은 바로 야구이다.

6 주말마다 할머니 댁에 가면, 할머니는 종종 과거 1940년대의 야구 경기에 관해 흥미로운 이야기를 내게 들려주신다.

7 그녀는 야구를 무척 좋아했던 게 분명하다.

8 나는 이 이야기들을 몇 번이고 듣는다.

9 그녀는 항상 "네가 원하는 것을 이루려고 노력하렴, Sarah.

10 새로운 것이나 도전적인 것을 시도해 보기를 두려워하지 말거라.

11 실패하는 것을 부끄러워하지 마라."라고 말씀하신다.

12 1943년, 전미 여자 프로야구 리그가 창립되었다.

13 미국의 청년 중 많은 사람들이 제2차 세계대전에 참전해 있었기 때문에 이 리그가 야구 팬들을 위해 만들어졌다.

14 Helen 할머니는 지역 심사가 바로 South Bend에서 있을 거라고 들었다.

15 그녀는 "야구 팀에 들어가서 고향을 위해 결승전까지 진출한다는 건 어떤 기분일까?"라며 궁금해했다.

16 그녀는 Helen Baker라는 이름이 포함된 큰 현수막이 야구장에 걸려 있는 것을 상상했다.

17 On the day of the tryouts, all the rules _____ _____ by an old man _____ _____ _____, who sounded very _____ and unkind.

18 She thought that _____ _____ _____ in the hot sun _____ _____ _____ him _____.

19 On that day, Helen played baseball _____ _____ with many _____ young _____.

20 She was excited _____ _____ _____ her baseball dreams!

21 About a week _____, Helen _____ _____ _____ in the mailbox.

22 _____ _____ _____ people who worked for the girls' baseball league in Chicago.

23 _____ _____ that she _____ _____ _____ to the _____ _____ _____ in Chicago!

24 _____ the days _____ _____, however, Helen became _____ that she might fail.

25 She also became _____ _____ traveling alone to Chicago, _____ was _____ _____ _____ home.

26 When the day of the _____ _____ came, she was _____ afraid _____ go.

27 My grandmother _____ _____ the rest of her life _____ her decision.

28 When she watches a baseball game on TV, she often says, "I _____ _____ _____ to Chicago.

29 You know, all your dreams _____ _____ _____, _____ _____ you catch only a fcw of them.

30 _____ _____ an _____."

17 심사 당일 모든 규칙이 정장을 입은 나이 든 남자에 의해 설명 되었는데, 그는 무척 진지하고 불친절하게 들렸다.

18 뜨거운 태양 아래 정장을 입고 있는 것이 그를 짜증나게 만들 었을지도 모른다고 그녀는 생각 했다.

19 그날, Helen 할머니는 다른 젊은 여성들과 함께 몇 시간 동안 야구를 했다.

20 그녀는 자신의 야구 꿈을 좇아 가게 되어 신이 났다!

21 일주일쯤 지나, Helen 할머니는 우편함에서 편지 한 통을 발견 했다.

22 그것은 시카고에 있는 여자 야 구리그에서 일하는 사람들이 보 낸 것이었다.

23 그 편지에는 그녀가 시카고에서 열리는 리그의 본심사에 초청되 었다고 적혀 있었다!

24 하지만 하루하루 갈수록, Helen 할머니는 심사에 떨어질까봐 걱 정되었다.

25 그녀는 또한 시카고까지 혼자 여행하는 것이 걱정되었는데, 시카고는 집에서 멀리 떨어진 곳이었다.

26 본심사가 있는 날이 되었을 때, 그녀는 너무 두려워서 갈 수 없 었다.

27 할머니는 남은 인생을 자신의 결정을 후회하며 보내셨다.

28 텔레비전에서 야구 경기를 볼 때, 그녀는 종종 "난 시카고에 갔어야 해.

29 너도 알겠지만, 모든 꿈은 추구 할 가지가 있단다. 비록 일부만 이루게 되더라도 말이야.

30 절대 기회를 놓치지 마라."라고 말씀하신다.

※ 다음 문장을 우리말로 쓰시오.

1 MY GRANDMOTHER'S BASEBALL DREAMS

➡ _____

2 My grandmother Helen used to be a cook in a restaurant in a small town near South Bend, Indiana.

➡ _____

3 She does not work anymore, but she still enjoys making delicious food, which I love so much.

➡ _____

4 Food is one of the many things that connect us.

➡ _____

5 What connects us most strongly, however, is baseball.

➡ _____

6 When I visit her on weekends, my grandmother often tells me exciting stories about playing baseball back in the 1940s.

➡ _____

7 She must have loved the sport very much.

➡ _____

8 I listen to these stories over and over.

➡ _____

9 She always says, "Go after what you want, Sarah.

➡ _____

10 Don't be afraid of trying something new or challenging.

➡ _____

11 Don't be ashamed of failing."

➡ _____

12 In 1943, the All-American Girls Professional Baseball League was founded.

➡ _____

13 This league was created for baseball fans because many of America's young men were fighting in World War II.

➡ _____

14 Helen was told that there would be local tryouts right in South Bend.

➡ _____

15 She wondered, "What would it be like to be on a baseball team and to make it to the finals for my hometown?"

➡ _____

16 She imagined a large banner hanging at the baseball field which included the name Helen Baker.

➡ _____

17 On the day of the tryouts, all the rules were explained by an old man in a suit, who sounded very serious and unkind.

➡ _____

18 She thought that wearing a suit in the hot sun might have made him impatient.

➡ _____

19 On that day, Helen played baseball for hours with many other young women.

➡ _____

20 She was excited to go after her baseball dreams!

➡ _____

21 About a week later, Helen found a letter in the mailbox.

➡ _____

22 It was from people who worked for the girls' baseball league in Chicago.

➡ _____

23 It read that she had been invited to the league's main tryouts in Chicago!

➡ _____

24 As the days went by, however, Helen became worried that she might fail.

➡ _____

25 She also became worried about traveling alone to Chicago, which was far away from home.

➡ _____

26 When the day of the main tryouts came, she was too afraid to go.

➡ _____

27 My grandmother has spent the rest of her life regretting her decision.

➡ _____

28 When she watches a baseball game on TV, she often says, "I should have gone to Chicago.

➡ _____

29 You know, all your dreams are worth chasing, even if you catch only a few of them.

➡ _____

30 Never miss an opportunity."

➡ _____

※ 다음 괄호 안의 단어들을 우리말에 맞도록 바르게 배열하시오.

1 (GRANDMOTHER'S / MY / DREAMS / BASEBALL)
➡ _____

2 (grandmother / my / used / Helen / be / to / cook / a / a / in / in / restarant / a / small / near / town / Bend, / South / Indiana.)
➡ _____
_____

3 (does / she / work / not / anymore, / she / but / enjoys / still / delicious / making / food, / I / which / so / love / much.)
➡ _____
_____

4 (is / food / of / one / many / the / things / connect / that / us.)
➡ _____

5 (connects / what / most / us / however, / strongly, / baseball. / is)
➡ _____

6 (I / when / visit / on / her / weekends, / grandmother / my / often / me / tells / stories / exciting / playing / about / back / baseball / the / in / 1940s.)
➡ _____
_____

7 (must / she / loved / have / sport / the / much. / very)
➡ _____

8 (listen / I / these / to / over / stories / over. / and)
➡ _____

9 (always / she / says, / after / "go / you / what / Sarah. / want,)
➡ _____

10 (be / don't / of / afraid / something / trying / or / new / challenging.)
➡ _____
_____

11 (be / don't / of / ashamed / failing.")
➡ _____

12 (1943, / in / All-American / the / Professional / Girls / League / Baseball / founded. / was)
➡ _____

13 (league / this / created / was / baseball / for / because / fans / of / many / young / America's / were / men / in / fighting / War / World / II.)
➡ _____

14 (was / Helen / that / told / would / there / local / be / right / tryouts / in / Bend. / South)
➡ _____

15 (wondered, / she / would / "what / be / it / to / like / on / be / a / team / baseball / and / make / to / it / the / to / for / finals / hometown?" / my)
➡ _____
_____

1 할머니의 야구 꿈

2 우리 할머니 Helen은 Indiana주 South Bend 근처 작은 마을에 있는 식당의 요리사였다.

3 할머니는 더 이상 일을 하지 않지만 여전히 맛있는 음식을 즐겨 만드시고, 나는 그 음식들을 무척 좋아한다.

4 음식은 우리를 연결하는 많은 것 가운데 하나이다.

5 하지만 우리를 가장 강하게 연결하는 것은 바로 야구이다.

6 주말마다 할머니 댁에 가면, 할머니는 종종 과거 1940년대의 야구 경기에 관해 흥미로운 이야기를 내게 들려주신다.

7 그녀는 야구를 무척 좋아했던 게 분명하다.

8 나는 이 이야기들을 몇 번이고 듣는다.

9 그녀는 항상 "네가 원하는 것을 이루려고 노력하렴, Sarah.

10 새로운 것이나 도전적인 것을 시도해 보기를 두려워하지 말거라.

11 실패하는 것을 부끄러워하지 마라."라고 말씀하신다.

12 1943년, 전미 여자 프로야구 리그가 창립되었다.

13 미국의 청년 중 많은 사람들이 제2차 세계대전에 참전해 있었기 때문에 이 리그가 야구 팬들을 위해 만들어졌다.

14 Helen 할머니는 지역 심사가 바로 South Bend에서 있을 거라고 들었다.

15 그녀는 "야구 팀에 들어가서 고향을 위해 결승전까지 진출한다는 건 어떤 기분일까?"라며 궁금해했다.

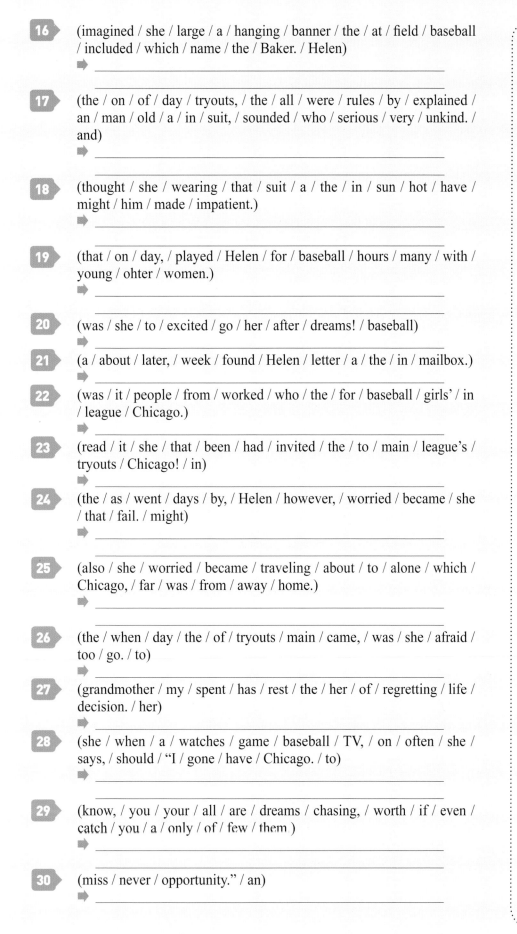

16 (imagined / she / large / a / hanging / banner / the / at / field / baseball / included / which / name / the / Baker. / Helen)
➡ _____
_____

17 (the / on / of / day / tryouts, / the / all / were / rules / by / explained / an / man / old / a / in / suit, / sounded / who / serious / very / unkind. / and)
➡ _____
_____

18 (thought / she / wearing / that / suit / a / the / in / sun / hot / have / might / him / made / impatient.)
➡ _____
_____

19 (that / on / day, / played / Helen / for / baseball / hours / many / with / young / ohter / women.)
➡ _____
_____

20 (was / she / to / excited / go / her / after / dreams! / baseball)
➡ _____

21 (a / about / later, / week / found / Helen / letter / a / the / in / mailbox.)
➡ _____

22 (was / it / people / from / worked / who / the / for / baseball / girls' / in / league / Chicago.)
➡ _____

23 (read / it / she / that / been / had / invited / the / to / main / league's / tryouts / Chicago! / in)
➡ _____

24 (the / as / went / days / by, / Helen / however, / worried / became / she / that / fail. / might)
➡ _____

25 (also / she / worried / became / traveling / about / to / alone / which / Chicago, / far / was / from / away / home.)
➡ _____

26 (the / when / day / the / of / tryouts / main / came, / was / she / afraid / too / go. / to)
➡ _____

27 (grandmother / my / spent / has / rest / the / her / of / regretting / life / decision. / her)
➡ _____

28 (she / when / a / watches / game / baseball / TV, / on / often / she / says, / should / "I / gone / have / Chicago. / to)
➡ _____

29 (know, / you / your / all / are / dreams / chasing, / worth / if / even / catch / you / a / only / of / few / them)
➡ _____
_____

30 (miss / never / opportunity." / an)
➡ _____

16 그녀는 Helen Baker라는 이름이 포함된 큰 현수막이 야구장에 걸려 있는 것을 상상했다.

17 심사 당일 모든 규칙이 정장을 입은 나이 든 남자에 의해 설명되었는데, 그는 무척 진지하고 불친절하게 들렸다.

18 뜨거운 태양 아래 정장을 입고 있는 것이 그를 짜증나게 만들었을지도 모른다고 그녀는 생각했다.

19 그날, Helen 할머니는 다른 젊은 여성들과 함께 몇 시간 동안 야구를 했다.

20 그녀는 자신의 야구 꿈을 좇아가게 되어 신이 났다!

21 일주일쯤 지나, Helen 할머니는 우편함에서 편지 한 통을 발견했다.

22 그것은 시카고에 있는 여자 야구리그에서 일하는 사람들이 보낸 것이었다.

23 그 편지에는 그녀가 시카고에서 열리는 리그의 본심사에 초청되었다고 적혀 있었다!

24 하지만 하루하루 갈수록, Helen 할머니는 심사에 떨어질까봐 걱정되었다.

25 그녀는 또한 시카고까지 혼자 여행하는 것이 걱정되었는데, 시카고는 집에서 멀리 떨어진 곳이었다.

26 본심사가 있는 날이 되었을 때, 그녀는 너무 두려워서 갈 수 없었다.

27 할머니는 남은 인생을 자신의 결정을 후회하며 보내셨다.

28 텔레비전에서 야구 경기를 볼 때, 그녀는 종종 "난 시카고에 갔어야 해.

29 너도 알겠지만, 모든 꿈은 추구할 가치가 있단다, 비록 일부만 이루게 되더라도 말이야.

30 절대 기회를 놓치지 마라."라고 말씀하신다.

※ 다음 우리말을 영어로 쓰시오.

1 할머니의 야구 꿈

➡ _____

2 우리 할머니 Helen은 Indiana주 South Bend 근처 작은 마을에 있는 식당의 요리사였다.

➡ _____

3 할머니는 더 이상 일을 하지 않지만 여전히 맛있는 음식을 즐겨 만드시고, 나는 그 음식들을 무척 좋아한다.

➡ _____

4 음식은 우리를 연결하는 많은 것 가운데 하나이다.

➡ _____

5 하지만 우리를 가장 강하게 연결하는 것은 바로 야구이다.

➡ _____

6 주말마다 할머니 댁에 가면, 할머니는 종종 과거 1940년대의 야구 경기에 관해 흥미로운 이야기를 내게 들려주신다.

➡ _____

_____

7 그녀는 야구를 무척 좋아했던 게 분명하다.

➡ _____

8 나는 이 이야기들을 몇 번이고 듣는다.

➡ _____

9 그녀는 항상 "네가 원하는 것을 이루려고 노력하렴, Sarah.

➡ _____

10 새로운 것이나 도전적인 것을 시도해 보기를 두려워하지 말거라.

➡ _____

11 실패하는 것을 부끄러워하지 마라."라고 말씀하신다.

➡ _____

12 1943년, 전미 여자 프로야구 리그가 창립되었다.

➡ _____

13 미국의 청년 중 많은 사람들이 제2차 세계대전에 참전해 있었기 때문에 이 리그가 야구 팬들을 위해 만들어졌다.

➡ _____

_____

14 Helen 할머니는 지역 심사가 바로 South Bend에서 있을 거라고 들었다.

➡ _____

15 그녀는 "야구 팀에 들어가서 고향을 위해 결승전까지 진출한다는 건 어떤 기분일까?"라며 궁금해했다.

➡ _____

_____

16 그녀는 Helen Baker라는 이름이 포함된 큰 현수막이 야구장에 걸려 있는 것을 상상했다.

➡ _____

_____

17 심사 당일 모든 규칙이 정장을 입은 나이 든 남자에 의해 설명되었는데, 그는 무척 진지하고 불친절하게 들렸다.

➡ _____

_____

18 뜨거운 태양 아래 정장을 입고 있는 것이 그를 짜증나게 만들었을지도 모른다고 그녀는 생각했다.

➡ _____

19 그날, Helen 할머니는 다른 젊은 여성들과 함께 몇 시간 동안 야구를 했다.

➡ _____

20 그녀는 자신의 야구 꿈을 좇아가게 되어 신이 났다!

➡ _____

21 일주일쯤 지나, Helen 할머니는 우편함에서 편지 한 통을 발견했다.

➡ _____

22 그것은 시카고에 있는 여자 야구 리그에서 일하는 사람들이 보낸 것이었다.

➡ _____

23 그 편지에는 그녀가 시카고에서 열리는 리그의 본심사에 초청되었다고 적혀 있었다!

➡ _____

24 하지만 하루하루 갈수록, Helen 할머니는 심사에 떨어질까봐 걱정되었다.

➡ _____

25 그녀는 또한 시카고까지 혼자 여행하는 것이 걱정되었는데, 시카고는 집에서 멀리 떨어진 곳이었다.

➡ _____

26 본심사가 있는 날이 되었을 때, 그녀는 너무 두려워서 갈 수 없었다.

➡ _____

27 할머니는 남은 인생을 자신의 결정을 후회하며 보내셨다.

➡ _____

28 텔레비전에서 야구 경기를 볼 때, 그녀는 종종 "난 시카고에 갔어야 해.

➡ _____

29 너도 알겠지만, 모든 꿈은 추구할 가치가 있단다. 비록 일부만 이루게 되더라도 말이야.

➡ _____

30 절대 기회를 놓치지 마라."라고 말씀하신다.

➡ _____

※ 다음 우리말과 일치하도록 빈칸에 알맞은 말을 쓰시오.

After You Read Graphic Organizer

Cause

1. The Second World War _____ _____.

2. She loved baseball _____ _____.

3. She _____ not _____ _____ her success. Also, she _____ _____ _____ _____ _____.

Effect

4. In 1943, the All-American Girls Professional Baseball League was _____.

5. She _____ _____ _____ _____ in South Bend.

6. She didn't go to the _____ _____.

My Writing Portfolio

1. JANE GOODALL, _____ _____ _____ _____

2. Jane Goodall _____ _____ _____ _____ _____, _____, in 1934.

3. _____ _____ _____ chimpanzees began _____ _____ _____ _____ about Tarzan.

4. She _____ _____ _____ wild chimpanzees in Africa _____ _____ _____.

5. She _____ also _____ _____ for the _____ _____.

6. In 1995, she _____ the Hubbard Medal _____ _____ _____ _____.

7. _____ _____ _____ _____, we have _____ _____ _____ a lot about chimpanzees.

8. Jane Goodall is _____ _____ _____ _____ _____ in history.

Words in Action

1. The Cheetahs _____ _____ the game, and their fans _____ _____ _____.

2. _____ Jason _____ _____ and _____ the ball, the game ends.

3. Oh my! He _____ the ball!

4. The Ducks _____ _____ _____, and the _____ _____.

5. Jason _____ _____ and _____.

6. The Ducks fans are _____ _____, _____ the Cheetahs fans _____ _____ and _____.

원인
1. 제2차 세계대전이 발발했다.
2. 그녀는 야구를 무척 좋아했다.
3. 그녀는 자신의 성공을 확신하지 못했다. 또한 그녀는 혼자 여행하는 것을 두려워했다.
결과
4. 1943년, 전미 여자 프로야구 리그가 창립되었다.
5. 그녀는 South Bend의 지역 심사에 참가했다.
6. 그녀는 본심사에 가지 않았다.

1. Jane Goodall, 침팬지의 어머니
2. Jane Goodall은 1934년 영국 런던에서 태어났다.
3. 침팬지에 대한 관심은 그녀가 타잔에 관해 읽었을 때 시작되었다.
4. 그녀는 20대 때부터 아프리카에서 야생 침팬지를 연구해 오고 있다.
5. 그녀는 침팬지 보호를 위해서도 노력해 오고 있다.
6. 1995년에 그녀는 야생 동물 보호에 대한 공로를 인정받아 허버드상을 받았다.
7. 일생을 바친 그녀의 연구 덕분에, 우리는 침팬지에 관해 많이 알게 되었다.
8. Jane Goodall은 역사상 가장 위대한 과학자 중 한 명이다.

1. Cheetahs가 경기를 이기고 있고, 팬들이 신나는 노래를 부르고 있습니다.
2. Jason이 침착함을 유지해서 공을 잡으면 경기가 끝납니다.
3. 오, 이럴수가! 그가 공을 놓칩니다!
4. Ducks는 2루로 진루하고, 경기는 계속됩니다.
5. Jason은 창피하고 긴장한 것처럼 보입니다.
6. Ducks 팬들은 열광하고 있는 반면, Cheetahs 팬들은 두렵고 걱정스러운 것처럼 보입니다.

※ 다음 우리말을 영어로 쓰시오.

After You Read Graphic Organizer

원인
1. 제2차 세계대전이 발발했다.
  ➡ _____

2. 그녀는 야구를 무척 좋아했다.
  ➡ _____

3. 그녀는 자신의 성공을 확신하지 못했다. 또한 그녀는 혼자 여행하는 것을 두려워했다.
  ➡ _____

결과
4. 1943년, 전미 여자 프로야구 리그가 창립되었다.
  ➡ _____

5. 그녀는 South Bend의 지역 심사에 참가했다.
  ➡ _____

6. 그녀는 본심사에 가지 않았다.
  ➡ _____

My Writing Portfolio

1. Jane Goodall, 침팬지의 어머니
  ➡ _____

2. Jane Goodall은 1934년 영국 런던에서 태어났다.
  ➡ _____

3. 침팬지에 대한 관심은 그녀가 타잔에 관해 읽었을 때 시작되었다.
  ➡ _____

4. 그녀는 20대 때부터 아프리카에서 야생 침팬지를 연구해 오고 있다.
  ➡ _____

5. 그녀는 침팬지 보호를 위해서도 노력해 오고 있다.
  ➡ _____

6. 1995년에 그녀는 야생 동물 보호에 대한 공로를 인정받아 허버드상을 받았다.
  ➡ _____

7. 일생을 바친 그녀의 연구 덕분에, 우리는 침팬지에 관해 많이 알게 되었다.
  ➡ _____

8. Jane Goodall은 역사상 가장 위대한 과학자 중 한 명이다.
  ➡ _____

Words in Action

1. Cheetahs가 경기를 이기고 있고, 팬들이 신나는 노래를 부르고 있습니다.
  ➡ _____

2. Jason이 침착함을 유지해서 공을 잡으면 경기가 끝납니다.
  ➡ _____

3. 오, 이럴수가! 그가 공을 놓칩니다!
  ➡ _____

4. Ducks는 2루로 진루하고, 경기는 계속됩니다.
  ➡ _____

5. Jason은 창피하고 긴장한 것처럼 보입니다.
  ➡ _____

6. Ducks 팬들은 열광하고 있는 반면, Cheetahs 팬들은 무섭고 걱정스러운 것처럼 보입니다.
  ➡ _____

※ 다음 영어를 우리말로 쓰시오.

01	shout	_____
02	relief	_____
03	safety product	_____
04	actually	_____
05	hurt	_____
06	lesson	_____
07	cycle	_____
08	throughout	_____
09	dirt	_____
10	entrance	_____
11	though	_____
12	wooden	_____
13	breathe	_____
14	gateway	_____
15	cast	_____
16	manager	_____
17	thumping	_____
18	opening	_____
19	particular	_____
20	would	_____

21	record	_____
22	scream	_____
23	thick	_____
24	whisper	_____
25	as usual	_____
26	set off	_____
27	in reply	_____
28	reach out	_____
29	day in and day out	_____
30	inch by inch	_____
31	after a while	_____
32	side by side	_____
33	as soon as	_____
34	at first	_____
35	in other words	_____
36	all of a sudden	_____
37	manage to	_____
38	thanks to	_____
39	used to	_____
40	stop ~ from -ing	_____

※ 다음 우리말을 영어로 쓰시오.

01 나무로 된, 목재의

02 안전 제품

03 ~하곤 했다
   (과거의 불규칙적 습관)

04 석고붕대, 깁스

05 그러나, 그래도

06 비명

07 자전거를 타다

08 흙, 먼지

09 입구, 입장

10 ~ 내내, ~ 동안 쭉

11 교훈

12 경영자, 관리자

13 열린 구멍, 틈

14 입구, 관문

15 특별한

16 기록

17 쿵쾅거리는

18 고통을 주다, 아프다

19 속삭이다

20 안도, 안심

21 외치다, 소리[고함]치다

22 실제(로)는, 사실은

23 숨 쉬다

24 두터운, 빽빽한

25 처음에는

26 (손·팔·다리 등을) 뻗다

27 조금씩

28 ~가 …하는 것을 막다

29 ~ 덕분에

30 출발하다

31 얼마 후에

32 나란히

33 매일

34 다시 말해서, 즉

35 ~하자마자

36 대답으로

37 여느 때처럼

38 간신히 ~하다

39 갑자기

40 ~하곤 했다(과거의 규칙적
   이고 반복적인 동작이나 상태)

※ 다음 영영풀이에 알맞은 단어를 <보기>에서 골라 쓴 후, 우리말 뜻을 쓰시오.

1 _____ : to take a breath: _____

2 _____ : to ride a bicycle: _____

3 _____ : loose or packed soil or sand: _____

4 _____ : the way you go in: _____

5 _____ : close-packed with units or individuals: _____

6 _____ : a loud sharp cry or noise: _____

7 _____ : removal of something painful: _____

8 _____ : an opening for a gate: _____

9 _____ : a large amount of water covering an area that is usually dry: _____

10 _____ : during the whole period of: _____

11 _____ : something learned through experience: _____

12 _____ : worthy of notice; special; unusual: _____

13 _____ : hitting something in a heavy, continuous way: _____

14 _____ : a person who is responsible for running part of a business organization: _____

15 _____ : a written account of something that is kept so that it can be looked at and used in the future: _____

16 _____ : to speak very quietly to somebody so that other people cannot hear what you are saying: _____

particular	breathe	whisper	dirt
lesson	scream	record	gateway
manager	thick	relief	cycle
flood	entrance	throughout	thumping

※ 다음 우리말과 일치하도록 빈칸에 알맞은 것을 골라 쓰시오.

1 _____ _____

A. Keep   B. Out

2 Every summer, my family _____ _____ _____ on holiday to the _____.

A. go   B. used   C. coast   D. to

3 We always went to the same _____ and _____ _____ the _____ small guesthouse.

A. place   B. at   C. same   D. stayed

4 We would _____ for two weeks, _____ in the sea and _____ around the _____ town.

A. walking   B. swimming   C. little   D. stay

5 In _____ _____, we never did _____ special, and nothing ever really _____ on these vacations.

A. words   B. happened   C. other   D. anything

6 _____ _____ _____ this story I was twelve years old.

A. time   B. at   C. of   D. the

7 Most people can remember this _____ summer, _____ it was the hottest summer England _____ had _____ records began.

A. since   B. had   C. particular   D. as

8 It did not rain _____ June and July, and the sun _____ day _____ and day _____.

A. shone   B. throughout   C. out   D. in

9 _____ Ron and I _____ the _____ and the _____.

A. heat   B. sun   C. but   D. loved

10 Every day, we would _____ our bicycles _____ and further _____ _____ the guesthouse.

A. ride   B. further   C. from   D. away

11 One day Ron _____ that we should _____ our bikes _____ the old train tracks to see where they would _____ us.

A. take   B. along   C. decided   D. ride

12 I was happy to follow Ron, _____ _____, and we _____ _____ after breakfast.

A. usual   B. off   C. as   D. set

13 At first, the tracks were _____ to _____, and we _____ along side _____ side.

A. follow   B. easy   C. by   D. cycled

1 들어가지 마시오

2 여름마다 나의 가족은 해안으로 휴가를 가곤 했다.

3 우리는 항상 같은 곳에 가서 똑같은 작은 게스트하우스에 묵었다.

4 우리는 2주 가량 머물며 바다에서 수영하고 작은 마을 주위를 돌아다니곤 했다.

5 다시 말해서, 그런 휴가에서 우리는 특별한 일을 하지 않았고 정말 아무 일도 일어나지 않았다.

6 이 이야기는 내가 12살 때 일이다.

7 관측 이래 영국이 겪은 가장 더운 여름이었기 때문에, 대부분의 사람들은 이 특별한 여름을 기억할 수 있다.

8 6월과 7월 내내 비가 오지 않았고 태양은 연일 쨍쨍했다.

9 하지만 Ron과 나는 그 더위와 태양을 사랑했다.

10 매일 우리는 게스트하우스에서 조금씩 먼 곳으로 자전거를 타고 가곤 했다.

11 어느 날, Ron은 낡은 철로가 우리를 어디로 데려다줄지 알아보려고 그 철로를 따라 자전거를 타기로 결정했다.

12 난 늘 그랬듯 Ron을 따르는 게 즐거웠고, 아침 식사 후에 우리는 출발했다.

13 처음에는 철길을 따라가는 게 어렵지 않아 우리는 나란히 자전거를 타고 갔다.

14 After a _____, the grass grew _____, and we had to ride one _____ the _____.
  A. behind   B. while   C. other   D. thicker

15 Ron _____ _____.
  A. ahead   B. was

16 The tracks went _____ the woods and it grew _____ as the trees stood tall and _____ a _____ over the tracks.
  A. formed   B. toward   C. darker   D. roof

17 Ron _____ _____. "Look _____!" he _____.
  A. shouted   B. suddenly   C. ahead   D. stopped

18 I stopped next _____ him and saw a white, _____ gateway _____ a black _____.
  A. across   B. to   C. opening   D. wooden

19 "It's _____ _____," I _____.
  A. tunnel   B. said   C. a

20 "Yes, and it says, '_____ _____' on the _____," _____ Ron.
  A. Out   B. gate   C. Keep   D. replied

21 "Do you want to _____ _____ _____ _____?"
  A. inside   B. a   C. have   D. look

22 _____, I did _____ to go _____.
  A. actually   B. inside   C. want   D. not

23 I felt a _____ cold all of a _____, and I wanted to go _____ _____ the sunlight.
  A. sudden   B. into   C. little   D. back

24 But I _____, "Sure," and _____ _____.
  A. moved   B. answered   C. ahead

25 We _____ our bikes at the _____ and _____ _____.
  A. left   B. over   C. gate   D. climbed

26 We _____ the _____ _____.
  A. tunnel   B. entered   C. cool

27 The _____ _____ was _____.
  A. heavy   B. inside   C. air

28 _____ our heads there was a _____ that _____ _____ and louder.
  A. sound   B. above   C. louder   D. grew

29 "What's that?" I _____ _____.
  A. out   B. called

30 "Bats," said Ron, "_____ your head _____." Then he _____ _____.
  A. on   B. keep   C. moved   D. down

31 "_____ go so _____." I _____ _____ him.
  A. after   B. fast   C. called   D. don't

---

14 한참 후, 풀이 점점 우거져서 우리는 한 사람이 앞서가고 다른 사람이 뒤에서 가야 했다.

15 Ron이 앞서가고 있었다.

16 철길은 숲으로 이어졌고 나무가 높이 자라 철길 위로 지붕을 형성하며 점점 더 어두워졌다.

17 Ron이 갑자기 멈췄다. "앞을 봐!"라고 그가 외쳤다.

18 나는 그의 옆에 멈춰서 캄캄한 입구를 가로지르는 흰색 나무문을 보았다.

19 "터널이네." 내가 말했다.

20 "맞아. 그리고 문에 '들어가지 마시오'라고 적혀 있어." Ron이 대답했다.

21 "안을 보고 싶니?"

22 사실, 난 안으로 들어가고 싶지 않았다.

23 갑자기 나는 한기를 살짝 느꼈고 햇빛 속으로 되돌아가고 싶었다.

24 그렇지만 나는 "물론이지."라고 답하며 앞으로 움직였다.

25 우리는 문 앞에 자전거를 남겨두고 넘어갔다.

26 우리는 서늘한 터널로 들어갔다.

27 안의 공기는 묵직했다.

28 우리 머리 위로 점점 더 커지는 소리가 났다.

29 "저게 뭐야?"라고 내가 소리쳤다.

30 "박쥐야." Ron이 말했다. "머리를 숙여." 그러고 나서 그는 계속 움직였다.

31 "너무 빨리 가지 마." 나는 그를 부르며 뒤쫓았다.

32 I _____ , "Don't _____ me _____ " but I didn't say _____ .

   A. behind   B. meant   C. leave   D. so

33 The next thing I heard was a _____ noise right above us, a _____ sound like an _____ train and then a _____ .

   A. thumping   B. scream   C. loud   D. express

34 "Ron!" I _____ . "Ron, what's _____ ? Can you _____ me?" No _____ .

   A. up   B. reply   C. shouted   D. hear

35 "_____ to me, Ron. _____ me _____ _____ ."

   A. happened   B. speak   C. what's   D. tell

36 I slowly walked _____ _____ Ron had _____ and found only _____ and small rocks.

   A. dirt   B. toward   C. been   D. where

37 As I _____ _____ my hands, I felt _____ _____ — Ron's face!

   A. out   B. wet   C. reached   D. something

38 His eyes _____ _____ , and he was _____ _____ .

   A. weakly   B. were   C. breathing   D. closed

39 "It's okay, Ron," I _____ . "I'll _____ you _____ ."

   A. whispered   B. out   C. get

40 "I think I've _____ my leg. It really _____ . Just go and _____ _____ , Ben."

   A. hurts   B. broken   C. help   D. get

41 "No," I _____ . "I'll _____ you _____ of here to _____ first."

   A. out   B. replied   C. safety   D. get

42 I started _____ the _____ and rocks _____ my hands.

   A. with   B. moving   C. dirt   D. away

43 I _____ _____ , and I felt _____ _____ .

   A. control   B. calm   C. in   D. felt

44 It _____ a long time to _____ _____ the earth _____ Ron.

   A. covering   B. took   C. away   D. clear

45 _____ , I _____ _____ _____ his body.

   A. free   B. managed   C. finally   D. to

46 _____ him under the arms, I pulled him _____ , inch by inch, _____ the tunnel _____ .

   A. toward   B. backward   C. holding   D. entrance

47 It _____ to take _____ , but finally I was _____ to get Ron _____ of the tunnel.

   A. ages   B. able   C. seemed   D. out

48 He didn't _____ _____ _____ , _____ .

   A. though   B. well   C. too   D. look

---

32 '나를 두고 가지 마'라고 말하고 싶었지만, 나는 그렇게 말하지 않았다.

33 그다음 내가 들은 것은 바로 앞에서 나는 큰 소음이었는데, 그것은 마치 고속열차 같은 쿵쾅거리는 소리였다. 이어서 비명이 들렸다.

34 "Ron!" 나는 외쳤다. "Ron, 무슨 일이야? 내 말 들려?" 아무 응답이 없었다.

35 "Ron, 나에게 말해 봐. 무슨 일이 생겼는지 말해 줘."

36 나는 천천히 Ron이 있던 곳으로 걸어갔고 흙과 작은 자갈만을 발견했다.

37 손을 뻗었을 때 나는 축축한 무언가를 느꼈다. Ron의 얼굴이었다!

38 그의 눈은 감겨 있었고 약하게 숨을 쉬고 있었다.

39 "괜찮아, Ron." 나는 속삭였다. "내가 꺼내 줄게."

40 "다리가 부러진 것 같아. 정말 아파. 그냥 가서 도움을 요청해, Ben."

41 "안 돼." 나는 대답했다. "우선 안전한 곳까지 여기에서 형을 꺼낼 거야."

42 나는 손으로 흙과 자갈을 치우기 시작했다.

43 나는 침착했고 내가 잘할 수 있다고 느꼈다.

44 Ron을 뒤덮은 흙을 치우는 데에 오랜 시간이 걸렸다.

45 드디어 나는 그의 몸을 자유롭게 할 수 있었다.

46 팔 밑으로 그를 안고서 그를 터널 입구 쪽으로 조금씩 뒤로 끌어당겼다.

47 오랜 시간이 걸린 듯했지만 결국 나는 Ron을 터널 밖으로 데리고 나올 수 있었다.

48 그는 별로 좋아 보이지 않았다.

49 His face was white, and he was trying hard to _____ himself _____ _____ _____ from crying out.

    A. crying   B. out   C. stop   D. from

50 I _____ our bikes and _____ the two _____ _____ to Ron.

    A. brought   B. found   C. bottles   D. water

51 "Here, drink these," I said. "I'll go and _____ _____ . I'll be as _____ _____ I can."

    A. quick   B. help   C. as   D. get

52 _____ _____ , Ron _____ _____ my hands.

    A. pressed   B. reply   C. simply   D. in

53 I got on my bicycle and _____ _____ along the tracks _____ I got to the _____ farmhouse.

    A. nearest   B. back   C. until   D. raced

54 I ran _____ the _____ and found a woman _____ some _____ in the kitchen.

    A. washing   B. past   C. dishes   D. gate

55 _____ to her, Ron was _____ to the hospital, where his leg was _____ in a _____ .

    A. put   B. cast   C. thanks   D. taken

56 As _____ as our parents _____ at the hospital and saw us, my mother cried _____ _____ .

    A. relief   B. soon   C. with   D. arrived

57 But all my father said was, "_____ that _____ a _____ to you."

    A. lesson   B. let   C. be

58 And what was the _____ ? It was "*Keep* _____ means _____ *out of* _____ ."

    A. lesson   B. trouble   C. out   D. stay

59 Ron is now the _____ of a big company which _____ helmets and other _____ _____ .

    A. safety   B. manager   C. produces   D. products

60 And me? I _____ a _____ _____ .

    A. fighter   B. fire   C. am

49 그의 얼굴은 창백했고 울음을 터뜨리지 않으려고 몹시 애쓰고 있었다.

50 나는 우리 자전거를 찾아서 Ron 에게 물병 두 개를 가져다주었다.

51 "여기, 이거 마셔." 나는 말했다. "내가 가서 도움을 구할게. 최대한 빨리 올게."

52 대답으로 Ron은 그저 내 손을 꽉 잡았다.

53 나는 자전거를 타고 왔던 철길을 따라 달려, 마침내 가장 가까운 농가에 도착했다.

54 대문을 지나 달려가 나는 부엌에서 설거지를 하고 있는 부인을 발견했다.

55 그 부인 덕분에 Ron은 병원으로 이송되었고, 병원에서 다리에 석고붕대를 했다.

56 부모님이 병원에 도착해서 우리를 보자마자, 어머니는 안도감에 울음을 터뜨리셨다.

57 하지만 아버지가 하신 말씀은 "이 일이 너희에게 교훈이 되기를 바란다."가 전부였다.

58 그래서 교훈이 무엇이었을까? 그것은 '들어가지 마시오'라는 말은 '곤경을 멀리하라'는 뜻이라는 것이다.

59 Ron은 지금 안전모와 여러 안전 제품을 생산하는 큰 회사의 관리자이다.

60 그럼 나는? 나는 소방관이다.

※ 다음 우리말과 일치하도록 빈칸에 알맞은 말을 쓰시오.

1 _____ _____

2 _____ summer, my family _____ _____ _____ on holiday to the coast.

3 We always went to the same place and _____ _____ the same small _____.

4 We would _____ _____ two weeks, _____ in the sea and _____ around the little town.

5 _____ _____ _____, we never did _____ _____, and nothing ever really happened on these vacations.

6 _____ _____ _____ _____ this story I was twelve years old.

7 Most people can remember this particular summer, as it was the hottest summer England _____ _____ since records began.

8 It did not rain _____ June and July, and the sun _____ _____ _____ _____ _____ _____.

9 But Ron and I loved _____ _____ and the sun.

10 Every day, we would ride our bicycles _____ _____ _____ _____ _____ the guesthouse.

11 One day Ron decided that we should ride our bikes along the old train tracks to see where they would _____ _____.

12 I was happy _____ _____ Ron, _____ _____, and we _____ _____ after breakfast.

13 At first, the tracks were easy to follow, and we _____ _____ _____ _____ _____.

1 들어가지 마시오
2 여름마다 나의 가족은 해안으로 휴가를 가곤 했다.
3 우리는 항상 같은 곳에 가서 똑같은 작은 게스트하우스에 묵었다.
4 우리는 2주 가량 머물며 바다에서 수영하고 작은 마을 주위를 돌아다니곤 했다.
5 다시 말해서, 그런 휴가에서 우리는 특별한 일을 하지 않았고 정말 아무 일도 일어나지 않았다.
6 이 이야기는 내가 12살 때 일이다.
7 관측 이래 영국이 겪은 가장 더운 여름이었기 때문에, 대부분의 사람들은 이 특별한 여름을 기억할 수 있다.
8 6월과 7월 내내 비가 오지 않았고 태양은 연일 쨍쨍했다.
9 하지만 Ron과 나는 그 더위와 태양을 사랑했다.
10 매일 우리는 게스트하우스에서 조금씩 먼 곳으로 자전거를 타고 가곤 했다.
11 어느 날, Ron은 낡은 철로가 우리를 어디로 데려다줄지 알아보려고 그 철로를 따라 자전거를 타기로 결정했다.
12 난 늘 그랬듯 Ron을 따르는 게 즐거웠고, 아침 식사 후에 우리는 출발했다.
13 처음에는 철길을 따라가는 게 어렵지 않아 우리는 나란히 자전거를 타고 갔다.

14 After a while, the grass _____ _____, and we had to ride _____ _____ _____ _____.

15 Ron was _____.

16 The tracks went toward the woods and it _____ as the trees stood tall and _____ _____ _____ over the tracks.

17 Ron stopped suddenly. "_____ _____!" he _____.

18 I stopped _____ _____ _____ and saw a white, wooden gateway across a _____ _____.

19 "It's _____ _____," I said.

20 "Yes, and it says, '_____ _____' on the gate," replied Ron.

21 "Do you want to _____ _____ _____ inside?"

22 _____, I did not want to _____ _____.

23 I felt a little cold _____ _____ _____ _____, and I wanted to _____ _____ _____ the sunlight.

24 But I answered, "Sure," and _____ _____.

25 We _____ our bikes at the gate and _____ _____.

26 We _____ the cool tunnel.

27 The air _____ was _____.

28 Above our heads there was a sound that _____ _____ _____ _____.

29 "What's that?" I _____ _____.

30 "Bats," said Ron, "_____ your head _____." Then he _____ _____.

31 "_____ _____ so fast." I _____ _____ him.

14 한참 후, 풀이 점점 우거져서 우리는 한 사람이 앞서가고 다른 사람이 뒤에서 가야 했다.

15 Ron이 앞서가고 있었다.

16 철길은 숲으로 이어졌고 나무가 높이 자라 철길 위로 지붕을 형성하며 점점 더 어두워졌다.

17 Ron이 갑자기 멈췄다. "앞을 봐!"라고 그가 외쳤다.

18 나는 그의 옆에 멈춰서 캄캄한 입구를 가로지르는 흰색 나무문을 보았다.

19 "터널이네." 내가 말했다.

20 "맞아. 그리고 문에 '들어가지 마시오'라고 적혀 있어." Ron이 대답했다.

21 "안을 보고 싶니?"

22 사실, 난 안으로 들어가고 싶지 않았다.

23 갑자기 나는 한기를 살짝 느꼈고 햇빛 속으로 되돌아가고 싶었다.

24 그렇지만 나는 "물론이지."라고 답하며 앞으로 움직였다.

25 우리는 문 앞에 자전거를 남겨 두고 넘어갔다.

26 우리는 서늘한 터널로 들어갔다.

27 안의 공기는 묵직했다.

28 우리 머리 위로 점점 더 커지는 소리가 났다.

29 "저게 뭐야?"라고 내가 소리쳤다.

30 "박쥐야." Ron이 말했다. "머리를 숙여." 그러고 나서 그는 계속 움직였다.

31 "너무 빨리 가지 마." 나는 그를 부르며 뒤쫓았다.

32 I meant, "Don't _____ me _____" but I didn't say so.

33 The next thing I heard was a _____ _____ right above us,
a _____ sound _____ _____ _____ _____ and then
a _____.

34 "Ron!" I shouted. "Ron, _____ _____? Can you hear me?"
No _____.

35 "Speak to me, Ron. Tell me _____ _____."

36 I slowly walked toward _____ _____ _____ _____ and
found only dirt and small rocks.

37 As I _____ _____ my hands, I felt _____ _____ —
Ron's face!

38 His eyes _____ _____, and he was _____ _____.

39 "It's okay, Ron," I whispered. "I'll _____ _____ _____."

40 "I think I'_____ _____ my leg. It really hurts. Just _____
_____ _____ _____, Ben."

41 "No," I replied. "I'll _____
to safety first."

42 I started _____ _____ the dirt and rocks with my hands.

43 I _____ _____, and I felt _____ _____.

44 It took a long time to _____ _____ the earth _____ Ron.

45 Finally, I _____ _____ _____ his body.

46 _____ him under the arms, I pulled him backward, _____
_____ _____, toward the _____ _____.

47 It seemed _____ _____ _____, but finally I was able to
get Ron _____ _____ the tunnel.

48 He didn't _____ _____ _____ _____, _____.

---

32 '나를 두고 가지 마'라고 말하고 싶었지만, 나는 그렇게 말하지 않았다.

33 그다음 내가 들은 것은 바로 앞에서 나는 큰 소음이었는데, 그것은 마치 고속열차 같은 쿵쾅거리는 소리였다. 이어서 비명이 들렸다.

34 "Ron!" 나는 외쳤다. "Ron, 무슨 일이야? 내 말 들려?" 아무 응답이 없었다.

35 "Ron, 나에게 말해 봐. 무슨 일이 생겼는지 말해 줘."

36 나는 천천히 Ron이 있던 곳으로 걸어갔고 흙과 작은 자갈만을 발견했다.

37 손을 뻗었을 때 나는 축축한 무언가를 느꼈다. Ron의 얼굴이었다!

38 그의 눈은 감겨 있었고 약하게 숨을 쉬고 있었다.

39 "괜찮아, Ron." 나는 속삭였다. "내가 꺼내 줄게."

40 "다리가 부러진 것 같아. 정말 아파. 그냥 가서 도움을 요청해, Ben."

41 "안 돼." 나는 대답했다. "우선 안전한 곳까지 여기에서 형을 꺼낼 거야."

42 나는 손으로 흙과 자갈을 치우기 시작했다.

43 나는 침착했고 내가 잘할 수 있다고 느꼈다.

44 Ron을 뒤덮은 흙을 치우는 데에 오랜 시간이 걸렸다.

45 드디어 나는 그의 몸을 자유롭게 할 수 있었다.

46 팔 밑으로 그를 안고서 그를 터널 입구 쪽으로 조금씩 뒤로 끌어당겼다.

47 오랜 시간이 걸린 듯했지만 결국 나는 Ron을 터널 밖으로 데리고 나올 수 있었다.

48 그는 별로 좋아 보이지 않았다.

49 His face was white, and he was trying hard to _____ himself _____ _____ _____ from _____ _____.

50 I found our bikes and brought the _____ _____ _____ to Ron.

51 "Here, drink these," I said. "I'll _____ _____ _____ _____. I'll be _____ _____ _____ I _____."

52 _____ _____, Ron simply _____ _____ _____.

53 I got on my bicycle and _____ _____ along the tracks until I got to _____ _____ _____.

54 I _____ _____ the gate and found a woman _____ _____ _____ in the kitchen.

55 _____ _____ _____, Ron was taken to the hospital, _____ his leg was _____ in a _____.

56 _____ _____ _____ our parents arrived at the hospital and saw us, my mother cried _____ _____.

57 But all my father said was, "_____ _____ _____ _____ _____ to you."

58 And what was the _____? It was "*Keep out* means _____ _____ _____ _____."

59 Ron is now the manager of a big company which produces helmets and _____ _____ _____.

60 And me? I am a _____ _____.

49 그의 얼굴은 창백했고 울음을 터뜨리지 않으려고 몹시 애쓰고 있었다.

50 나는 우리 자전거를 찾아서 Ron에게 물병 두 개를 가져다주었다.

51 "여기, 이거 마셔." 나는 말했다. "내가 가서 도움을 구할게. 최대한 빨리 올게."

52 대답으로 Ron은 그저 내 손을 꽉 잡았다.

53 나는 자전거를 타고 왔던 철길을 따라 달려, 마침내 가장 가까운 농가에 도착했다.

54 대문을 지나 달려가 나는 부엌에서 설거지를 하고 있는 부인을 발견했다.

55 그 부인 덕분에 Ron은 병원으로 이송되었고, 병원에서 다리에 석고붕대를 했다.

56 부모님이 병원에 도착해서 우리를 보자마자, 어머니는 안도감에 울음을 터뜨리셨다.

57 하지만 아버지가 하신 말씀은 "이 일이 너희에게 교훈이 되기를 바란다."가 전부였다.

58 그래서 교훈이 무엇이었을까? 그것은 '들어가지 마시오'라는 말은 '곤경을 멀리하라'는 뜻이라는 것이다.

59 Ron은 지금 안전모와 여러 안전 제품을 생산하는 큰 회사의 관리자이다.

60 그럼 나는? 나는 소방관이다.

※ 다음 문장을 우리말로 쓰시오.

1 Keep Out

➡ _____

2 Every summer, my family used to go on holiday to the coast.

➡ _____

3 We always went to the same place and stayed at the same small guesthouse.

➡ _____

4 We would stay for two weeks, swimming in the sea and walking around the little town.

➡ _____

5 In other words, we never did anything special, and nothing ever really happened on these vacations.

➡ _____

6 At the time of this story I was twelve years old.

➡ _____

7 Most people can remember this particular summer, as it was the hottest summer England had had since records began.

➡ _____

8 It did not rain throughout June and July, and the sun shone day in and day out.

➡ _____

9 But Ron and I loved the heat and the sun.

➡ _____

10 Every day, we would ride our bicycles further and further away from the guesthouse.

➡ _____

11 One day Ron decided that we should ride our bikes along the old train tracks to see where they would take us.

➡ _____

12 I was happy to follow Ron, as usual, and we set off after breakfast.

➡ _____

13 At first, the tracks were easy to follow, and we cycled along side by side.

➡ _____

14 After a while, the grass grew thicker, and we had to ride one behind the other.

➡ _____

15 Ron was ahead.

➡ _____

16 The tracks went toward the woods and it grew darker as the trees stood tall and formed a roof over the tracks.

➡ _____

17 Ron stopped suddenly. "Look ahead!" he shouted.

➡ _____

18 I stopped next to him and saw a white, wooden gateway across a black opening.

➡ _____

19 "It's a tunnel," I said.

➡ _____

20 "Yes, and it says, 'Keep Out' on the gate," replied Ron.

➡ _____

21 "Do you want to have a look inside?"

➡ _____

22 Actually, I did not want to go inside.

➡ _____

23 I felt a little cold all of a sudden, and I wanted to go back into the sunlight.

➡ _____

24 But I answered, "Sure," and moved ahead.

➡ _____

25 We left our bikes at the gate and climbed over.

➡ _____

26 We entered the cool tunnel.

➡ _____

27 The air inside was heavy.

➡ _____

28 Above our heads there was a sound that grew louder and louder.

➡ _____

29 "What's that?" I called out.

➡ _____

30 "Bats," said Ron, "Keep your head down." Then he moved on.

➡ _____

31 "Don't go so fast." I called after him.

➡ _____

32 I meant, "Don't leave me behind" but I didn't say so.

➡ _____

33 The next thing I heard was a loud noise right above us, a thumping sound like an express train and then a scream.

➡ _____

_____

34 "Ron!" I shouted. "Ron, what's up? Can you hear me?" No reply.

➡ _____

35 "Speak to me, Ron. Tell me what's happened."

➡ _____

36 I slowly walked toward where Ron had been and found only dirt and small rocks.

➡ _____

37 As I reached out my hands, I felt something wet — Ron's face!

➡ _____

38 His eyes were closed, and he was breathing weakly.

➡ _____

39 "It's okay, Ron," I whispered. "I'll get you out."

➡ _____

40 "I think I've broken my leg. It really hurts. Just go and get help, Ben."

➡ _____

41 "No," I replied. "I'll get you out of here to safety first."

➡ _____

42 I started moving away the dirt and rocks with my hands.

➡ _____

43 I felt calm, and I felt in control.

➡ _____

44 It took a long time to clear away the earth covering Ron.

➡ _____

45 Finally, I managed to free his body.

➡ _____

46 Holding him under the arms, I pulled him backward, inch by inch, toward the tunnel entrance.

➡ _____

47 It seemed to take ages, but finally I was able to get Ron out of the tunnel.

➡ _____

48 He didn't look too well, though.

➡ _____

49 His face was white, and he was trying hard to stop himself from crying out.

➡ _____

50 I found our bikes and brought the two water bottles to Ron.

➡ _____

51 Here, drink these," I said. "I'll go and get help. I'll be as quick as I can."

➡ _____

52 In reply, Ron simply pressed my hands.

➡ _____

53 I got on my bicycle and raced back along the tracks until I got to the nearest farmhouse.

➡ _____

54 I ran past the gate and found a woman washing some dishes in the kitchen.

➡ _____

55 Thanks to her, Ron was taken to the hospital, where his leg was put in a cast.

➡ _____

56 As soon as our parents arrived at the hospital and saw us, my mother cried with relief.

➡ _____

57 But all my father said was, "Let that be a lesson to you."

➡ _____

58 And what was the lesson? It was "*Keep out* means *Stay out of trouble*."

➡ _____

59 Ron is now the manager of a big company which produces helmets and other safety products.

➡ _____

60 And me? I am a fire fighter.

➡ _____

※ 다음 괄호 안의 단어들을 우리말에 맞도록 바르게 배열하시오.

1 (Out / Keep)
➡ _____

2 (summer, / every / family / my / to / used / on / go / holiday / to / coast. / the)
➡ _____

3 (always / we / to / went / same / the / place / and / at / stayed / the / small / same / guesthouse.)
➡ _____

4 (would / we / for / stay / weeks, / two / in / swimming / the / and / sea / around / walking / little / the / town.)
➡ _____

5 (other / in / words, / never / we / anything / did / special, / and / ever / nothing / really / happened / these / on / vacations.)
➡ _____

6 (the / at / of / time / story / this / was / I / twelve / old. / years)
➡ _____

7 (people / most / can / this / remember / summer, / particular / it / as / the / was / summer / hottest / had / England / since / had / began. / records)
➡ _____

8 (did / it / rain / not / June / throughout / July, / and / the / and / sun / shone / in / day / and / out. / day)
➡ _____

9 (Ron / but / and / loved / I / heat / the / and / sun. / the)
➡ _____

10 (day, / every / would / we / our / ride / further / bicycles / and / from / away / further / guesthoue. / the)
➡ _____

11 (day / one / decided / Ron / that / should / we / our / ride / along / bikes / old / the / tracks / train / see / to / they / where / take / would / us.)
➡ _____

12 (was / I / to / happy / Ron, / follow / usual, / as / and / set / we / off / breakfast. / after)
➡ _____

13 (first, / at / tracks / the / easy / were / follow, / to / we / and / along / cycled / by / side / side.)
➡ _____

1 들어가지 마시오

2 여름마다 나의 가족은 해안으로 휴가를 가곤 했다.

3 우리는 항상 같은 곳에 가서 똑같은 작은 게스트하우스에 묵었다.

4 우리는 2주 가량 머물며 바다에서 수영하고 작은 마을 주위를 돌아다니곤 했다.

5 다시 말해서, 그런 휴가에서 우리는 특별한 일을 하지 않았고 정말 아무 일도 일어나지 않았다.

6 이 이야기는 내가 12살 때 일이다.

7 관측 이래 영국이 겪은 가장 더운 여름이었기 때문에, 대부분의 사람들은 이 특별한 여름을 기억할 수 있다.

8 6월과 7월 내내 비가 오지 않았고 태양은 연일 쨍쨍했다.

9 하지만 Ron과 나는 그 더위와 태양을 사랑했다.

10 매일 우리는 게스트하우스에서 조금씩 먼 곳으로 자전거를 타고 가곤 했다.

11 어느 날, Ron은 낡은 철로가 우리를 어디로 데려다줄지 알아보려고 그 철로를 따라 자전거를 타기로 결정했다.

12 난 늘 그랬듯 Ron을 따르는 게 즐거웠고, 아침 식사 후에 우리는 출발했다.

13 처음에는 철길을 따라가는 게 어렵지 않아 우리는 나란히 자전거를 타고 갔다.

14 (a / after / while, / grass / the / thicker, / grew / we / and / to / had / one / ride / behind / other. / the)
➡ _____

15 (was / Ron / ahead.)
➡ _____

16 (tracks / the / toward / went / woods / the / and / grew / it / as / darker / the / stood / trees / and / tall / a / formed / roof / the / over / tracks.)
➡ _____

17 (stopped / Ron / suddenly. // ahead!" / "look / shouted. / he)
➡ _____

18 (stopped / I / to / next / and / him / a / saw / white, / gateway / wooden / a / across / opening. / black)
➡ _____

19 (a / "it's / I / tunnel," / said.)
➡ _____

20 (and / "yes, / says, / it / Out' / 'Keep / the / on / gate," / Ron. / replied)
➡ _____

21 (you / "do / to / want / a / have / inside?" / look)
➡ _____

22 (I / actually, / not / did / to / want / inside. / go)
➡ _____

23 (felt / I / little / a / cold / a / of / all / sudden, / and / wanted / I / go / to / into / back / sunlight. / the)
➡ _____

24 (I / but / anwered, / "sure," / moved / and / ahead.)
➡ _____

25 (left / we / bikes / our / the / at / and / gate / over. / climbed)
➡ _____

26 (entered / we / the / tunnel. / cool)
➡ _____

27 (air / the / inside / heavy. / was)
➡ _____

28 (our / above / there / heads / was / sound / a / grew / that / and / louder / louder.)
➡ _____

29 (that?" / "what's / called / I / out.)
➡ _____

30 (Ron, / said / "bats, / "keep / head / your / down." // he / then / on. / moved)
➡ _____

31 (go / "don't / fast." / so // called / I / him. / after)
➡ _____

14 한참 후. 풀이 점점 우거져서 우리는 한 사람이 앞서가고 다른 사람이 뒤에서 가야 했다.

15 Ron이 앞서가고 있었다.

16 철길은 숲으로 이어졌고 나무가 높이 자라 철길 위로 지붕을 형성하며 점점 더 어두워졌다.

17 Ron이 갑자기 멈췄다. "앞을 봐!"라고 그가 외쳤다.

18 나는 그의 옆에 멈춰서 캄캄한 입구를 가로지르는 흰색 나무문을 보았다.

19 "터널이네." 내가 말했다.

20 "맞아. 그리고 문에 '들어가지 마시오'라고 적혀 있어." Ron이 대답했다.

21 "안을 보고 싶니?"

22 사실. 난 안으로 들어가고 싶지 않았다.

23 갑자기 나는 한기를 살짝 느꼈고 햇빛 속으로 되돌아가고 싶었다.

24 그렇지만 나는 "물론이지."라고 답하며 앞으로 움직였다.

25 우리는 문 앞에 자전거를 남겨 두고 넘어갔다.

26 우리는 서늘한 터널로 들어갔다.

27 안의 공기는 묵직했다.

28 우리 머리 위로 점점 더 커지는 소리가 났다.

29 "저게 뭐야?"라고 내가 소리쳤다.

30 "박쥐야." Ron이 말했다. "머리를 숙여." 그러고 나서 그는 계속 움직였다.

31 "너무 빨리 가지 마." 나는 그를 부르며 뒤쫓았다.

32 (meant, / I / leave / "don't / behind" / me / I / but / didn't / so. / say)

➡ _____

33 (next / the / I / thing / was / heard / a / noise / loud / above / right / us, / a / sound / thumping / like / express / an / and / train / then / scream. / a)

➡ _____

34 ("Ron!" / shouted. / I // what's / Ron, / up? // you / can / me? / hear // reply. / no)

➡ _____

35 (to / "speak / Ron. / me, // me / tell / happened." / what's)

➡ _____

36 (slowly / I / toward / walked / Ron / where / been / had / and / only / found / dirt / small / and / rocks.)

➡ _____

37 (I / as / out / reached / hands, / my / felt / I / wet / something / — / face! / Ron's)

➡ _____

38 (eyes / his / closed, / were / he / and / breathing / was / weakly.)

➡ _____

39 (okay, / "it's / Ron," / whispered. / I // get / "I'll / out." / you)

➡ _____

40 (think / "I / broken / I've / leg. / my // really / it / hurts. // go / just / and / help, / get / Ben.")

➡ _____

41 ("no," / repiled. / I / get / "I'll / out / you / here / of / safety / to / first.")

➡ _____

42 (started / I / away / moving / dirt / the / and / with / rocks / hands. / my)

➡ _____

43 (felt / I / calm, / I / and / in / felt / control.)

➡ _____

44 (took / it / long / a / to / time / away / clear / earth / the / Ron. / covering)

➡ _____

45 (I / finally, / to / managed / his / body. / free)

➡ _____

46 (him / holding / the / under / arms, / pulled / I / backward, / him / by / inch / inch, / toward / tunnel / the / entrance.)

➡ _____
_____

47 (seemed / it / take / to / ages, / finally / but / was / I / to / able / Ron / get / of / out / tunnel. / the)

➡ _____

48 (didn't / he / too / look / though. / well,)

➡ _____

32 '나를 두고 가지 마'라고 말하고 싶었지만, 나는 그렇게 말하지 않았다.

33 그다음 내가 들은 것은 바로 앞에서 나는 큰 소음이었는데, 그것은 마치 고속열차 같은 쿵쾅거리는 소리였다. 이어서 비명이 들렸다.

34 "Ron!" 나는 외쳤다. "Ron, 무슨 일이야? 내 말 들려?" 아무 응답이 없었다.

35 "Ron, 나에게 말해 봐. 무슨 일이 생겼는지 말해 줘."

36 나는 천천히 Ron이 있던 곳으로 걸어갔고 흙과 작은 자갈만을 발견했다.

37 손을 뻗었을 때 나는 축축한 무언가를 느꼈다. Ron의 얼굴이었다!

38 그의 눈은 감겨 있었고 약하게 숨을 쉬고 있었다.

39 "괜찮아, Ron." 나는 속삭였다. "내가 꺼내 줄게."

40 "다리가 부러진 것 같아. 정말 아파. 그냥 가서 도움을 요청해, Ben."

41 "안 돼." 나는 대답했다. "우선 안전한 곳까지 여기에서 형을 꺼낼 거야."

42 나는 손으로 흙과 자갈을 치우기 시작했다.

43 나는 침착했고 내가 잘할 수 있다고 느꼈다.

44 Ron을 뒤덮은 흙을 치우는 데에 오랜 시간이 걸렸다.

45 드디어 나는 그의 몸을 자유롭게 할 수 있었다.

46 팔 밑으로 그를 안고서 그를 터널 입구 쪽으로 조금씩 뒤로 끌어당겼다.

47 오랜 시간이 걸린 듯했지만 결국 나는 Ron을 터널 밖으로 데리고 나올 수 있었다.

48 그는 별로 좋아 보이지 않았다.

49 (face / his / white, / was / he / and / trying / was / to / hard / stop / from / himself / out. / crying)

➡ _____

50 (found / I / bikes / our / and / the / brought / water / two / to / bottles / Ron.)

➡ _____

51 (drink / "here, / these," said. / I // go / "I'll / get / and / help. // be / I'll / quick / as / I / as / can.")

➡ _____

52 (reply, / in / simply / Ron / my / pressed / hands.)

➡ _____

53 (got / I / my / on / bicycle / and / back / raced / the / along / tracks / I / until / to / got / nearest / the / farmhouse.)

➡ _____

54 (ran / I / the / past / gate / and / a / found / woman / some / washing / dishes / the / in / kitchen.)

➡ _____

55 (to / thanks / her, / was / Ron / to / taken / the / where / hospital, / his / was / leg / put / cast. / a / in)

➡ _____

56 (soon / as / our / as / parents / at / arrived / the / and / hospital / saw / my / us, / mother / with / cried / relief.)

➡ _____

57 (all / but / father / my / was, / said, / that / "let / a / be / to / lesson / you.")

➡ _____

58 (what / and / the / was / lesson? // was / it / *out* / "*Keep* / *Stay* / means / *of* / *out* / *trouble*.")

➡ _____

59 (is / Ron / the / now / of / manager / big / a / company / produces / which / helmets / other / and / products. / safety)

➡ _____

60 (me? / and / am / I / fire / fighter. / a)

➡ _____

49 그의 얼굴은 창백했고 울음을 터뜨리지 않으려고 몹시 애쓰고 있었다.

50 나는 우리 자전거를 찾아서 Ron에게 물병 두 개를 가져다주었다

51 "여기, 이거 마셔." 나는 말했다. "내가 가서 도움을 구할게. 최대한 빨리 올게."

52 대답으로 Ron은 그저 내 손을 꽉 잡았다.

53 나는 자전거를 타고 왔던 철길을 따라 달려, 마침내 가장 가까운 농가에 도착했다.

54 대문을 지나 달려가 나는 부엌에서 설거지를 하고 있는 부인을 발견했다.

55 그 부인 덕분에 Ron은 병원으로 이송되었고, 병원에서 다리에 석고붕대를 했다.

56 부모님이 병원에 도착해서 우리를 보자마자, 어머니는 안도감에 울음을 터뜨리셨다.

57 하지만 아버지가 하신 말씀은 "이 일이 너희에게 교훈이 되기를 바란다."가 전부였다.

58 그래서 교훈이 무엇이었을까? 그것은 '들어가지 마시오'라는 말은 '곤경을 멀리하라'는 뜻이라는 것이다.

59 Ron은 지금 안전모와 여러 안전 제품을 생산하는 큰 회사의 관리자이다.

60 그럼 나는? 나는 소방관이다.

※ 다음 우리말을 영어로 쓰시오.

1 들어가지 마시오

➡ _____

2 여름마다 나의 가족은 해안으로 휴가를 가곤 했다.

➡ _____

3 우리는 항상 같은 곳에 가서 똑같은 작은 게스트하우스에 묵었다.

➡ _____

4 우리는 2주 가량 머물며 바다에서 수영하고 작은 마을 주위를 돌아다니곤 했다.

➡ _____

5 다시 말해서, 그런 휴가에서 우리는 특별한 일을 하지 않았고 정말 아무 일도 일어나지 않았다.

➡ _____

_____

6 이 이야기는 내가 12살 때 일이다.

➡ _____

7 관측 이래 영국이 겪은 가장 더운 여름이었기 때문에, 대부분의 사람들은 이 특별한 여름을 기억할 수 있다.

➡ _____

_____

8 6월과 7월 내내 비가 오지 않았고 태양은 연일 쨍쨍했다.

➡ _____

9 하지만 Ron과 나는 그 더위와 태양을 사랑했다.

➡ _____

10 매일 우리는 게스트하우스에서 조금씩 먼 곳으로 자전거를 타고 가곤 했다.

➡ _____

11 어느 날, Ron은 낡은 철로가 우리를 어디로 데려다줄지 알아보려고 그 철로를 따라 자전거를 타기로 결정했다.

➡ _____

_____

12 난 늘 그랬듯 Ron을 따르는 게 즐거웠고, 아침 식사 후에 우리는 출발했다.

➡ _____

13 처음에는 철길을 따라가는 게 어렵지 않아 우리는 나란히 자전거를 타고 갔다.

➡ _____

14 한참 후, 풀이 점점 우거져서 우리는 한 사람이 앞서가고 다른 사람이 뒤에서 가야 했다.

➡ _____

15 Ron이 앞서가고 있었다.

➡ _____

16 철길은 숲으로 이어졌고 나무가 높이 자라 철길 위로 지붕을 형성하며 점점 더 어두워졌다.

➡ _____

_____

17 Ron이 갑자기 멈췄다. "앞을 봐!"라고 그가 외쳤다.

➡ _____

18 나는 그의 옆에 멈춰서 캄캄한 입구를 가로지르는 흰색 나무문을 보았다.

➡ _____

19 "터널이네." 내가 말했다.

➡ _____

20 "맞아. 그리고 문에 '들어가지 마시오'라고 적혀 있어." Ron이 대답했다.

➡ _____

21 "안을 보고 싶니?"

➡ _____

22 사실, 난 안으로 들어가고 싶지 않았다.

➡ _____

23 갑자기 나는 한기를 살짝 느꼈고 햇빛 속으로 되돌아가고 싶었다.

➡ _____

24 그렇지만 나는 "물론이지."라고 답하며 앞으로 움직였다.

➡ _____

25 우리는 문 앞에 자전거를 남겨 두고 넘어갔다.

➡ _____

26 우리는 서늘한 터널로 들어갔다.

➡ _____

27 안의 공기는 묵직했다.

➡ _____

28 우리 머리 위로 점점 더 커지는 소리가 났다.

➡ _____

29 "저게 뭐야?"라고 내가 소리쳤다.

➡ _____

30 "박쥐야." Ron이 말했다. "머리를 숙여." 그러고 나서 그는 계속 움직였다.

➡ _____

31 "너무 빨리 가지 마." 나는 그를 부르며 뒤쫓았다.

➡ _____

32 '나를 두고 가지 마.'라고 말하고 싶었지만, 나는 그렇게 말하지 않았다.

➡ _____

33 그다음 내가 들은 것은 바로 앞에서 나는 큰 소음이었는데, 그것은 마치 고속열차 같은 쿵쾅거리는 소리였다. 이어서 비명이 들렸다.

➡ _____

34 "Ron!" 나는 외쳤다. "Ron, 무슨 일이야? 내 말 들려?" 아무 응답이 없었다.

➡ _____

35 "Ron, 나에게 말해 봐. 무슨 일이 생겼는지 말해 줘."

➡ _____

36 나는 천천히 Ron이 있던 곳으로 걸어갔고 흙과 작은 자갈만을 발견했다.

➡ _____

37 손을 뻗었을 때 나는 축축한 무언가를 느꼈다. Ron의 얼굴이었다!

➡ _____

38 그의 눈은 감겨 있었고 약하게 숨을 쉬고 있었다.

➡ _____

39 "괜찮아, Ron." 나는 속삭였다. "내가 꺼내 줄게."

➡ _____

40 "다리가 부러진 것 같아. 정말 아파. 그냥 가서 도움을 요청해, Ben."

➡ _____

41 "안 돼." 나는 대답했다. "우선 안전한 곳까지 여기에서 형을 꺼낼 거야."

➡ _____

42 나는 손으로 흙과 자갈을 치우기 시작했다.

➡ _____

43 나는 침착했고 내가 잘할 수 있다고 느꼈다.

➡ _____

44 Ron을 뒤덮은 흙을 치우는 데에 오랜 시간이 걸렸다.

➡ _____

45 드디어 나는 그의 몸을 자유롭게 할 수 있었다.

➡ _____

46 팔 밑으로 그를 안고서 그를 터널 입구 쪽으로 조금씩 뒤로 끌어당겼다.

➡ _____

47 오랜 시간이 걸린 듯했지만 결국 나는 Ron을 터널 밖으로 데리고 나올 수 있었다.

➡ _____

48 그는 별로 좋아 보이지 않았다.

➡ _____

49 그의 얼굴은 창백했고 울음을 터뜨리지 않으려고 몹시 애쓰고 있었다.

➡ _____

50 나는 우리 자전거를 찾아서 Ron에게 물병 두 개를 가져다주었다.

➡ _____

51 "여기, 이거 마셔." 나는 말했다. "내가 가서 도움을 구할게. 최대한 빨리 올게."

➡ _____

52 대답으로 Ron은 그저 내 손을 꽉 잡았다.

➡ _____

53 나는 자전거를 타고 왔던 철길을 따라 달려, 마침내 가장 가까운 농가에 도착했다.

➡ _____

54 대문을 지나 달려가 나는 부엌에서 설거지를 하고 있는 부인을 발견했다.

➡ _____

55 그 부인 덕분에 Ron은 병원으로 이송되었고, 병원에서 다리에 석고붕대를 했다.

➡ _____

56 부모님이 병원에 도착해서 우리를 보자마자, 어머니는 안도감에 울음을 터뜨리셨다.

➡ _____

57 하지만 아버지가 하신 말씀은 "이 일이 너희에게 교훈이 되기를 바란다."가 전부였다.

➡ _____

58 그래서 교훈이 무엇이었을까? 그것은 '들어가지 마시오'라는 말은 '곤경을 멀리하라'는 뜻이라는 것이다.

➡ _____

59 Ron은 지금 안전모와 여러 안전 제품을 생산하는 큰 회사의 관리자이다.

➡ _____

60 그럼 나는? 나는 소방관이다.

➡ _____

영어 기출 문제집

적중 100

2학기

정답 및 해설

천재 | 이재영

중 3

적중 100

영어 기출 문제집

적중100

2학기

정답 및 해설

천재 | 이재영

중 **3**

Watch Out

시험대비 실력평가 p.08

01 effective 　　　　02 ① 　　　03 ③
04 (1) flooded　(2) occurred　(3) overnight
05 (1) on his way back　(2) have, in common
　　(3) solar system　(4) do harm　(5) shot, into
06 ③

01 주어진 관계는 명사와 형용사의 관계를 나타낸다. active: 활동 중인, effective: 효과적인
02 '꼭대기에 용암이 솟아나오는 구멍이 있는 산'을 가리키는 말은 volcano(화산)이다.
03 destroy: 파괴하다
04 flood: 홍수가 나다, occur: 발생하다, overnight: 하룻밤 동안
05 shoot ~ into: ~을 …으로 내뿜다, solar system: 태양계, on one's way back home: 집으로 돌아오는 길에, have ~ in common: ~을 공통점으로 가지다, do harm: 해를 끼치다
06 have in common: ~을 공통점으로 갖다, have an effect on: ~에 영향을 미치다, get hurt: 다치다, get stuck in: 갇히다, take care of: ~을 돌보다, take off: ~을 벗다

서술형 시험대비 p.09

01 entire
02 (1) have, in common　(2) in harmony with
　　(3) named after
03 (1) scenery　(2) threaten　(3) prevent　(4) warnings
　　(5) volume
04 (1) Stretching is a good way to relieve your neck pain.
　　(2) My family likes to visit hot springs in winter.
　　(3) Germs can spread through the air.
05 (1) You should wear a helmet when you ride a bike.
　　(2) Heatwave warnings were issued.
　　(3) The app helps you locate your child.
　　(4) The thief threatened the shopkeeper and stole cash.

01 주어진 관계는 반의어 관계를 나타낸다. sudden: 갑작스러운, entire: 전체의

02 have ~ in common: ~을 공통으로 가지다, in harmony with: ~와 조화를 이루어, name after: ~을 따서 이름 짓다
03 prevent: 막다, 예방하다 scenery: 경치, 풍경 threaten: 위협하다 volume: 부피 warning: 주의, 경고
04 relieve: 완화하다, hot spring: 온천, spread: 퍼지다, germ: 세균
05 helmet: 헬멧, 안전모, issue: 발효하다, locate: ~의 위치를 찾아내다, threaten: 위협하다, thief: 도둑

Conversation

핵심 Check p.10~11

1 Please make sure you wear a life jacket.
2 ②

교과서 대화문 익히기

Check(√) True or False p.12

1 T　2 F　3 F　4 T

교과서 확인학습 p.14~15

Listen - Listen & Answer Talk 1
hit, warning, issued, rainfall, flooding, inside, make sure

Listen - Listen & Answer Dialog 2
favor / typhoon, bring in / No, bike / care, dishes / typhoon / stay home

Listen - Listen More
sandwiches / ride my bike / good, a favor / on your way back / problem / make sure, wear, no / worry

Speak - Talk in pairs.
Wash your hands / more, you don't play with the knives / mind

Wrap Up 5
having a good time / cool, going / fishing / wear a life jacket / keep, in mind

Wrap Up 6

do me a favor / on Christmas, tickets / tickets do you want

시험대비 기본평가   p.16

01 ⓓ → wear   02 ⑤

03 She wants to go to the Tom Dylan concert.

04 She wants him to buy some concert tickets for her.

01 make sure 뒤에 접속사 that이 생략된 절이므로 동사 wear가 적절하다.

02 위 대화를 통해 아빠가 무엇을 명심해야 하는지 알 수 없다.

03 할머니는 크리스마스에 Tom Dylan 콘서트에 가고 싶어 하신다.

04 할머니는 Jack이 콘서트 표를 사주기를 원한다.

시험대비 실력평가   p.17~18

01 ③   02 He asks her to wash her hands first.   03 칼을 가지고 놀지 말 것.   04 ⑤
05 ⑤   06 typhoon   07 ⑤   08 ③
09 ③   10 ①, ④   11 ⑤   12 ④

01 위 대화는 부엌에서 주의해야 할 사항에 대해 이야기하고 있다.

02 남자는 여자에게 먼저 손을 씻을 것을 요청한다.

03 남자는 여자에게 'Make sure you don't play with the knives.'라고 하고 있다.

04 (A)는 부탁하기를 나타내는 표현이지만, ⑤번은 도움을 주려는 의미를 나타낸다.

05 위 대화를 통해 소라가 할머니에게 무엇을 가져갈지는 알 수 없다.

06 '강한 바람을 동반한 강한 열대성 폭풍'을 가리키는 말은 typhoon(태풍)이다.

07 (A)는 당부하는 표현으로 ⑤번과 바꾸어 쓰기에 어색하다.

08 태풍주의보가 발효되었다.

09 주어진 문장은 부탁하는 표현으로 다음에 이어지는 응답으로 부탁 내용이 무엇인지 묻고 있는 (C)가 적절하다.

10 지민은 '최가네 샌드위치' 가게와 '아이스크림' 가게를 방문할 것이다.

11 어떻게 Brian이 지민을 도울 수 있을지는 알 수 없다.

12 부탁하는 표현에 '그 말을 들으니 유감이다'라는 말은 어색하다.

서술형 시험대비   p.19

01 (B) → (C) → (E) → (D) → (A)

02 (A) stay home   (B) a typhoon is coming tonight

03 It is going to hit Jejudo tonight.

04 It will cause lots of rainfall with a high chance of flooding in some areas.

05 He asks the listeners to stay inside and keep listening to the reports.

06 (C) → (E) → (B) → (D) → (A)

01 (B) 부탁하기 → (C) 부탁 내용 질문 → (E) 부탁 내용 설명 → (D) 반응 및 구체적인 질문 → (A) 구체적인 질문에 대한 대답

03 태풍 도니는 오늘밤 제주도를 강타할 것이다.

04 태풍 도니는 일부 지역에 많은 비를 동반한 홍수를 야기할 것이다.

05 남자는 청취자들에게 실내에 머무르고 계속 보도를 청취해 주기를 부탁한다.

06 (C) 아빠와 좋은 시간을 보냈음을 설명 → (E) 반응 및 내일 계획 질문 → (B) 내일 계획 설명 → (D) 당부하기 → (A) 대답하기

〔교과서〕
Grammar

핵심 Check   p.20~21

1 (1) Living   (2) Being

2 (1) might be reformed   (2) could be done

시험대비 기본평가   p.22

01 ④

02 (1) Feeling   (2) not knowing
    (3) will be delivered   (4) should be kept

03 ⑤   04 ③

01 접속사 없이 '주어+동사'가 이어지고 있으므로 빈칸에는 '접속사+주어+동사'의 역할을 할 수 있는 현재분사로(그가 배고픈 것은 능동이므로) 분사구문이 되어야 한다.

02 (1) 접속사가 없으므로 '접속사+주어+동사'의 역할을 할 수 있는 Feeling이 적절하다. (2) 분사구문의 부정은 분사 앞에 'not'이나 'never'를 쓴다. (3) 의자가 배달되는 것이므로 수동태로 나타내는 것이 적절하다. (4) 조동사가 있는 문장의 수동태는 '조동사+be+과거분사'의 형태로 나타낸다.

03 접속사 없이 '주어+동사'가 이어지고 있으므로 '접속사+주어+동사'의 역할을 할 수 있는 분사구문으로 나타내는 것이 적절하다.

3

04 조동사가 있는 문장의 수동태는 '조동사+be+과거분사'의 형태로 나타낸다.

01 ③   02 ⑤   03 ②   04 ②

05 (1) can be borrowed   (2) cannot be   (3) appear

    (4) took place   (5) Finishing   (6) waiting

    (7) not feeling   (8) It being

06 ①   07 ⑤   08 Walking

09 ③   10 ④

11 (1) can be read   (2) should not be accepted

12 ②   13 ⑤

14 (1) he was   (2) she was   (3) you were

15 ④   16 ①   17 ③

01 dance라는 동사가 있고 접속사가 없으므로 listen을 listening으로 분사구문으로 만들어야 한다. Every Friday evening, we dance together, listening to music.

02 조동사가 있는 문장의 수동태는 '조동사+be+과거분사'의 형태로 나타낸다.

03 첫 번째 빈칸에는 접속사가 없으므로 '접속사+주어+동사'의 역할을 할 수 있는 knowing이 적절하다. 두 번째 빈칸에는 수동태가 나와야 하므로 'be taught'가 적절하다.

04 앞에 give라는 동사가 있고 접속사가 없으므로 know를 knowing으로 분사구문으로 만들어야 한다.

05 (1) 조동사가 있는 문장의 수동태는 '조동사+be+과거분사'의 형태로 나타내며, 책은 '빌려지는 것'이므로 수동태가 적절하다. (2) 조동사가 있는 문장의 수동태의 부정문은 '조동사+not+be+과거분사'의 형태로 쓴다. (3) appear는 자동사이므로 수동태로 쓰이지 않는다. (4) took place는 자동사로 쓰이므로 수동태로 쓰이지 않는다. (5) 접속사가 없으므로 '접속사+주어+동사'의 역할을 할 수 있는 분사구문으로 쓰는 것이 적절하다. (6) 분사구문의 뜻을 명확히 하기 위해 접속사 While을 생략하지 않고 남겨둔 경우이다. (7) 분사구문의 부정은 분사 앞에 'not'이나 'never'를 쓴다. (8) 부사절과 주절의 주어가 다르므로 부사절의 주어를 생략하지 않고 써야 한다.

06 The work should be finished by 7 p.m. 조동사가 있는 문장의 수동태는 '조동사+be+과거분사'의 형태로 나타낸다.

07 '접속사+주어+동사'의 부사절을 분사구문으로 바꾸어 쓸 수 있다. 분사구문의 뜻을 명확히 하기 위해 접속사를 생략하지 않기도 하지만 필요한 주어를 생략하지는 않는다.

08 한 문장으로 쓰면 'While he was walking around the park, he met his neighbor Ms. Marple.'이고, 분사구문으로 바꾸면 'While he was walking'을 현재분사 Walking으로 써야 한다.

09 동물들이 이용되는 것이므로 수동태로 쓰고, 부정문을 만들기 위해서는 조동사 뒤에 not을 쓴다.

10 'Because she felt very cold, she drank a cup of hot tea.'를 분사구문으로 바르게 바꾼 것은 ④번이다.

11 (1) 조동사가 있는 문장의 수동태는 '조동사+be+과거분사'의 형태로 나타낸다. (2) 조동사가 있는 문장의 수동태의 부정문은 '조동사+not+be+과거분사'의 형태로 나타낸다.

12 주어진 문장과 ②번은 '이유'를 나타낸다. ① 양보, ③ 시간, ④ 동시동작, ⑤ 조건

13 조동사가 있는 문장의 수동태는 '조동사+be+과거분사'의 형태로 나타낸다.

14 부사절에서 주어가 주절의 주어와 같을 때 '주어+be동사'를 생략할 수 있으며 이것은 분사구문으로 고쳤을 때 being을 생략하고 접속사를 남겨둔 것과 같다.

15 조동사가 있는 문장의 수동태는 '조동사+be+과거분사'의 형태로 나타낸다.

16 부사절의 시제가 주절보다 앞선 경우에는 완료분사구문(having+과거분사)으로 쓴다.

17 부사절과 주절의 주어가 다를 때는 부사절의 주어를 생략하지 않고 사용하며 이것을 독립분사구문이라고 한다.

01 (1) Getting up late, she was late for school yesterday.

    (2) The girl got off the bus, saying goodbye to her friend.

    (3) Climbing to the top of the hill, you can see the garden well.

    (4) Studying hard, she failed the exam.

    (5) Not knowing the way to the theater, I asked the girl sitting next to me to tell me the way.

    (6) It being fine tomorrow, I'll go hiking Dobong Mountain.

    (7) Having lost her job, she had to leave the office.

    (8) (Being) Interested in history, she likes her history class.

02 (1) New books should be returned in a week by you.

    (2) This song will be loved for a long time (by people).

    (3) The population growth has to be slowed down (by us).

    (4) The sincerity of his decision may be doubted by her.

    (5) 불가. 이유: resemble은 상태를 나타내는 동사로 수동태로 쓰이지 않는다.

(6) 불가. 이유: '소유'를 나타내는 타동사는 수동태로 쓰이지 않는다.

03 (1) Embarrassing → Embarrassed

(2) Meeting → Having met

04 must be cooled   05 breaking

06 (1) Arriving at the train station, Mike began to look for his friends.

(2) Not knowing what to do, she asked for my advice.

(3) More gold can be found in this region.

(4) The cooking room should be kept clean at all times.

07 (1) Knives must be kept in a safe place.

(2) The department denies responsibility for what occurred.

(3) Arriving home, he cleaned the whole house.

(4) It being chilly outside, I wanted to stay home.

(5) (Having been) Written in haste, the book has many mistakes.

01 '접속사+주어+동사'로 이루어진 부사절의 주어가 주절의 주어와 일치할 때 접속사와 주어를 생략하고 동사를 분사(동사원형+-ing)로 만든다. (1) '이유', (2) '연속동작' (3) '조건' (4) '양보' (5) 분사구문의 부정은 'not+현재분사'이다. (6) 주절의 주어와 부사절의 주어가 다르므로 주어를 생략하면 안 된다.(독립분사구문) (7) 부사절의 시제가 주절보다 앞선 경우에는 완료분사구문(having+과거분사)으로 쓴다. (8) 과거분사로 시작되는 분사구문은 being이 생략된 것으로 수동의 의미를 갖는다.

02 조동사가 있는 문장의 수동태는 '조동사+be+과거분사'의 형태로 나타낸다. 행위자가 일반인이거나 강조할 필요가 없을 때에는 'by+행위자'를 생략하고 쓸 수 있다. (3)번의 경우 주어의 수사 복수에서 단수로 바뀌므로 'have to'가 'has to'로 되어야 함에 주의한다.

03 (1) 당황하게 한 것이 아니라 '당황하게 된'이라는 '수동'의 의미가 되어야 하므로 Embarrassed로 고쳐야 한다. (2) 몇 번 만난 것은 기억하는 것보다 먼저 일어난 일이므로 완료분사구문으로 쓴다.

04 조동사가 있는 문장의 수동태는 '조동사+be+과거분사'의 형태로 나타낸다. 행위자가 일반인이거나 강조할 필요가 없을 때에는 'by+행위자'를 생략하고 쓸 수 있다.

05 'and broke'를 분사구문 breaking으로 쓴다. = Mike fell down the steps and broke his arm.(연속 동작)

06 (1) 현재분사가 분사구문을 이끌도록 한다. (2) 분사구문의 부정은 분사 앞에 'not'이나 'never'를 쓴다. (3), (4) 조동사가 있는 문장의 수동태는 '조동사+be+과거분사'의 형태로 나타내며 행위자가 일반인이거나 강조할 필요가 없을 때에는 'by+행위자'를 생략하고 쓸 수 있다.

07 (1) Knives가 주어이므로 수동태로 써야 하고, 조동사가 있는 문장의 수동태는 '조동사+be+과거분사'의 형태로 쓴다. (2) occur는 자동사이므로 수동태로 쓰이지 않는다. (3) 도착하는 것은 능동이므로 현재분사를 쓰쓰는 것이 적절하다. (4) 주절의 주어와 부사절의 주어가 다르므로 독립분사구문으로 써야 한다. (5) 책이 쓰여지는 것이므로 수동의 의미인 과거분사가 나와야 하며, 책이 쓰여진 시제가 앞서므로 완료분사구문으로 써야 한다. Having been written에서 Having been을 생략하여 써도 좋다.

교과서
Reading

확인문제   p.28

1 T   2 F   3 T

확인문제   p.29

1 T   2 F

확인문제   p.30

1 T   2 F

교과서 확인학습 A   p.31~32

01 Power   02 have in common

03 of course   04 volcanic eruptions

05 are named after

06 make big islands appear

07 should be studied and understood

08 how many volcanoes there are

09 According to, above sea level

10 hard to locate

11 a large number of   12 are located

13 home to   14 alone, lies on

15 where, occur   16 Sudden

17 something surprising   18 appeared overnight

19 grow

20 kept growing, stopped growing

21 can be found   22 have been discovered

23 the largest known

24 100 times greater than that of

25 do harm to   26 get hurt

27 may be destoryed, can be threatened

28 have serious effects on

29 shoots, into, preventing, from reaching, disturbing

30 Deadly

31 erupted

32 eruption

33 unusually

34 What volcanoes do, not always

35 is good for

36 tourist attraction

37 Looking for

38 can be used

39 turns, into

40 greater harmony with

교과서 확인학습 B
p.33~34

1 The Power of Volcanoes

2 What do Jejudo, Sicily, and Hawaii have in common?

3 They are islands, of course.

4 In fact, they are all islands made from volcanic eruptions.

5 Volcanoes are very powerful, so they are named after Vulcan, the Roman god of fire.

6 They can make big islands appear or destroy entire cities like Pompeii.

7 Therefore, they should be studied and understood.

8 Nobody knows for sure how many volcanoes there are in the world.

9 According to scientists, there are about 1,500 active volcanoes above sea level.

10 Many more are underwater, and they are hard to locate.

11 Still, scientists have discovered a large number of them so far.

12 Many of the volcanoes on Earth are located along the Ring of Fire that circles the Pacific Ocean.

13 The ring is about 40,000 kilometers long, and it is home to around 75% of the world's active volcanoes.

14 Indonesia alone has over 120 active volcanoes since the country lies on the Ring of Fire.

15 This ring is also the area where most of the world's earthquakes occur.

16 A Sudden Volcano

17 Working on a cornfield one day in 1943, farmers in Mexico found something surprising.

18 A volcano appeared overnight on a flat cornfield.

19 Residents watched the volcano grow over 100 meters tall within a week.

20 The volcano, called Paricutin, kept growing, and it finally stopped growing at 424 meters in 1952.

21 You may think volcanoes can be found only on Earth.

22 However, they have been discovered on other planets, too, such as Mars and Jupiter.

23 In fact, "Olympus Mons" on Mars is the largest known volcano in the solar system.

24 Its volume is about 100 times greater than that of Mauna Loa, the largest volcano on Earth.

25 Being very powerful and dangerous, volcanoes do harm to people in many ways.

26 Sometimes people get hurt, or they may lose their houses.

27 Crops may be destoryed, and air traffic can be threatened.

28 Volcanoes can also have serious effects on world weather.

29 A volcanic eruption shoots lots of ash and dust into the air, preventing some of the sunlight from reaching Earth and thus disturbing usual weather patterns.

30 A Deadly Volcano

31 Mt. Tambora, an active volcano on the island of Sumbawa, Indonesia, erupted in 1815.

32 The eruption killed more than 10,000 residents.

33 It also caused an unusually cold summer around the world the following year.

34 What volcanoes do is not always bad for humans, however.

35 The soil near a volcano is good for farming.

36 Volcanoes are also a great tourist attraction.

37 Looking for fantastic scenery, millions of tourists visit Mt. Halla in Jejudo, Mt. Etna in Sicily, or Diamond Head in Hawaii every year.

38 Volcanoes can be used to produce electricity, too.

39 Iceland, for example, actively turns its volcanoes' heat energy into electricity.

40 Today people around the world are studying ways to live in greater harmony with volcanoes, and they are hopeful that more ways will be found soon.

시험대비 실력평가
p.35~39

01 ⑤   02 ①   03 volcanic eruptions

04 ②   05 According as → According to

06 ②

07 While they were working on a cornfield one day in

1943 또는 When[As] they worked on a cornfield one day in 1943

08 to grow → growing　　　09 Olympus Mons

10 ③　　　　11 (A) in the solar system　(B) on Earth

12 ②　　　　13 The eruption　　　14 ④

15 ①, ④

16 preventing some of the sunlight from reaching Earth and thus disturbing usual weather patterns

17 ③　　　　18 ⑤　　　　19 ②

20 have discovered　　　21 ④　　　　22 ⑤

23 (A) surprising　(B) grow　(C) called　　24 ④

01 앞의 내용의 결과가 나오고 있으므로 Therefore가 가장 적절하다. therefore: 그러므로, ② 게다가, 더욱이, ③ 다시 말해서

02 ⓐ과 ⓑ: 'Jejudo, Sicily, and Hawaii', ⓒ~ⓔ: '화산'

03 제주도, 시칠리아, 하와이는 모두 '화산 분출'에 의해 형성된 섬이다.

04 이 글은 '세계에 얼마나 많은 화산이 있는지 누구도 정확히 알지 못하고 해수면 위에 대략 1,500개의 활화산이 있는데, 그것보다 더 많이 존재하는 해저 화산들은 정확한 위치를 파악하기가 어렵다'는 내용의 글이므로, 제목으로는 ②번 '세계에 얼마나 많은 화산이 있는가?'가 적절하다.

05 'according as+주어+동사'이므로 'According to'로 고치는 것이 적절하다.

06 ⓑ와 ①, ③: 부사적 용법, ②, ⑤: 명사적 용법, ④: 형용사적 용법

07 '때'를 나타내는 부사절로 바꿔 쓸 수 있다.

08 '1952년에 424m로 '드디어 성장을 멈추었다'고 해야 하므로 to grow를 growing으로 고치는 것이 적절하다. stop+~ing: ~하는 것을 멈추다, stop+to부정사: ~하기 위해 멈추다

09 '올림푸스 몬스'를 가리킨다.

10 ⓑ와 ③: [앞에서 말한 명사의 반복을 피하기 위해] (~의) 그것(지시대명사), ① 지시형용사, ② 저것(말하는 사람과 가까이에 있지 않은 사람이나 사물을 가리킴), ④ 관계대명사, ⑤ [수량·정도를 나타내는 말을 한정하여] 그만큼(지시부사)

11 Olympus Mons는 '태양계에서' 가장 크다고 알려진 화산이고, Mauna Loa는 '지구에서' 가장 큰 화산이다.

12 이 글은 'Tambora 산의 분출이 주민 1만 명 이상을 죽음에 이르게 했다'는 내용의 글이므로, 제목으로는 ②번 '목숨을 앗아가는 화산'이 적절하다. ① definition: 정의

13 (Tambora 산의) '분출'을 가리킨다.

14 Tambora 산이 1815년에 분출했을 때 '얼마나 오래' 분출했는지는 알 수 없다. ① It's on the island of Sumbawa, Indonesia. ② It erupted in 1815. ③ It killed more than 10,000 residents. ⑤ It was unusually cold.

15 ⓐ와 ①, ④: 이유, ② 양보, ③ 조건, ⑤ 때

16 preventing과 disturbing은 부대상황을 나타내는 분사 구문이다. prevent A from -ing: A가 ~하는 것을 막다

17 이 글은 '화산이 매우 강력하고 위험하기 때문에, 여러 면에서 사람들에게 해를 끼친다'는 내용의 글이므로, 주제로는 ③번 '인간 생활에 끼치는 화산의 해로운 영향'이 적절하다.

18 앞의 내용의 예가 나오고 있으므로 for example이 가장 적절하다. ① 게다가, 더욱이, ② 그 결과, ④ 다른 한편으로는, 반면에

19 주어진 문장의 also에 주목한다. ②번 앞 문장에서 화산이 인류에게 항상 나쁜 것만은 아닌 첫 번째 예로 화산 인근의 토양이 농사에 좋다고 말한 다음에, '또한' 화산은 매우 훌륭한 관광 명소라는 설명을 하는 것이므로 ②번이 적절하다.

20 과학자들이 (과거부터) 지금까지 해저에 존재하는 많은 수의 화산을 '발견해 왔다'라고 해야 하므로 '현재완료시제'로 쓰는 것이 적절하다.

21 주어진 문장의 They에 주목한다. ①번 앞 문장의 Volcanoes를 받고 있으므로 ④번이 적절하다.

22 과학자들에 따르면, '해수면 위에' 대략 1,500개의 활화산이 있다.

23 (A) 감정을 나타내는 동사는 감정을 유발할 때 현재분사를 쓰는 것이 적절하므로 surprising이 적절하다. (B) watch는 지각동사이므로 목적격보어 자리에 동사원형인 grow가 적절하다. (C) Paricutin(파리쿠틴)'이라 '불리는' 화산이라고 해야 하므로 called가 적절하다.

24 1943년에 생기기 시작해서 1952년에 드디어 성장을 멈추었다고 했으므로 '10년 이상 동안' 계속 자랐다는 것은 옳지 않다.

🦉 **서술형 시험대비**　　　　　p.40~41

01 eruptions

02 As a matter of fact / Actually / To tell the truth

03 Because they can make big islands appear or destroy entire cities like Pompeii.

04 the Ring of Fire　　　05 three-fourths

06 There are over 120 active volcanoes in Indonesia.

07 (A) other　(B) is　(C) known

08 Mauna Loa → that of Mauna Loa

09 Olympus Mons.

10 What volcanoes do is not always bad for humans

11 be used

12 ⑴ 화산 인근의 토양은 농사에 좋다.
　⑵ 화산은 또한 매우 훌륭한 관광 명소이다.
　⑶ 화산은 또한 전기를 생산하는 데에도 이용될 수 있다.

13 explosive power → heat energy

14 like　　　15 as great as

16 other planets

01 eruption: 분출, 증기와 화산 물질의 강력한 방출이 갑작스럽게 발생하는 것

02 In fact / As a matter of fact / Actually / To tell the truth: 사실

03 화산은 큰 섬이 생겨나게 하거나 폼페이 같은 도시 전체를 파멸시킬 수도 있기 때문이다.

04 '불의 고리(환태평양조산대)'를 가리킨다.

05 75%는 4분의 3이다. 분수를 읽을 때 분자는 '기수', 분모는 '서수'로 읽는 것이 적절하다. 분자와 분모는 하이픈으로 연결하여 쓰고, 분자가 2 이상인 경우 분모 끝에 s를 붙인다.

06 인도네시아에는 120개가 넘는 활화산이 있다.

07 (A) another 뒤에는 단수 명사가 와야 하므로 other가 적절하다. (B) "Olympus Mons"가 주어이므로 is가 적절하다. (C) 태양계에서 가장 크다고 '알려진' 화산이라고 해야 하므로 known이 적절하다.

08 그것의 부피는 지구에서 가장 큰 화산 Mauna Loa의 '부피'보다 약 100배 더 크다고 해야 하므로, that of Mauna Loa로 고치는 것이 적절하다. 대명사 that은 the volume을 대신한다.

09 'Olympus Mons'는 'Mauna Loa'의 부피보다 약 100배 더 크다.

10 선행사를 포함하는 관계대명사 what을 주어로 하여 쓰는 것이 적절하다. not always는 '언제나 ~인 것은 아닌'이라는 의미로 부분 부정을 나타낸다.

11 화산은 또한 전기를 생산하는 데에도 '이용될 수' 있다고 해야 하므로 수동태로 쓰는 것이 적절하다.

12 화산이 인류에게 항상 나쁜 것만은 아니라고 말하면서 예로 든 세 가지를 쓰는 것이 적절하다.

13 아이슬란드는 적극적으로 화산의 '열에너지'를 전기로 바꾼다. explosive power: 폭발력

14 such as = like: ~와 같은

15 ~ times+비교급+than A = ~ times+as+원급+as A: A보다 ~ 배 더 ···한

16 화산은 지구뿐만 아니라 '다른 행성'에서도 발견되어 왔다.

영역별 핵심문제
p.43~47

01 discovery 02 ④

03 (1) There may be life on other planets.
   (2) Heavy rainfall is expected this summer.
   (3) There are eight planets in our solar system.

04 ③

05 (1) Everything in the house turned into ash after the fire.
   (2) The floor of the room was covered with dust.
   (3) This year farmers expect to have a good crop.

06 ①   07 ⓓ → inside   08 ④

09 life jacket 10 ①   11 ③

12 Can you give me a hand?   13 ⑤

14 ②   15 ③   16 ⑤   17 ②
18 ⑤   19 The electricity being   20 ③
21 ③   22 ②, ⑤   23 until now 24 ③
25 growing 26 ⑤
27 Because[As] they are very powerful and dangerous
28 ④   29 ②   30 ⑤

01 주어진 단어의 관계는 동사와 명사의 관계를 나타낸다. destroy: 파괴하다, discover: 발견하다

02 주어진 문장에서 issue는 '발표하다'를 의미한다.

03 (1) planet: 행성 (2) rainfall: 강우(량) (3) solar system: 태양계

04 주어진 문장에서 volume은 '부피'를 의미하며 이와 같은 의미로 쓰인 것은 ③번이다. ① '책, (책의) 권 ②,④,⑤ 음량, 볼륨

05 (1) turn into: ~로 변하다 (2) be covered with: ~로 덮이다 (3) expect: 기대하다

06 주어진 문장에서 issue는 '발표하다'를 의미하며 이와 같은 의미로 쓰인 것은 ①번이다. 나머지는 모두 '주제, 쟁점, 문제'를 의미한다.

07 태풍이 오니 실내에 머물러 있을 것을 조언하는 것이 자연스러우므로 inside가 적절하다.

08 태풍 도니는 강한 바람과 많은 비를 동반할 것이다.

10 당부하는 말에 '명심할게요.'라는 대답이 적절하다.

11 위 대화에서 준호가 신난 것을 알 수 있다. frightened: 겁먹은

12 'Can you give me a hand?'는 '저를 도와주시겠어요?'라고 도움을 요청하는 표현이다.

13 위 대화에서 할머니가 누구와 콘서트를 갈지는 알 수 없다.

14 상대방의 당부하는 말에 '신경 쓰지 마. 기운 내!'라는 대답은 어색하다.

15 Lions and tigers belong to the cat family. 'belong to'는 '~에 속하다'라는 뜻으로 수동태로 쓰이지 않는다.

16 주어진 문장은 '이유'를 나타내는 분사구문으로 볼 수 있다.

17 조동사 will이 있으므로 'will+be+과거분사'의 형태로 쓴다.

18 ① Riding in a flying car, you will be able to go places faster. ② Not having much work to do, I have time to see a movie. ③ The sun rising, we made wishes. ④ Singing and dancing together, we had a great time. ⑤ 'Because it appeared overnight, Paricutin is a sudden volcano.'를 분사구문으로 쓴 것이다.

19 'When the electricity was out, ~'을 부사구문으로 고쳐 쓴 것이다. 주절의 주어와 부사절의 주어가 다르므로 주어를 생략하면 안 된다.(독립분사구문)

20 첫 번째 문장에서는 접속사가 없으므로 '접속사+주어+동사'의 역할을 할 수 있는 분사구문 watching이 적절하다. 두 번째 문장에서는 수동태가 나와야 하고 조동사가 있으므로 '조동사+be+과거분사'의 형태로 쓴다.

21 ⓐ와 ③: 그럼에도 불구하고(부사), ①과 ⑤: 아직(도)(부사), ② (비교급을 강조하여) 훨씬(부사), ④ 가만히 있는, 고요한(형용사)

22 ⓑ와 ②, ⑤: 계속 용법, ① 완료 용법, ③ 결과 용법, ④ 경험 용법

23 so far = until now: 지금까지

24 이 글은 '밤사이에 평평한 옥수수 밭 위로 화산이 생겨난 것'에 관한 글이므로, 제목으로는 ③번 '갑작스럽게 생겨난 화산'이 적절하다.

25 keep ~ing: 계속해서 ~하다

26 ⑤ prevent A from -ing: A가 ~하는 것을 막다, ① do harm to: ~에 해를 끼치다, ② in many ways: 여러 면에서, ③ have effects on: ~에 영향을 끼치다, ④ shoot ~ into ...: ~을 …으로 내뿜다

27 '이유'를 나타내는 부사절로 바꿔 쓸 수 있다.

28 '다량의 용암을 분출시킨다.'는 말은 위 글에 없다.

29 위 글은 '감상문'이다. review (책, 연극, 영화 등에 대한) 논평[비평], 감상문, ① (신문, 잡지의) 글, 기사, ③ 수필, ④ 요약, 개요, ⑤ 독후감

30 '글쓴이가 누구와 함께 영화를 보았는지'는 알 수 없다. ① It is *The Perfect Storm*. ② Wolfgang Petersen. ③ It came out in 2000. ④ It is about a big storm in the Atlantic Ocean that put a fishing boat in danger.

단원별 예상문제 p.48~51

01 ②

02 (1) earthquake destroyed (2) effect, physical
  (3) volcano, erupt

03 ③ **04** ⑤

05 He visited Dokdo with his father.

06 He should make sure to wear a life jacket.

07 ⓔ → wear

08 ④ **09** can you do me a favor? **10** ②

11 should be done **12** ②

13 Listening to music, he read the novel he had bought the other day.

14 ⓓ, ⓕ **15** ② **16** occurs → occur

17 ③ **18** ⑤ **19** ① **20** ④

21 use → be used **22** ①

23 a hot spring

01 '지구 표면의 갑작스러운 흔들림'을 나타내는 말은 earthquake(지진)이다.

02 earthquake: 지진, destroy: 파괴하다, effect: 영향, 효과, physical: 신체의, volcano: 화산, erupt: 분출하다

03 (A) '발표하다'를 뜻하며 수동태로 issued, (B) because of+

명사(구), because+주어+동사, (C) keep ~ing: 계속 ~하다

04 위 대화를 통해 언제 비가 그칠지는 알 수 없다.

05 준호는 아빠와 독도를 방문했다.

06 준호는 낚시 갈 때 구명조끼를 꼭 입을 것을 명심해야 한다.

07 make sure (that) 주어+동사 ~: 꼭 ~해라, 반드시 ~해라

10 아빠는 바깥에 있는 옷가지들을 안으로 가져올 것을 부탁하였다.

11 be동사가 주어졌으므로 조동사가 있는 수동태인 '조동사+be+과거분사'의 형태로 쓴다.

12 조동사가 있는 문장의 수동태는 '조동사+be+과거분사'의 형태로 나타낸다.

13 접속사와 부사절의 주어를 생략하고 현재분사를 그대로 쓴다.

14 ⓐ Felt → Feeling. ⓑ Having not → Not having ⓒ Being → It being ⓔ design → be designed ⓖ discuss → be discussed ⓗ known → be known

15 ⓐ와 ②: 약, ~쯤, ① 사방에(서), 빙 둘러, ③ 둘레에, 주위에, ④ 이리저리, 여기저기, ⑤ (특정한 사람이나 사상 등에) 맞춰, (내가 모든 걸 당신 일정에 맞출 수는 없잖아요!)

16 'most+복수명사'는 복수로 취급해야 하므로 'occur'로 고치는 것이 적절하다.

17 '인도네시아에서 활화산이 얼마나 자주 분출하는지'는 대답할 수 없다. ① They are located along the Ring of Fire that circles the Pacific Ocean. ② It is about 40,000 kilometers long. ④ Because the country lies on the Ring of Fire. ⑤ They occur in the Ring of Fire that circles the Pacific Ocean.

18 ⓐ 앞에 나오는 내용과 상반되는 내용이 뒤에 이어지므로 However가 가장 적절하다. ⓑ 방금 한 말에 대해 자세한 내용을 덧붙이고 있으므로 In fact가 가장 적절하다. ① Therefore 그러므로, ② In addition 게다가, 더욱이, ④ on the other hand 다른 한편으로는, 반면에

19 화산은 화성이나 목성 같은 '다른 행성에서도' 발견되어 왔다.

20 선행사를 포함하는 관계대명사 what을 쓰는 것이 적절하다.

21 '조동사 can+be+p.p.'의 수동태가 되어야 한다.

22 주어진 문장은 ①번 앞 문장에서 말한 '화산에서 이 에너지를 볼 수 있다'는 것을 설명하는 문장이므로 ①번이 적절하다.

23 '온천'을 가리킨다.

서술형 실전문제 p.52~53

01 She is going to Choi's to buy some sandwiches.

02 He asks her to buy chocolate ice cream for him on her way back.

03 She should keep in mind that she wears a helmet and no ear phones.

04 (1) While he was walking home after school, Tom found a soccer ball on the street.

(2) Because[As/ Since] I slept on the bus, I missed my stop.

(3) He started to cry, admitting his fault.

(4) It not being so cold outside, she went out without a coat.

05 (1) She left home, waving at her parents.

(2) Feeling tired, I came home earlier than usual.

(3) This project cannot be finished by today.

(4) The concert will be held next week.

06 (1) All students must follow school rules.

(2) We should finish the project tonight.

(3) By whom will the problem be solved?

(4) Eggs and cheese can be added according to your taste.

07 Nobody knows for sure how many volcanoes there are in the world.

08 one thousand five hundred

09 them

10 influence

11 it prevents, disturbs

12 (A) crops   (B) air traffic

01 지민이는 지금 샌드위치를 사러 '최가네'에 간다.

02 Brian은 지민이에게 돌아오는 길에 초콜릿 아이스크림을 사다 줄 것을 요청한다.

03 지민이는 헬멧을 쓰고 이어폰을 끼지 말 것을 명심해야 한다.

04 (1) 의미상 '시간'을 나타내는 분사구문이다. (2) 의미상 '이유'를 나타내는 분사구문이다. (3) 의미상 '부대상황'을 나타내는 분사구문으로 바꾼다. (4) 주절의 주어와 다르므로 독립분사구문으로 바꾼다.

05 (1) 의미상 '동시동작'을 나타내는 분사구문이다. (2) 의미상 '이유'를 나타내는 분사구문이다. (3), (4) 조동사가 있는 문장의 수동태는 '조동사+be+과거분사'의 형태로 나타낸다.

06 조동사가 있는 수동태는 '조동사+be+과거분사'의 형태로 쓴다. (3)은 Who will the problem be solved by?로 바꿀 수도 있다.

07 동사 knows의 목적어로 '간접의문문의 순서(의문사+주어+동사)'로 쓰는 것이 적절하다.

08 'one thousand five hundreds'로 쓰지 않도록 조심해야 한다.

09 주어 they를 locate의 '목적어'로 바꾸는 것이 적절하다.

10 have an effect[influence/impact] on = influence = affect: ~에 영향을 미치다

11 ⓑ는 부대상황을 나타내는 분사구문으로, and it prevents ~ and thus disturbs ~로 바꾸어 쓸 수 있다.

12 화산은 사람들에게 해를 끼치고 집뿐만 아니라 '농작물'을 파괴할 수 있다. 또한 화산은 '항공 교통'을 위협하고 세계 날씨를 바꾼다.

|모범답안|

01 (A) bike   (B) some sandwiches
   (C) buy chocolate ice cream
   (D) wear a helmet and no ear phones

02 (A) *The Perfect Storm*   (B) in 2000
   (C) Wolfgang Petersen
   (D) a big storm in the Atlantic Ocean that put a fishing boat in danger
   (E) good acting   (F) natural disasters

01 지민이는 샌드위치를 사러 자전거로 '최가네'에 갈 것이다. Brian은 그녀에게 그를 위해 돌아오는 길에 초콜릿 아이스크림을 사다 달라고 요청한다. Brian은 그녀에게 헬멧을 쓰고 이어폰을 사용하지 말 것을 상기시킨다.

01 ②   02 ⑤

03 (1) flooding   (2) chance   (3) area
   (4) favor   (5) Volcanoe(s)

04 How many tickets do you want?   05 ⑤

06 He wants her to bring in the clothes from outside and call Grandma.

07 He is going to take care of the bike.

08 She will tell her to stay home.

09 (B) → (D) → (C) → (E) → (A)   10 ④

11 ⑤   12 (E) → (B) → (A) → (D) → (C)

13 (1) can be used   (2) should not be allowed
   (3) will be built

14 ②, ④

15 (1) The pizza will be delivered within 30 minutes.
   (2) The problem should be solved right now.
   (3) Dana came across her history teacher, walking to the market.
   (4) Feeling cold, Susan put on her coat.

16 ①, ④

17 (1) Food and drinks must not be brought into the library.
   (2) The computer should be fixed by Mr. Hinkle.
   (3) (Being) Tired after the game, the players took a rest for a while.
   (4) Not having any money, I borrowed some from my older brother.

18 ④   19 ②

20 (A) for   (B) produce   (C) harmony   21 ③

22 Residents watched the volcano grow over 100 meters tall within a week.

23 ①

01 '별 주변을 도는 우주에 있는 크고 둥근 물체'를 가리키는 것은 planet(행성)이다.

02 주어진 단어들 중 나머지는 모두 자연 재해를 나타내지만 ⑤번은 '태양계'를 나타낸다.

03 favor: 친절, 부탁, volcano: 화산, chance: 가능성, flooding: 홍수, area: 지역

05 할머니가 Jack의 크리스마스 계획을 찬성한다는 내용은 대화를 통해 알 수 없다.

06 아빠는 소라가 바깥에서 옷가지들을 들여오고 할머니께 전화를 하길 원하신다.

07 아빠는 설거지를 끝낸 후에 자전거를 처리하실 것이다.

08 소라는 할머니께 집안에 계시라고 말할 것이다.

09 (B) 걸어가지 않고 자전거를 탈 것이라고 설명 → (D) 부탁하기 → (C) 부탁 내용 질문 → (E) 부탁 내용 설명 → (A) 허락

10 (A)는 당부하는 표현이지만 ④번은 궁금증을 나타낸다.

11 준호는 내일 '아빠'와 보트를 탈 것이다.

12 (E) 부탁 내용 설명 → (B) 대답 및 자전거 관리 질문 → (A) 자전거 관리에 대한 대답 → (D) 요구 사항 확인 → (C) 대답

13 조동사가 있는 수동태는 '조동사+be+과거분사'의 형태로 쓴다.

14 ① Walked → Walking ③ Very → Being very ⑤ study → be studied

15 (1), (2) 조동사가 있는 수동태는 '조동사+be+과거분사'의 형태로 쓴다. (3) '시간'의 분사구문을 이용한다. (4) '이유'의 분사구문을 이용한다.

16 ① This medicine must be taken after meal. ④ Tina sat back on the sofa, closing her eyes.

17 (1) 조동사가 있는 수동태는 '조동사+be+과거분사'의 형태로 쓴다. (2) 컴퓨터가 주어이므로 수동태가 되어야 한다. 조동사가 있는 수동태는 '조동사+be+과거분사'의 형태로 쓴다. (3) 주어가 피곤하게 되는 수동의 관계이므로 being이 생략된 과거분사 Tired나 Being tired로 시작하는 문장으로 바꾼다. (4) 분사구문의 부정은 분사 앞에 'not'이나 'never'를 쓴다.

18 ④ This ring is also the area. + Most of the world's earthquakes occur in the area.를 합친 문장이므로, This ring is also the area 'where[in which]' most of the world's earthquakes occur.라고 하는 것이 적절하다.

19 (A)와 ②: ~때문에, ①, ③, ④, ⑤: ~한 이후로

20 (A) 화산 인근의 토양은 농사에 '좋다'고 해야 하므로 for가 적절하다. be good at: ~을 잘하다, be good for: ~에 좋다, (B) 화산은 또한 전기를 '생산하는 데에도' 이용될 수 있다고 해야 하므로 produce가 적절하다. be used to ~ing: ~하 데 익

숙하다, (C) 화산과 더 '조화롭게' 살 방법이라고 해야 하므로 harmony가 적절하다. conflict: 투쟁, 전투, 분쟁

21 화산은 또한 전기를 생산하는 데에도 이용될 수 있다.

22 watch는 지각동사로 목적격보어 자리에 동사원형인 grow를 쓰는 것이 적절하다.

23 ① all at once: 갑자기, finally / at last / eventually / in the end / in the long run: 마침내

Lesson 8

All Your Dreams Are Worth Chasing

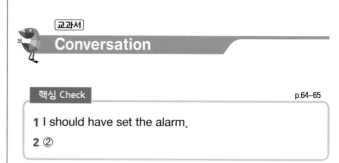

시험대비 실력평가   p.62

01 completely   02 ①   03 ③

04 (1) Harvard University was founded in 1636.

  (2) The writer's novel is worth reading over and over.

05 (1) went by   (2) deal with   (3) be ashamed of

  (4) do her hair   (5) hang out with

06 ③

01 주어진 관계는 동의어의 관계를 나타낸다. achieve: 이루다, 달성[성취]하다 accomplish: 이루다, 성취하다 entirely: 완전히 completely: 완전히, 전적으로

02 '추구하거나 뒤쫓다'를 가리키는 말은 'go after(~을 추구하다)'이다.

03 apply for: ~에 지원하다, ~을 신청하다

05 be ashamed of: ~을 부끄러워하다, deal with: ~을 다루다, do one's hair: 머리를 손질하다, hang out with: ~와 시간을 보내다, go by: 지나가다, 흐르다

06 break down: 고장나다, break out: 발발[발생]하다, go after: ~을 추구하다, go by: 지나가다, 흐르다

서술형 시험대비   p.63

01 include

02 (1) Go after   (2) was ashamed of   (3) deal with

03 (1) include   (2) impatient   (3) read   (4) opportunity

  (5) offer

04 (1) The book will help you expand your imagination.

  (2) She became a zookeeper by going after what she was interested in.

  (3) He is looking for a challenging and rewarding job.

05 (1) When monkeys play and chase each other, they laugh.

  (2) The price of all sandwiches in our store includes drinks.

  (3) The hospital was founded to treat poor people.

01 주어진 관계는 반의어 관계를 나타낸다. lend: 빌리다, borrow: 빌려주다, include: 포함하다, exclude: 제외[배제]하다

02 go after: ~을 추구하다, be ashamed of: ~을 부끄러워하다, deal with: ~을 다루다

03 impatient: 짜증 난, 참지 못하는 opportunity: 기회 offer: 제의, 제안 read: ~라고 적혀 있다 include: 포함하다

04 imagination: 상상, 상상력, go after: ~을 추구하다, challenging: 도전적인

05 chase: 쫓다, 추적하다, include: 포함하다, found: 설립하다

교과서

Conversation

핵심 Check   p.64~65

1 I should have set the alarm.

2 ②

교과서 대화문 익히기

Check(√) True or False   p.66

1 T   2 F   3 T   4 F

교과서 확인학습   p.68~69

Listen - Listen & Answer Dialog 1

What / for / are, when / On, left / How's, gojng / It, to draw what, should have practiced / make it

Listen - Listen & Answer Dialog 2

to meet, do well on / sure, did my best / What made, for / (I)'ve, loved, since / quite right / What, think / I'd say, completely

Speak - Talk in pairs.

saved / share, with

Listen - Listen More

to see / I'm afraid / hate to be / should have set / happens a lot, tired / What made / do my hair / We're stuck in, get off / you're mistaken, stay on / terribly

시험대비 기본평가
p.70

01 ⓓ must → should   02 ⑤

03 She wants to work with robots.

04 Because she thinks it'll be a good job in the future.

01 'must have p.p.'는 '~했음에 틀림없다'라는 의미이고, 'should have p.p.'는 '~했어야 한다'라는 의미이므로 must를 should로 고치는 것이 적절하다.

02 위 대화를 통해 소라가 왜 마나 애니메이션 고등학교에 입학하고 싶은지 알 수 없다.

03 소녀는 로봇과 관련된 일을 하고 싶어 한다.

04 소녀는 '그것이 미래에 좋은 직업이 될 거라고 생각하기 때문이야.'라고 말하고 있다.

시험대비 실력평가
p.71~72

01 ⑤   02 ③   03 I'd say imagination.

04 ②   05 ④   06 stuck   07 ③

08 ⑤   09 ①

10 How come your computer has viruses?

11 **모르는 사람에게서 온 이메일을 연 것.**

01 (A)에 이어서 '저는 게임 디자이너가 되고 싶습니다.'라고 하는 것으로 보아 상대방의 말을 수정할 때 쓰는 표현이 나오는 것이 적절하다.

02 위 대화의 M과 G는 면접[인터뷰] 하는 사람과 면접[인터뷰] 받는 사람의 관계이다.

03 I'd[I would] say ~: 내 생각엔 ~인 것 같다

04 'I should have+p.p. ~.'는 'I ought to have+p.p.', 'I'm sorry I didn't[wasn't] ~.' 또는 'I regret I didn't[wasn't] ~.' 등으로 바꿔 쓸 수 있다.

05 위 대화를 통해 지호와 Amber가 얼마나 늦었는지 알 수 없다.

06 '한 위치에서 다른 위치로 움직이기 힘든'을 가리키는 말은 stuck(갇힌, 꼼짝 못 하는)이다.

07 (A)는 후회하는 표현이 적절하다. (B)는 많은 책을 읽지 못한 것을 걱정하고 있으므로 afraid가 적절하다. (C) spend+시간/돈+on (동)명사: ~에 시간이나 돈을 쓰다

08 'G2는 휴대 전화에 너무 많은 시간을 썼다고 후회하고 있다.

09 상대방의 말을 수정해 주는 말에 '유감이다'라고 말하는 것은 어색하다.

10 'How come?'은 평서문의 어순이 이어지는 것에 주의해야 한다. 완전한 문장으로 쓸 때 뒤에 'your computer has viruses'라고 써야 한다.

11 '그러지 말았어야 해.'라고 말하고 있다. 즉, 모르는 사람에게서 온 이메일을 열지 말았어야 한다는 말이다.

서술형 시험대비
p.73

01 (B) → (C) → (A) → (E) → (D)

02 (A) repair   (B) a good job

03 I'm afraid you're mistaken

04 do you want to repair robots

05 She regrets that she didn't practice more.

06 She has the exam this Friday.

07 To draw[Drawing] what she wants to express is difficult.

08 (C) → (B) → (D) → (A)

01 '커서 무엇을 하고 싶은지' 묻는 주어진 글에 이어 (B)에서 답하고, (C)에서 추가적인 질문을 하고, (A)에서 추가적인 질문에 답하고, (E)에서 이유를 묻고, (D)에서 답하는 순서가 자연스럽다.

02 G는 그것이 미래에 좋은 직업이 될 거라 생각하기 때문에 로봇을 수리하는 일을 하고 싶어 한다.

03 That's not quite right.는 상대방의 말을 수정하기 위해 쓰는 표현으로 'I'm afraid you're mistaken.'으로 바꿔 쓸 수 있다.

04 왜 로봇을 수리하고 싶은지 묻는 말이다.

05 '더 연습했어야 해.'라고 하는 것으로 보아 더 연습하지 않았던 것을 후회하고 있음을 알 수 있다.

06 '금요일'이라고 하면서 '이틀밖에 안 남았다'고 했으므로 이번 금요일임을 알 수 있다.

07 '내가 표현하고 싶은 것을 그리기가 쉽지 않아.'라고 하고 있다.

08 (C)에서 무슨 일인지 묻고, (B)에서 배고프다며 식량을 저장해 놓지 않음을 후회하고, (D)에서 걱정하지 말라며 식량을 나눠 주겠다고 하자 (A)에서 고맙다고 답하는 순서가 적절하다.

교과서

Grammar

핵심 Check
p.74~75

1 (1) shouldn't have eaten   (2) must have put

2 (1) who   (2) which   (3) which

01 ①   02 (1) must (2) might (3) should

03 ③

04 (1) You shouldn't have eaten so much.

   (2) I'll visit you during the vacation, which begins tomorrow.

01 Mr. Decker를 선행사로 하는 계속적 용법의 주격 관계대명사 who가 와야 한다. that이나 what은 계속적 용법의 관계대명사로 쓸 수 없다.

02 (1) 문맥상 '~했음이 틀림없다'는 강한 추측의 표현이 적절하다. (2) 문맥상 '~했을지도 모른다'는 약한 추측의 표현이 적절하다. (3) 문맥상 '~했어야 한다'는 후회의 표현이 적절하다.

03 계속적 용법의 관계대명사에서 선행사가 My favorite writer로 사람이고 is의 주어가 필요한 주격이므로 who를 쓰는 것이 적절하다.

04 (1) should not[ought not to] have p.p.: ~하지 않았어야 했는데 (그런데 했다) (후회) (2) 우리말 해석이 순차적으로 되어 있으므로 관계대명사의 계속적 용법을 이용한다.

01 ②   02 ③   03 ①

04 (1) who (2) which (3) which (4) must (5) should (6) might

05 ⑤   06 ④   07 ④

08 (1) which (2) which (3) who (4) which

09 ②   10 ②   11 ③

12 My dad gave me a birthday present, from which I got much happiness.

13 ②   14 which   15 ②

16 (1) Yesterday I called my aunt, who lives in Mexico.

   (2) Tom also showed me a book, which had KenKuller's autograph on it.

   (3) You should not have broken the rule.

   (4) They must have left some messages with their own letters.

17 ④   18 ②

19 (1) Ms. Molly named her granddaughter Daisy, which is the name of a flower.

   (2) The writer might have finished his novel.

01 관계대명사 that은 계속적 용법으로 사용할 수 없다.

02 'should+have+p.p.' 형태가 되어야 한다. I should have built it with stronger material.

03 첫 번째 빈칸에는 'should+have+p.p.' 형태가 적절하다. 두 번째 빈칸에는 선행사가 사람이고 주어 역할을 하는 계속적 용법이므로 who가 적절하다.

04 (1) 선행사가 King Sejong으로 사람이고 주어 역할을 하는 계속적 용법이므로 who가 적절하다. (2) 선행사가 사물이고 주어 역할을 하는 계속적 용법이므로 which가 적절하다. (3) 선행사가 앞의 절 전체(Tom visited her)이므로 which가 적절하다. (4) must have p.p.: ~했음이 틀림없다 (강한 추측) (5) should have p.p.: ~했어야 한다 (그런데 하지 못했다) (후회) (6) might have p.p.: ~했을지도 모른다 (약한 추측)

05 'I'm sure+that 주어+과거동사(~을 확신한다, 분명히 ~하다)'은 강한 추측의 must have p.p.(~했음이 틀림없다)로 쓸 수 있다.

06 계속적 용법의 관계대명사는 '접속사+대명사'로 바꾸어 쓸 수 있다. 이것은 '감자 먹는 사람들'인데 Vincent van Gogh가 1885년에 그렸다'라는 것으로, 적절한 접속사는 and이다.

07 should not[ought not to] have p.p.: ~하지 않았어야 했는데 (그런데 했다) (후회)

08 계속적 용법에는 선행사가 사람이면 who, 동물이나 사물이면 which를 쓴다.

09 should have p.p.: ~했어야 한다(후회)

10 앞에 콤마가 있는 관계대명사의 계속적 용법에는 that을 쓰지 않는다.

11 '하루 종일 졸렸다'는 말로 보아 늦게까지 깨어 있으면 안 되었다는 후회의 말이 적절하다. should not[ought not to] have p.p.: ~하지 않았어야 했는데 (그런데 했다) (후회)

12 선행사가 앞 절 전체이므로 which를 이용한다. 전치사 from의 목적어로 쓰이는 것에 주의한다.

13 휴대폰을 잃어버린 것이므로 후회(~했어야 한다)의 의미를 가지는 should have p.p.가 적절하다.

14 계속적 용법의 관계대명사는 '접속사+대명사'로 바꾸어 쓸 수 있다.

15 첫 번째 빈칸에는 must have p.p.(~했음이 틀림없다)가 적절하다. 두 번째 빈칸에는 should not have p.p.(~하지 않았어야 했는데)가 적절하다.

16 (1) 선행사가 사람이므로 which가 아니라 who를 써야 한다. (2) 계속적 용법에는 that을 쓰지 않는다. (3) should는 조동사로 not이 바로 다음에 나와야 한다. (4) 'must have p.p.' 형태가 되어야 한다.

17 ① 계속적 용법에는 that을 쓰지 않는다. (that → which) ② 동사의 수의 일치가 부적절하다. (come → comes) ③ 주격 관계대명사가 나와야 하므로 whom을 who로 고쳐야 한다. ⑤ 선행사가 앞 절의 내용이므로 that을 which로 고쳐야 한다.

18 must have p.p.: ~했음이 틀림없다 (강한 추측)

19 (1) 관계대명사의 계속적 용법을 이용한다. 선행사를 Daisy로 하고 관계대명사 which가 수식하도록 쓴다. (2) might have p.p.: ~했을지도 모른다 (약한 추측)

01 (1) who   (2) which   (3) who   (4) which

02 (1) You shouldn't have played soccer in the rain.

  (2) The film, in which he plays the leading role, is a big hit.

  (3) The old lady, whom I saw on the subway, was a famous actress.

03 (1) should[ought to] have made

  (2) must have been sick   (3) can't have slept

04 해석: (1) Anne은 교사인 아들 두 명이 있다.

     (2) Anne은 아들 두 명이 있는데, 그들 모두 교사이다.

  차이: (1)은 관계대명사의 한정적 용법으로 선행사를 수식하는 형용사 역할을 하며 '교사인 아들 두 명'으로 해석한다. 아들이 몇 명인지 모르는데 그 중에 교사인 아들이 두 명이라는 의미이며, (2)는 관계대명사의 계속적 용법으로 선행사를 부연 설명하며 아들이 두 명으로 둘 다 교사이다.

05 I shouldn't have spent all my money on buying clothes.

06 who encouraged me to

07 (1) She should not[ought not to] have watched the movie.

  (2) She cannot have watched the movie.

  (3) She may[might] have watched the movie.

  (4) She must have watched the movie.

08 I'm fond of the actor, whose name is not known well.

09 (1) Harry invited Lindsey to the party, which made her feel happy.

  (2) Do you know Thomas Edison, who invented the light bulb?

  (3) The book, which is cheap, contains very good contents.

10 (1) who → which

  (2) which → who

  (3) that → who

  (4) must → should

  (5) cannot → may[might]

  (6) must → cannot

01   who와 which는 모두 계속적 용법에 쓰일 수 있고 선행사가 사람이면 who, 동물이나 사물이면 which를 쓴다. (1), (3) 앞의 선행사가 사람이므로 who를 쓴다. (2) 앞의 선행사가 사물이므로 which를 쓴다. (4) which는 앞의 절 전체를 선행사로 받을 수 있다.

02 (1) shouldn't have p.p.: ~하지 않았어야 했는데 (그런데 했다) (후회) (2) The film is a big hit. + He plays the leading role in the film.을 계속적 용법의 관계대명사 which로 연결한다. (3) The old lady was a famous actress. + I saw her on the subway.를 계속적 용법의 관계대명사 whom으로 연결한다. saw의 목적어 The old lady를 선행사로 하는 목적격 관계대명사 whom을 이용하여 'The old lady, whom I saw ~'로 쓴다.

03 (1) 'should[ought to] have p.p.'를 이용하여 '후회'를 나타낸다. (2) 'must have p.p.'를 이용하여 '추측'을 나타낸다. (3) 'can't have p.p.'를 이용하여 '부정의 추측'을 나타낸다.

05 '다 써버리지 말았어야 했는데'라고 후회하는 표현을 써야 하므로 'should have+과거분사'를 이용한다.

06 friend를 선행사로 하는 관계대명사 who를 이용하고, encourage는 목적격보어로 to부정사를 쓰는 것에 주의한다.

07 (1) should not[ought not to] have p.p.: ~하지 않았어야 했는데 (그런데 했다) (과거 사실에 대한 유감이나 후회) (2) cannot have p.p.: ~했을 리가 없다 (과거 사실에 대한 강한 부정의 추측) (3) may[might] have p.p.: ~했을지도 모른다 (과거 사실에 대한 약한 긍정의 추측) (4) must have p.p.: ~했음이 틀림없다 (과거 사실에 대한 강한 추측)

08 뒤에 나오는 name을 수식해 주는 소유격 whose가 적절하다.

09 (1) 앞에 나온 절 전체를 선행사로 받는 which를 이용한다. (2) 사람을 선행사로 받는 who를 이용한다. (3) 계속적 용법의 관계대명사는 '접속사(and, but, for, though 등)+대명사'로 고쳐 쓸 수 있다. 여기서는 'though+it'으로 생각할 수 있다.

10 (1) 선행사가 사물이므로 which로 나타낸다. (2) 선행사가 사람이므로 who로 나타낸다. (3) 계속적 용법의 관계대명사로는 that을 쓰지 않는다. (4) '후회'를 나타내는 'should have p.p.'가 적절하다. (5) 몇 명의 사람들이 나오고 있으므로 '약한 추측'을 나타내는 'may[might] have p.p.'가 적절하다. (6) '강한 부정의 추측'을 나타내는 'cannot have p.p.'가 적절하다.

교과서

Reading

확인문제   p.82

1 T   2 F   3 T   4 F

확인문제   p.83

1 T   2 F   3 T   4 F   5 T   6 F

01 DREAMS
02 used to be
03 anymore, which
04 that connect us
05 What, is
06 on weekends, back
07 must have loved
08 over and over
09 Go after
10 something new or challenging
11 Don't be ashamed of
12 was founded
13 was created, were fighting
14 there would be
15 What would it be like
16 hanging, which included
17 were explained, in a suit
18 wearing a suit, impatient
19 for hours
20 to go after
21 found a letter
22 It was from
23 It read, had been invited
24 As, worried
25 which, far away from
26 too, to
27 regretting
28 should have gone
29 are worth chasing
30 Never miss

1 MY GRANDMOTHER'S BASEBALL DREAMS

2 My grandmother Helen used to be a cook in a restaurant in a small town near South Bend, Indiana.

3 She does not work anymore, but she still enjoys making delicious food, which I love so much.

4 Food is one of the many things that connect us.

5 What connects us most strongly, however, is baseball.

6 When I visit her on weekends, my grandmother often tells me exciting stories about playing baseball back in the 1940s.

7 She must have loved the sport very much.

9 I listen to these stories over and over.

9 She always says, "Go after what you want, Sarah.

10 Don't be afraid of trying something new or challenging.

11 Don't be ashamed of failing."

12 In 1943, the All-American Girls Professional Baseball League was founded.

13 This league was created for baseball fans because many of America's young men were fighting in World War II.

14 Helen was told that there would be local tryouts right in South Bend.

15 She wondered, "What would it be like to be on a baseball team and to make it to the finals for my hometown?"

16 She imagined a large banner hanging at the baseball field which included the name Helen Baker.

17 On the day of the tryouts, all the rules were explained by an old man in a suit, who sounded very serious and unkind.

18 She thought that wearing a suit in the hot sun might have made him impatient.

19 On that day, Helen played baseball for hours with many other young women.

20 She was excited to go after her baseball dreams!

21 About a week later, Helen found a letter in the mailbox.

22 It was from people who worked for the girls' baseball league in Chicago.

23 It read that she had been invited to the league's main tryouts in Chicago!

24 As the days went by, however, Helen became worried that she might fail.

25 She also became worried about traveling alone to Chicago, which was far away from home.

26 When the day of the main tryouts came, she was too afraid to go.

27 My grandmother has spent the rest of her life regretting her decision.

28 When she watches a baseball game on TV, she often says, "I should have gone to Chicago.

29 You know, all your dreams are worth chasing, even if you catch only a few of them.

30 Never miss an opportunity."

01 (A) used to   (B) What   (C) must
02 ③
03 ④
04 ③
05 all your dreams
06 ②, ⑤
07 World War Two 또는 the Second World War
08 ④
09 (A) young men   (B) baseball fans
10 ④
11 ③
12 ④
13 ②
14 wearing a suit in the hot sun might have made him impatient
15 ③
16 ⑤
17 connect → connects

01 (A) 할머니는 식당의 '요리사였다'고 해야 하므로 used to가 적절하다. used to: 과거의 규칙적 습관이나 현재와 비교한 과거의 상태를 나타냄. would: 과거의 불규칙적 습관을 나타냄. (B) 우리를 가장 강하게 연결하는 '것'이라고 해야 하므로 선행사가 포함된 관계대명사 What이 적절하다. (C) 야구를 무척 '좋아했던 게 분명하다'고 해야 하므로 must가 적절하다. must have p.p.: ~했음에 틀림없다(과거에 대한 강한 추측), should have p.p.: ~했어야 했는데(과거 사실에 대한 후회나 유감을 나타냄.)

02 ③ 모험심이 강한, 할머니는 항상 "새로운 것이나 도전적인 것을 시도해 보기를 두려워하지 말거라."라고 말씀하시는 것으로 보아, 할머니의 성격은 '모험심이 강하다'라고 하는 것이 적절하다. ① 완고한, 고집스러운, ② 우유부단한, ④ 보수적인, ⑤ 소심한

03 'Sarah의 할머니'가 종종 과거 1940년대의 야구 경기에 관해 흥미로운 이야기를 'Sarah에게' 들려주신다. ③ common interest: 공통된 관심

04 ⓐ와 ③: ~할수록(접속사), ① ~한 대로(접속사), ② ~로서(전치사), ④ [보통 as ~ as ...로 형용사·부사 앞에서] ~와 같을 정도로, (as ~ as ...에서, 앞의 as가 지시부사, 뒤의 as는 접속사), ⑤ ~이므로, ~이기 때문에(접속사)

05 be worth ~ing = be worth while to 동사원형: ~할 만한 가치가 있다

06 이 글은 '본심사가 있는 날 할머니는 너무 두려워서 갈 수 없었고 남은 인생을 자신의 결정을 후회하며 보내셨으며, 종종 "절대 기회를 놓치지 마라."라고 말씀하셨다'는 내용의 글이므로, 어울리는 속담으로는 ②번 '기회를 놓치지 마라'와 ⑤번 '쇠뿔도 단김에 빼라.'가 적절하다. ① 급할수록 돌아가라. ③ 안 좋은 일은 겹쳐서 일어나기 마련이다. ④ 잘 생각해 보고 행동하라[돌다리도 두드려 보고 건너라].

07 'World War Ⅱ(제2차 세계대전)'는 World War Two 또는 the Second World War로 읽는다.

08 ⓑ와 ②: 명사적 용법, ①, ④: 부사적 용법, ③, ⑤: 형용사적 용법

09 미국의 '청년' 중 많은 수가 제2차 세계대전에 참전해 있었기 때문에 1943년, 전미 여자 프로야구 리그가 '야구 팬들'을 위해 창립되었다.

10 앞에 나오는 내용과 상반되는 내용이 뒤에 이어지므로 however가 가장 적절하다. ② 즉[말하자면], ③ 게다가, 더욱이, ⑤ 따라서, 그러므로

11 이 글은 'Helen은 리그의 본심사에 초청되었지만 심사에 떨어질까봐 걱정되기도 하고 시카고까지 혼자 여행하는 것도 걱정되어, 본심사가 있는 날이 되었을 때 너무 두려워서 갈 수 없었다.'

는 내용의 글이므로, 제목으로는 ③번 '두려움 때문에 이루지 못한 꿈'이 적절하다. unfulfilled: 이루지 못한, out of fear: 두려움 때문에, ④ What if ~?: ~면 어쩌지[~라면 어떻게 될까]?, ⑤ No way!: 절대로 안 되다, 싫다

12 Helen은 시카고까지 혼자 여행하는 것이 걱정되었는데, 시카고는 집에서 멀리 떨어진 곳이었다.

13 ⓐ in: '착의'를 나타내는 전치사, ⓑ go after: ~을 추구하다

14 might have p.p.: 과거에 대한 추측(~했을지도 모른다)

15 (B)의 Food는 주어진 글에서 말한 food를 가리키므로 제일 먼저 오고, (A)의 these stories가 (C)의 exciting stories about playing baseball back in the 1940s를 가리키므로 (C) 다음에 (A)가 와야 한다. 그러므로 (B)-(C)-(A)의 순서가 적절하다.

16 (A)와 ①, ②, ③, ④: 현재와 비교한 과거의 상태(would로 바꿔 쓸 수 없음.), ⑤ used to: 과거의 규칙적 습관(would로 바꿔 쓰면 과거의 불규칙적 습관을 나타내게 됨), call on: ~을 방문하다

17 우리를 가장 강하게 연결하는 것은 바로 '야구'라는 뜻으로 What은 단수인 The thing which를 대신한 것이기 때문에, connect를 connects로 고치는 것이 적절하다.

18 이 글은 'Sarah와 할머니를 연결하는 많은 것 가운데 하나가 요리지만 그들을 가장 강하게 연결하는 것은 야구라는 것과, 할머니께서 과거 1940년대의 야구 경기에 관한 흥미로운 이야기를 몇 번이고 반복해서 하시면서 Sarah를 격려해 주시는' 내용의 글이므로, 주제로는 ③번 'Sarah의 할머니의 야구에 대한 사랑'이 적절하다. ⑤ nursery story: 옛날 이야기

19 (A) 감각동사의 보어는 형용사를 써야 하므로, 'serious and unkind'가 적절하다. (B) 목적격 보어이므로 형용사 impatient가 적절하다. (C) 그 편지에는 그녀가 시카고에서 열리는 리그의 본심사에 초청되었다고 '적혀 있었다'고 해야 하므로 read가 적절하다. read: (~라고) 적혀[쓰여] 있다

20 'Helen이 리그의 본심사에 참가했는지는' 알 수 없다. ① An old man in a suit did. ② With many other young women. ③ People who worked for the girls' baseball league in Chicago did. ④ In Chicago.

서술형 시험대비   p.92~93

01 that → which   02 loved
03 (A) was   (B) Sarah   04 regretting
05 so, that, couldn't
06 must have gone → should have gone
07 (1) 심사에 떨어질까봐 걱정되었기 때문이었다.
   (2) 시카고까지 혼자 여행하는 것이 걱정되었는데, 시카고는 집에서 멀리 떨어진 곳이었기 때문이었다.
08 What connects us most strongly

09 every weekend

10 exciting stories about playing baseball back in the 1940s

11 and he　　12 had been invited

13 (A) wearing a suit　(B) serious and unkind

01 관계대명사 that은 계속적 용법으로 쓸 수 없기 때문에, which로 고치는 것이 적절하다.

02 must have p.p.는 과거에 대한 강한 추측을 나타내므로 'loved'로 쓰는 것이 적절하다.

03 Sarah의 할머니는 식당의 '요리사였지만', 지금은 더 이상 요리사가 아니다. 그렇기는 하지만, 그녀는 여전히 맛있는 음식을 즐겨 만드시고, 'Sarah'는 그 음식들을 무척 좋아한다.

04 spend+시간+~ing: ~하는 데 시간을 보내다

05 too ~ to ... = so ~ that 주어 can't ...: 너무 ~ 해서 …할 수 없다

06 '난 시카고에 갔어야 해.'라고 해야 하므로, must를 should로 고치는 것이 적절하다. must have p.p.: ~이었음에 틀림없다, should have p.p.: ~했어야 했는데(과거의 일에 대한 후회나 유감)

07 Helen은 '심사에 떨어질까 봐 걱정되었고' 또 '시카고까지 혼자 여행하는 것이 걱정되어', 본심사가 있는 날이 되었을 때, 그녀는 너무 두려워서 갈 수 없었다.

08 선행사가 포함된 관계대명사 What을 쓰는 것이 적절하다.

09 on weekends = every weekend: 주말마다

10 '과거 1940년대의 야구 경기에 관한 흥미로운 이야기'를 가리킨다.

11 계속적 용법의 관계대명사는 '접속사+대명사'로 바꿔 쓸 수 있다.

12 그 초청 편지에는 '그녀가 시카고에서 열리는 리그의 본심사에 초청되었다'는 사실이 적혀 있었다.

13 Helen은 뜨거운 태양 아래 '정장을 입고 있는 것'이 모든 규칙을 설명한 나이 든 남자를 짜증나게 만들었을지도 모르고, 그 결과 그는 무척 '진지하고 불친절하게' 들렸다고 생각했다.

영역별 핵심문제　　　　　p.95~99

01 decision　　02 ④　　03 ③

04 (1) How come Mr. Lee always works overtime?

　　(2) If you want to accomplish your dream, you should go after it.

　　(3) Does the recipe include eggs and milk?

05 ①　　06 ⑤　　07 ①

08 You're mistaken.　　09 ④

10 Because she thinks a good designer should create a completely new world in a game.

11 I shouldn't have done that.

12 How come?

13 If I were you, I'd get help from a computer service center right now.

14 ②　　15 ⑤　　16 ①, ③

17 with whom

18 (1) should have gone　(2) can't have gone
　　(3) must have gone　(4) shouldn't have gone
　　(5) might[may] have gone

19 ②　　20 ④　　21 ⓐ, ⓒ, ⓔ

22 ③　　23 ③

24 Don't be afraid of trying something new or challenging.

25 (A) founded　(B) wondered　(C) What　26 ④

27 ①, ⑤　　28 a letter

01 주어진 관계는 동의어의 관계이다. offer: 제의, 제안 proposal: 제안, 제의 determination: 결심, 결단(력) decision: 결정, 판단

02 tryout: 심사, 테스트

03 주어진 문장에서 apply는 '~에 지원하다, ~을 신청하다'를 의미하며 이와 같은 의미로 쓰인 것은 ③번이다. ① 가는 붓으로 물감을 칠해라. ② 그 규칙은 여기에서는 적용되지 않는다. ③ 저는 영업 이사직에 지원하고자 합니다. ④ 그는 문을 열기 위해 힘을 써야 했다. ⑤ 이 규정은 당신의 경우에는 해당되지 않습니다.

04 (1) How come: 왜. How come을 이용하여 의문문을 쓸 때는 평서문의 어순임에 주의해야 한다. (2) go after: ~을 추구하다, ~을 얻기 위해 노력하다 (3) include: 포함하다

05 주어진 문장에서 rest는 '나머지'를 의미하며 이와 같은 의미로 쓰인 것은 ①번이다. ② 쉬다, ③ 휴식, ④ 기대다, ⑤ 의지하다

06 '과거에 한 것에 대해 서운함을 느끼다'는 의미로 'regret(후회하다)'이 적절하다 ① 연습하다, 훈련하다 ② 이루다, 달성[성취]하다 ③ 향상시키다, 개선하다 ④ 연결하다

07 주어진 문장은 '면접을 시작합시다.'라는 말이다. ①번 다음부터 면접에 관련된 질문이 나오고 있으므로 ①번이 가장 적절하다.

08 상대방의 말을 수정하기 위해 'That's not right[true].', 'I don't think that's right.', 'That's wrong.', 'You're mistaken.' 등의 표현을 사용한다.

09 소라는 '만화가가 되고 싶나요?'라는 질문에 '꼭 그렇지는 않습니다. 저는 게임 디자이너가 되고 싶습니다.'라고 답하고 있다.

10 소라는 '게임 디자이너에게 필요한 가장 중요한 기량이 무엇이라고 생각하나요?'라는 질문에 '상상력이라고 말씀드리겠습니다. 훌륭한 게임 디자이너는 게임 속에서 완전히 새로운 세계를 창조해야 하거든요.'라고 답하고 있다.

11 shouldn't have p.p.: 하지 말았어야 하는 일을 한 것에 대한 후회를 나타낼 때 쓸 수 있다. 앞 문장에서 말한 내용을 that으로 받아 한 단어로 처리한다.

12 How come?: 왜 그렇지?, 어쩌다 그렇게 됐니?

13 가정법 과거를 이용한다. If I were you: 내가 너라면, I

would를 줄여서 I'd로 축약하여 단어 수를 맞춘다.

14 'My nose is getting longer.'에 이어 'I shouldn't have told lies.'라고 하는 것이 적절하다.

15 a picture를 선행사로 하는 계속적 용법의 목적격 관계대명사 which가 와야 한다. that은 계속적 용법의 관계대명사로 쓸 수 없다.

16 ① You should have come to the meeting on time. ③ He might[may] have been in Paris when Irene went to Finland.

17 앞에 콤마(,)가 있는 관계대명사의 계속적 용법을 이용한다. 함께 달린 것이므로 전치사 with와 목적격이므로 whom을 쓴다.

18 (1) should[ought to] have p.p.: ~했어야 한다 (그런데 하지 못했다) (후회) (2) cannot have p.p.: ~했을 리가 없다 (강한 부정의 추측) (3) must have p.p.: ~했음이 틀림없다 (강한 추측) (4) should not[ought not to] have p.p.: ~하지 않았어야 했는데 (그런데 했다) (후회) (5) may[might] have p.p.: ~했을지도 모른다 (약한 추측)

19 계속적 용법의 관계대명사는 '접속사(and, but, for, though 등)+대명사'로 고쳐 쓸 수 있다. 여기서는 'though she'가 적절하다.

20 앞에 콤마(,)가 있으므로 관계대명사의 계속적 용법으로 loved의 목적어 역할을 할 수 있는 whom이 적절하다.

21 ⓑ eat → eaten ⓓ should → shouldn't ⓕ that → who

22 주어진 문장의 however에 주목한다. ③번 앞 문장의 내용과 상반되는 내용이 뒤에 이어지고 있으므로 ③번이 적절하다.

23 이 글은 'Sarah와 할머니를 연결하는 많은 것 가운데 하나가 요리지만 그들을 가장 강하게 연결하는 것은 야구라는 것과, 할머니께서 과거 1940년대의 야구 경기에 관한 흥미로운 이야기를 몇 번이고 반복해서 하시면서 Sarah를 격려해 주시는' 내용의 글이므로, 제목으로는 ③번 '야구, 우리를 가장 강하게 연결하는 것'이 적절하다.

24 -thing이나 -body로 끝나는 부정대명사는 형용사가 뒤에서 꾸며 주어야 하므로, new or challenging이 뒤에서 something을 꾸며 주는 것이 적절하다.

25 (A) 전미 여자 프로야구 리그가 '창립되었다'고 해야 하므로 founded가 적절하다. found-founded-founded: 설립하다, find-found-found: 찾다[발견하다]. (B) "야구 팀에 들어가서 고향을 위해 결승전까지 진출한다는 건 어떤 기분일까?"라며 '궁금해 했다'고 해야 하므로 wondered가 적절하다. wonder: 궁금해 하다, wander: 거닐다, 돌아다니다, (C) like의 목적어에 해당하므로 의문대명사 What이 적절하다. 의문부사 How는 목적어 자리에 쓸 수 없다.

26 Helen은 야구 팀에 들어 간 것이 아니라, "야구 팀에 들어가서 고향을 위해 결승전까지 진출한다는 건 어떤 기분일까?"라며 궁금해 했다.

27 ⓐ와 ①, ⑤: 동명사, ②, ③, ④: 현재분사

28 Helen이 우편함에서 발견한 '편지 한 통'을 가리킨다.

01 ②
02 (1) curious (2) regretful (3) jealous
    (4) relieved (5) gloomy
03 ③   04 What made you apply for our school?
05 various subjects   06 do you? → are you?
07 ④   08 ④   09 That's not quite right.
10 ④   11 ④   12 ③, ⑤
13 and it   14 (1) should have spent (2) shouldn't
have wasted (3) should have brought   15 ②
16 making   17 ②   18 ③   19 ④
20 ④   21 ⑤   22 didn't go
23 all your dreams

01 '단체나 전체의 일부로 어떤 것을 갖다'를 나타내는 말은 include(포함하다)이다.

02 gloomy: 우울한, regretful: 후회하는, curious: 호기심 있는, jealous: 질투심이 많은, relieved: 안도하는

03 (A) 긍정문이므로 too가 적절하다. (B) because of+명사(구), because+주어+동사, (C) if는 불확실한 내용을 이끌 때 쓰이고, that은 확실한 내용을 이끌 때 쓰인다.

04 What made you ~? = Why did you ~?: 왜 ~했나요?

05 앞에서 말한 'various subjects'를 가리킨다.

06 앞에서 'I'm preparing for ~'라고 하고 있으므로 'do you'가 아닌 'are you'로 쓰는 것이 적절하다.

07 소라는 'I should have practiced more.'라고 후회하고 있다.

08 언제부터 소라가 게임 디자이너가 되고 싶었는지는 알 수 없다.

09 상대방의 말을 수정하기 위해 'That's not right[true].', 'I don't think that's right.', 'That's wrong.', 'You're mistaken.' 등의 표현을 사용한다.

10 내용상 'I shouldn't have made you wait.'라고 하는 것이 적절하다.

11 모두 관계대명사 who가 적절하지만 ④번은 선행사가 앞선 절의 일부(went on a trip to Africa)이므로 which가 적절하다.

12 ① I should have practiced more to improve my speaking skills. ② I think sending text messages might have been better. ④ It must have rained last night.

13 계속적 용법의 관계대명사는 '접속사(and, but, for, though 등)+대명사'로 고쳐 쓸 수 있다.

14 'should (not) have p.p.'가 '후회'의 의미로 쓰이지만 2인칭을 주어로 하여 '충고'하는 의미로도 쓰일 수 있다.

15 첫 번째 문장에서는 날이 더워서 티셔츠와 반바지를 '입었어야 한다'는 'should have p.p.'가 적절하다. 두 번째 문장에서는 선행사가 Sydney로 사물이고 계속적 용법이므로 which가 적절하다.

16 enjoy는 동명사를 목적어로 취하는 동사이므로, making으로 쓰는 것이 적절하다.

17 (A)와 ②: 관계대명사, the thing(s) which로 바꿀 수 있음.
①과 ④: 의문대명사, ③과 ⑤: 의문형용사

18 ③ 한 걸음 한 걸음, 점차로, ⓒ와 나머지: 반복해서

19 ④번 다음 문장의 It이 주어진 문장의 a letter를 가리키는 것이므로 ④번이 적절하다.

20 이 글은 'Helen이 자신의 야구 꿈을 좇아가기 위해 선수 선발 테스트를 받고 시카고에서 열리는 리그의 본심사에 초청되는' 내용의 글이므로, 주제로는 ④번 '자신의 야구 꿈을 좇아가는 것에서부터 오는 Helen의 흥분'이 적절하다.

21 중반부의 'She was excited to go after her baseball dreams!'를 통해 'excited'를 찾을 수 있다. ① 후회하는, ② 두려운, ③ 어리둥절해 하는, ④ 실망한

22 should have p.p.는 '~했어야 한다'라는 뜻으로 과거의 일에 대한 후회나 유감을 나타내므로, '나는 시카고에 가지 않아서 유감이다.'로 고치는 것이 적절하다.

23 '모든 꿈'을 가리킨다.

서술형 실전문제   p.104~105

01 They are going to the school festival.

02 Because he got up early but it took him some time to do his hair.

03 Because she thought (that) they were stuck in a heavy traffic jam.

04 (1) This book is about Abraham Lincoln, who was the 16th President of the U.S.
(2) My grandmother's house, which was built 100 years ago, is still nice to live in.
(3) She enjoys making delicious food, from which she finds satisfaction.

05 (1) Fallen leaves are on the ground. It might[may 또는 must] have been windy.
(2) Sam looks very tired this morning. He must [또는 shouldn't] have stayed up late last night.
(3) His favorite place is his house, which is next to mine.
(4) My brother, whose major was history, is a professor of the university.

06 (1) The train may[might] have arrived at the station.
(2) He cannot have done this by himself.
(3) This smartphone, which I bought last month, has a great design.

07 and I love it so much   **08** nineteen forties

09 what she wants   **10** had been invited

11 an old man in a suit explained all the rules

12 (A) letter   (B) main tryouts

---

01 지호가 '학교 축제에 늦고 싶지 않은데.'라고 하고 있다.

02 '무슨 일로 늦었'는지 묻는 Amber의 질문에 지호는 '난 일찍 일어났어. 그런데 머리를 손질하느라 시간이 좀 걸렸어.'라고 답하고 있다.

03 Amber가 '우리 교통 체증에 갇혔어. 버스에서 내려서 뛰어가자.'라고 하고 있다.

04 (1) 선행사가 사람이므로 who를 이용한다. (2) 선행사가 사물이므로 which를 이용한다. (3) 선행사가 앞 절의 일부(making delicious food)이므로 which를 이용한다. 전치사 from의 목적어로 쓰이는 것에 주의한다.

05 (1) 낙엽이 떨어져 있는 것이므로 '추측'을 나타내는 표현이 적절하다. (2) 매우 피곤해 보이는 것이므로 '단정적인 추측이나 후회'를 나타내는 표현이 적절하다. (3) 계속적 용법에는 that을 사용하지 않는다. which가 적절하다. (4) 뒤에 나오는 major(전공)를 수식해 주는 소유격 whose가 적절하다. 내 동생은 전공이 역사였는데 그 대학의 교수이다.

06 (1) may[might] have p.p.: ~했을지도 모른다 (약한 추측) (2) cannot have p.p.: ~했을 리가 없다 (강한 부정의 추측) by himself: 혼자서 (3) 선행사가 사물이므로 which를 이용한다.

07 계속적 용법의 관계대명사는 '접속사+대명사'로 바꿔 쓸 수 있고, 본문에서 which는 delicious food를 추가 설명하기 위해 쓰인 목적격 관계대명사이므로, 접속사 and와 대명사 it을 사용하여 고치는 것이 적절하다.

08 연도는 두 자씩 끊어서 읽고, 1940s(1940년대)는 복수이므로 뒷부분을 forties로 읽는 것이 적절하다.

09 Sarah의 할머니는 Sarah에게 '그녀가 원하는 것'을 이루려고 노력하라고 항상 말씀하신다.

10 본심사에 초청된 것은 편지를 읽은 것보다 앞선 시제이므로 '과거완료(had p.p.)'로, 그리고 '초청된' 것이므로 '수동태'로 쓰는 것이 적절하다.

11 'an old man in a suit'를 주어로 해서 고치는 것이 적절하다.

12 Helen은 리그의 '본심사'가 열리게 될 시카고에 있는 여자야구리그에서 일하는 사람들이 보낸 초청 '편지'를 받았다.

창의사고력 서술형 문제   p.106

|모범답안|

01 (1) 더 많은 책을 읽었어야 했다.
(2) 온라인 게임을 그렇게 많이 하지 말았어야 했다.
(3) 선생님들과 반 친구들에게 더 친절했어야 했다.
(4) 패스트푸드를 그렇게 많이 먹지 말았어야 했다.

02 (1) It must have rained last night.
(2) She may have gone out for dinner.
(3) I should have studied math harder.

03 (A) in London, England   (B) wild chimpanzees

(C) the protection of chimpanzees

(D) the Hubbard Medal

01 ②   02 ③

03 (1) imagination   (2) confident   (3) disappointed

04 You can make it!

05 She will have the exam for Mana Animation High School this Friday.

06 ④   07 She forgot to set her alarm.

08 Because she thought they were stuck in a heavy traffic jam.

09 (B) → (A) → (D) → (C)   10 ④

11 It's because she thinks it'll be a good job in the future.

12 (1) Mina got her finger burned while making coffee, which is her favorite drink. She ought to have been more careful.

(2) Mina got her finger burned while making coffee, and it is her favorite drink. She should have been more careful.

13 ③, ⑤, ⑥   14 must have been   15 ④

16 ①

17 (1) She does not work anymore, but she still enjoys making delicious food, which I love so much.

(2) She is my friend, Nida, who[whom] I met in Germany.

(3) Gogh met Gauguin in Arles, which changed his life.

(4) The rabbit shouldn't have slept during the race to beat the turtle.

(5) Hanju must have lost his umbrella in the subway. He doesn't have it now.

18 ⑤

19 exciting stories about playing baseball back in the 1940s

20 ③   21 ②   22 ①   23 ④

24 ①   25 ②

01 '어떤 것에 대해 좋거나 충분히 중요한'을 가리키는 것은 worth(~할 가치가 있는)이다.

02 even if: 비록 ~하더라도 / 싫더라도 꼭 해야 한다.

03 imagination: 상상, 상상력, confident: 확신하는, 자신만만한, disappointed: 실망한, 낙담한

04 You can make it!: 넌 해낼 수 있어!

05 ' When is the exam?'이라는 남자의 질문에 소라는 'On Friday'라고 답하고 있고 이틀 남았다고 했으므로 이번 금요일임을 알 수 있다.

06 '버스에서 내려서 뛰어가자.'라는 Amber의 말에 ④번 다음에 '차들이 다시 움직이기 시작해. 내리지 말자.'라고 하고 있으므로 '네가 잘못 생각하는 거야.'라는 주어진 글은 ④번에 들어가는 것이 가장 적절하다.

07 Amber는 '알람을 맞출걸. 내가 깜빡했어.'라고 후회하고 있다.

08 Amber는 '우리 교통 체증에 갇혔어. 버스에서 내려서 뛰어가자.'라고 하고 있다.

09 긴장했는지 질문하는 문장에 이어 (B)에서 약간이라고 답하고 (A)에서 면접을 시작하자고 하면서 지원한 이유를 묻고 (D)에서 이유를 대답하고 (C)에서 행운을 빌자, 마지막에 주어진 문장에서 감사를 표하는 순서가 자연스럽다.

10 (A)는 상대방의 말을 수정하기 위해 쓰는 표현이지만, ④번은 상대방이 맞다고 말하는 것이다.

11 G는 '왜?'라고 묻는 질문에 '그것이 미래에 좋은 직업이 될 거라고 생각하기 때문이야.'라고 하고 있다.

12 and it is her favorite drink =, which is her favorite drink. should have p.p. = ought to have p.p.: ~했어야 한다 (그런데 하지 못했다) (후회). to를 추가한다.

13 ① He is my son, who works at the amusement park. ② I got up late. I should have set my alarm. ④ One of my friends, who wants to be a teacher, is Abigail. ⑦ She also became worried about traveling alone to Chicago, which was far away from home.

14 'must have p.p. ~했음이 틀림없다'를 이용하여 '강한 추측'을 나타낸다.

15 첫 번째 빈칸에는 'should have p.p.: ~했어야 한다 (그런데 하지 못했다) (후회)'를 이용하고, 두 번째 빈칸에는 'should not have p.p.: ~하지 않았어야 했는데 (그런데 했다) (후회)'를 이용한다.

16 which는 앞 문장 전체를 선행사로 받을 수 있으므로 접속사 and와 it 대신에 쓸 수 있다.

17 (1) 관계대명사의 계속적 용법으로 that을 쓰지 않으며, 관계대명사는 접속사와 대명사의 역할을 하므로 목적어로 쓰인 it을 삭제해야 한다. (2) 선행사가 사람이고 목적격이므로 which를 who나 whom으로 고치는 것이 적절하다. (3) 관계대명사의 계속적 용법으로 that을 쓰지 않으며 앞에 나오는 절을 선행사로 받는 which가 적절하다. (4) should not[ought not to] have p.p.: ~하지 않았어야 했는데 (그런데 했다) (후회) (5) must have p.p.: ~했음이 틀림없다 (강한 추측)

18 앞에 나오는 내용과 상반되는 내용이 뒤에 이어지므로 however가 적절하다. ① 그러므로, ② 게다가, 더욱이, ③ 다시 말해서, ④ 그 결과

21

19 '과거 1940년대의 야구 경기에 관한 흥미로운 이야기'를 가리킨다.

20 ⓐ for baseball fans: 야구 팬들을 위해, ⓑ on: '소속'을 나타내는 전치사, be on ~: ~의 일원이다

21 (A)와 ②: '바로'라는 뜻으로 뒤의 내용을 강조하는 표현, ① (의견, 판단이) 옳은[맞는], ③ (법적, 도덕적) 권리[권한], ④ 오른쪽의, 우측의, ⑤ (도덕적으로) 옳은, 올바른

22 ⓐ와 ①: ~라고 적혀 있다, 그 표지판에는 '입장 금지'라고 적혀 있었다. ②와 ④: 읽어 주다, ③과 ⑤: (글, 기호 등을) 읽다

23 '시카고에 있는 여자 야구 리그에서 일하는 사람들'이 초청 편지를 보냈다.

24 주어진 문장의 also에 주목한다. ①번 앞 문장에 이어 또 다른 걱정을 말하는 것이므로 ①번이 적절하다.

25 should have p.p.는 '~했어야 한다'라는 뜻으로 과거의 일에 대한 후회나 유감을 나타내는 표현이므로 ②번 regretful이 적절하다. regretful: 유감스러워[애석해] 하는, 후회하는, ① 혼란스러워 하는, ③ 부끄러운, ④ 초조한, ⑤ 우울한

Keep Out

교과서
Reading

확인문제 p.116

1 T 2 F 3 T 4 F 5 T 6 F

확인문제 p.117

1 T 2 F 3 T 4 F 5 T 6 F

확인문제 p.118

1 T 2 F 3 T 4 T 5 F

확인문제 p.119

1 T 2 F 3 T 4 F 5 T 6 F

교과서 확인학습 A		p.120~123
01 Keep Out	02 used to go	
03 stayed at	04 swimming, walking	
05 In other words, anything special		
06 At the time of	07 had had	
08 day in and day out	09 the heat	
10 further and further	11 take us	
12 as usual, set off	13 side by side	
14 one behind the other	15 ahead	
16 grew darker, formed a roof		
17 Look ahead	18 next to him	
19 a tunnel	20 Keep Out	
21 have a look	22 Actually	
23 all of a sudden	24 moved ahead	
25 left	26 entered	
27 heavy		

28 grew louder and louder 29 called out

30 Keep, down 31 called after

32 leave, behind

33 thumping, like an express train

34 what's up 35 what's happened

36 where Ron had been 37 something wet

38 were closed 39 get you out

40 (I')ve broken, go and get help

41 get you out of here 42 moving away

43 in control 44 covering

45 managed to free

46 Holding, inch by inch 47 to take ages

48 look too well

49 stop, from crying out 50 two water bottles

51 go and get help

52 In reply, pressed my hands

53 raced back

54 washing some dishes

55 Thanks to her, where 56 with relief

57 Let that be a lesson 58 *Stay out of trouble*

59 safety products 60 fire fighter

교과서 확인학습 B
p.124~127

1 Keep Out

2 Every summer, my family used to go on holiday to the coast.

3 We always went to the same place and stayed at the same small guesthouse.

4 We would stay for two weeks, swimming in the sea and walking around the little town.

5 In other words, we never did anything special, and nothing ever really happened on these vacations.

6 At the time of this story I was twelve years old.

7 Most people can remember this particular summer, as it was the hottest summer England had had since records began.

8 It did not rain throughout June and July, and the sun shone day in and day out.

9 But Ron and I loved the heat and the sun.

10 Every day, we would ride our bicycles further and further away from the guesthouse.

11 One day Ron decided that we should ride our bikes along the old train tracks to see where they would take us.

12 I was happy to follow Ron, as usual, and we set off after breakfast.

13 At first, the tracks were easy to follow, and we

cycled along side by side.

14 After a while, the grass grew thicker, and we had to ride one behind the other.

15 Ron was ahead.

16 The tracks went toward the woods and it grew darker as the trees stood tall and formed a roof over the tracks.

17 Ron stopped suddenly. "Look ahead!" he shouted.

18 I stopped next to him and saw a white, wooden gateway across a black opening.

19 "It's a tunnel," I said.

20 "Yes, and it says, 'Keep Out' on the gate," replied Ron.

21 "Do you want to have a look inside?"

22 Actually, I did not want to go inside.

23 I felt a little cold all of a sudden, and I wanted to go back into the sunlight.

24 But I answered, "Sure," and moved ahead.

25 We left our bikes at the gate and climbed over.

26 We entered the cool tunnel.

27 The air inside was heavy.

28 Above our heads there was a sound that grew louder and louder.

29 "What's that?" I called out.

30 "Bats," said Ron, "Keep your head down." Then he moved on.

31 "Don't go so fast." I called after him.

32 I meant, "Don't leave me behind" but I didn't say so.

33 The next thing I heard was a loud noise right above us, a thumping sound like an express train and then a scream.

34 "Ron!" I shouted. "Ron, what's up? Can you hear me?" No reply.

35 "Speak to me, Ron. Tell me what's happened."

36 I slowly walked toward where Ron had been and found only dirt and small rocks.

37 As I reached out my hands, I felt something wet — Ron's face!

38 His eyes were closed, and he was breathing weakly.

39 "It's okay, Ron," I whispered. "I'll get you out."

40 "I think I've broken my leg. It really hurts. Just go and get help, Ben."

41 "No," I replied. "I'll get you out of here to safety first."

42 I started moving away the dirt and rocks with my hands.

43 I felt calm, and I felt in control.

44 It took a long time to clear away the earth covering Ron.

45 Finally, I managed to free his body.

46 Holding him under the arms, I pulled him backward, inch by inch, toward the tunnel entrance.

47 It seemed to take ages, but finally I was able to get Ron out of the tunnel.

48 He didn't look too well, though.

49 His face was white, and he was trying hard to stop himself from crying out from crying out.

50 I found our bikes and brought the two water bottles to Ron.

51 "Here, drink these," I said. "I'll go and get help. I'll be as quick as I can."

52 In reply, Ron simply pressed my hands.

53 I got on my bicycle and raced back along the tracks until I got to the nearest farmhouse.

54 I ran past the gate and found a woman washing some dishes in the kitchen.

55 Thanks to her, Ron was taken to the hospital, where his leg was put in a cast.

56 As soon as our parents arrived at the hospital and saw us, my mother cried with relief.

57 But all my father said was, "Let that be a lesson to you."

58 And what was the lesson? It was "*Keep out* means *Stay out of trouble*."

59 Ron is now the manager of a big company which produces helmets and other safety products.

60 And me? I am a fire fighter.

서술형 실전문제
p.128~129

01 (t)hin

02 (1) thumping (2) In other words (3) managed to (4) All of a sudden

03 (1) as usual (2) at first (3) As soon as

04 ⑤, There being no objection, the meeting was put off.

05 (1) would → used to (2) covered → covering (3) which → where (4) that → what

06 had had 07 (1) going (2) to go

08 Because it was the hottest summer England had had since records began.

09 (A) where (B) calm (C) to free

10 It took a long time to clear away the earth covering Ron.

11 a shovel → his hands

01 주어진 단어의 관계는 반의어 관계이다. entrance: 입구, exit: 출구, thick: 두꺼운, thin: 얇은

02 all of a sudden: 갑자기, thumping: 쿵쾅거리는, manage to: 간신히 ~하다, in other words: 다시 말해서, 즉

03 as usual: 여느 때처럼, at first: 처음에는, as soon as: ~하자마자

04 주절의 주어와 부사절의 주어(유도부사, 허위 주어: there)가 다르므로 부사절의 유도부사 there를 써 주어야 한다. As there was no objection, the meeting was put off.를 분사구문으로 쓴 것이다.

05 (1) used to: ~하곤 했다(과거의 규칙적이고 반복적인 동작이나 상태), would: ~하곤 했다(과거의 불규칙적 습관) (2) while 뒤에 '주어+be동사'가 생략된 문장이다. 분사구문에서 접속사 while을 남겨 두었다고 보아도 좋다. this case로 목적어가 있으므로 covering이 적절하다. (3) happen은 자동사로 which 다음의 절이 완전하므로 which를 관계부사 where로 고쳐야 한다. (4) Tell의 직접목적어와 has happened의 주어 역할을 하도록 that을 what으로 고쳐야 한다.

06 주절보다 먼저 있었던 일을 언급하므로 과거완료 (had had)로 쓰는 것이 적절하다.

07 used to는 '~하곤 했다'라는 뜻으로 과거의 규칙적이고 반복적인 동작이나 상태를 나타낸다. used to 동사원형 = be in the habit of ~ing = make it a rule to 동사원형

08 '관측 이래 영국이 겪은 가장 더운 여름이었기 때문'이었다.

09 (A) Ron이 있던 '곳'으로 걸어갔다고 해야 하므로 where가 적절하다. 관계부사 where 앞에 선행사 the place가 생략되어 있다. (B) 감각동사의 보어는 형용사로 써야 하므로 calm이 적절하다. (C) manage는 to부정사를 목적어로 취하므로 to free가 적절하다.

10 take+시간+to부정사의 순서로 쓰는 것이 적절하다.

11 Ben은 '손으로' 흙과 자갈을 치우기 시작했다. shovel: 삽

단원별 예상문제
p.130~134

01 (1) wooden (2) cast (3) thanks to (4) After a while (5) relief

02 ①   03 ④   04 ⑤   05 hurt

06 (1) She leaned over and whispered something in his ear.

(2) I would often practice reading the scripts in the empty recording room.

(3) I wanted to show that I could improve my

acting inch by inch.

07 (1) I'm so tired of eating at the same restaurant day in and day out.

(2) Please keep out of that room.

(3) As I reached out my hand, I felt something wet.

08 ①

09 (1) It did not rain throughout June and July, the sun shining day in and day out.

(2) It having been the hottest summer England had had since records began, most people can remember this particular summer.

(3) Ron decided that we should ride our bikes along the old train tracks to see where they would take us.

(4) I'd like to see if she can give me a hand.

10 (1) The book is a detailed piece of work covering all aspects of the subject.

(2) The two men were walking quickly, one behind the other.

(3) Ron was taken to the hospital, where[in which] his leg was put in a cast.

(4) It took her some time to realize the dangers of her situation.

11 ④   12 ②, ⑤   13 ⑤

14 the old train tracks   15 ③   16 ②

17 all of a sudden

18 saw a white, wooden gateway across a black opening

19 Keep Out   20 ④   21 ②   22 ⑤

23 there, in the hospital   24 being → be

25 *Stay out of trouble*

01 thanks to: ~ 덕분에, wooden: 나무로 된, 목재의, relief: 안도, 안심, after a while: 얼마 후에, cast: 석고붕대, 깁스

02 '크고 날카로운 울음이나 소음'을 의미하는 말은 'scream(비명)'이다.

03 '고통스러운 어떤 것의 제거'를 의미하는 말은 'relief(안도, 안심)'이다.

04 side by side: 나란히

05 • 나는 그가 다치지 않은 것이 감사했다. (동사) • 승객 중 심하게 다친 사람은 아무도 없었다. (형용사) • 그녀의 목소리에는 상처와 진짜 분노가 서려 있었다. (명사)

06 (1) whisper: 속삭이다, (2) would: ~하곤 했다(과거의 불규칙적 습관), (3) inch by inch: 조금씩

07 day in and day out: 매일, keep out of: ~에 들어가지 않다, reach out: (손·팔·다리 등을) 뻗다

08 ② has had → had had ③ to ache seeing → ache to see

④ to cry → from crying ⑤ other → the other

09 (1) 주절과 부사절의 주어가 다르므로 부사절의 주어를 생략하면 안 되며, 부사절의 시제가 앞서므로 완료분사구문으로 써야 한다. (2) 주절과 부사절의 주어가 다르므로 부사절의 주어를 생략하지 않은 독립분사구문으로 써야 한다. (3) 목적을 나타내는 'so that ~ can'은 to부정사를 이용하여 부사적 용법(목적)으로 바꿔 쓸 수 있다. (4) 의문사가 없는 간접의문문은 'if+주어+동사'의 형태로 써야 한다.

10 (1) work를 수식하는 현재분사가 적절하다. (2) 둘 중에서 하나는 one으로 나타내고 나머지 하나는 the other로 나타낸다. (3) where 다음의 절이 완전하므로 in을 생략하거나 where를 which로 고쳐야 한다. (4) it takes+시간+to부정사: ~하는 데 …의 시간이 걸리다

11 as와 as 사이에 be동사의 보어로 형용사가 나와야 한다. I'll be as quick as I can.

12 ⓐ와 ②, ⑤: 계속 용법, ① 경험 용법, ③ 완료 용법, ④ 결과 용법

13 매일 Ron과 글쓴이는 게스트하우스에서 '조금씩 먼 곳으로' 자전거를 타고 가곤 했다.

14 '낡은 철로'를 가리킨다.

15 ③번 다음 문장 'Ron was ahead.'에 주목한다. 주어진 문장의 'one behind the other'를 더 자세히 설명하는 것이므로 ③번이 적절하다.

16 ⓑ와 ②, ④: 부사적 용법, ①: 형용사적 용법, ③, ⑤: 명사적 용법

17 all of a sudden 갑자기

18 '색깔+재료'의 순서로 쓰는 것이 적절하다.

19 문에는 '들어가지 마시오'라고 적혀 있었다.

20 ⓐ, ⓒ, ⓓ: 글쓴이, ⓑ, ⓔ: Ron

21 위 글의 분위기로는 '긴급한'이 적절하다. ③ 축제의, 축하하는, ④ 우울한, ⑤ (지루할 정도로) 단조로운

22 'Ron에게 무슨 일이 생겼는지'는 대답할 수 없다. ① They left their bikes at the gate. ② They entered the cool tunnel. ③ There were bats above their heads. ④ Ron said it.

23 관계부사 where는 계속적 용법으로 쓰여 and there, 즉 and in the hospital의 의미이다.

24 사역동사 let 뒤에는 목적보어로 동사원형을 쓴다.

25 그들은 '들어가지 마시오'라는 말은 '곤경을 멀리하라'는 뜻이라는 것을 배웠다. stay out of trouble: '재난[곤란, 어려움, 문젯거리 등]으로부터 벗어나다'

교과서 파헤치기

단어 TEST Step 1 , p.02

01 먼지
02 방해하다
03 지진
04 완화하다, 줄이다
05 모래 폭풍
06 가뭄
07 영향, 효과, 결과
08 분출하다
09 농작물
10 자원
11 분출
12 파괴하다
13 발표하다, 발행하다
14 범람하다; 홍수
15 태풍
16 부피, 용적
17 경치, 풍경
18 산불
19 막다, 예방하다
20 황사
21 주의, 경고
22 화산
23 해일
24 전체의, 온
25 갑작스러운
26 위협하다
27 산사태
28 강우, 강우량
29 ~의 위치를 찾아내다
30 근처의; 근처에
31 일어나다, 발생하다
32 재
33 가능성
34 둘러싸다
35 A를 위험하게 하다
36 ~을 이용하다
37 다치다
38 ~을 따라 이름 짓다
39 ~을 명심하다
40 ~에 영향을 미치다
41 A가 ~하지 못하게 하다
42 ~을 …으로 내뿜다
43 ~와 조화를 이루어

단어 TEST Step 2 p.03

01 rainfall
02 drought
03 active
04 crop
05 destroy
06 earthquake
07 disturb
08 eruption
09 relieve
10 threaten
11 tsunami
12 flood
13 occur
14 dust
15 volume
16 scenery
17 warning
18 landslide
19 effect
20 ash
21 wildfire
22 yellow dust
23 entire
24 resource
25 sandstorm
26 typhoon
27 volcano
28 sudden
29 erupt
30 prevent
31 issue
32 soil
33 circle
34 overnight
35 millions of
36 shoot ~ into …
37 get stuck in
38 name after
39 have an effect on
40 make use of
41 put A in danger
42 in harmony with
43 on one's way back

단어 TEST Step 3 p.04

1 eruption, 분출   2 active, 활동 중인   3 circle, 둘러싸다
4 traffic, 교통   5 earthquake, 지진   6 flat, 평평한
7 prevent, 막다, 예방하다   8 ash, 재   9 flood, 홍수

10 rainfall, 강우량   11 crop, 농작물   12 dust, 먼지
13 planet, 행성   14 disturb, 방해하다
15 volcano, 화산   16 landslide, 산사태

대화문 TEST Step 1 p.05~06

Listen - Listen & Answer Talk 1

hit, warning, issued, rainfall, flooding, inside, make sure, keep listening to

Listen - Listen & Answer Dialog 2

do, a favor / typhoon, bring in, outside / No, bike / take care of, dishes / typhoon / tell, to stay home

Listen - Listen More

going out / sandwiches / ride my bike / good, a favor / on your way back / problem / make sure, wear, no / Don't worry

Speak - Talk in pairs.

Wash your hands / problem / more, you don't play with the knives / keep, mind

Wrap Up 5

having a good time / cool, going / going fishing / make sure, wear a life jacket / keep, in mind

Wrap Up 6

do me a favor / Sure / on Christmas, buy, tickets / problem, tickets do you want

대화문 TEST Step 2 p.07~08

Listen - Listen & Answer Talk 1

M: Hi, this is Cha Gisang from the Weather Station. Here is today's weather. Typhoon Doni is moving north and is going to hit Jejudo tonight. A typhoon warning has been issued. There will be lots of rainfall with a high chance of flooding in some areas. Please stay inside because Typhoon Doni will come with strong winds. Also, please make sure you keep listening to our reports. Thank you.

Listen - Listen & Answer Dialog 2

M: Sora, can you do me a favor?

G: What is it, Dad?

M: A typhoon is coming tonight. Can you bring in the clothes from outside?

G: No problem. What about your bike?

M: I'll take care of it after I finish the dishes.

G: Okay. Do you want me to call Grandma and tell her about the typhoon?

M: Yes. Please tell her to stay home.

G: Okay, Dad.

Listen - Listen More

B: Jimin, are you going out?

G: Yeah. I'm going to buy some sandwiches at Choi's.

B: Are you walking there?

G: No. I'll ride my bike.

B: That's good. Can you do me a favor?

G: Sure. What is it?

B: Can you buy chocolate ice cream for me on your way back?

G: No problem.

B: Thanks. Please make sure you wear a helmet and no ear phones!

G: Don't worry about that.

Speak - Talk in pairs.

A: Can I start now?

B: Wash your hands before you start.

A: Okay. No problem.

B: One more thing. Make sure you don't play with the knives.

A: I'll keep that in mind.

Wrap Up 5

B: Hi, Mom.

W: Hi, Junho. Are you having a good time with Dad?

B: Yeah. Today we visited Dokdo.

W: That sounds cool. What are you going to do tomorrow?

B: We're going fishing on a boat.

W: Great. Please make sure you wear a life jacket.

B: Okay, Mom. I'll keep that in mind.

Wrap Up 6

W: Can you do me a favor?

B: Sure, Grandma. What is it?

W: I want to go to the Tom Dylan concert on Christmas. Can you buy some tickets for me?

B: No problem. How many tickets do you want?

W: Two tickets, please.

01 Power, Volcanoes
02 have in common
03 islands, of course
04 fact, islands, volcanic eruptions
05 powerful, so, named after
06 make, appear, destroy entire
07 Therefore, should, studied, understood
08 for sure, volcanoes there
09 According, active, above, level
10 underwater, hard to locate
11 Still, discovered, number, far
12 volcanoes, located along, circles
13 about, long, home, around
14 alone, since, lies on
15 area, most, earthquakes occur
16 Sudden, Volcano
17 Working, cornfield, something surprising
18 appeared overnight, flat cornfield
19 Residents, grow over, within
20 called, kept, stopped growing
21 may, can be found
22 been discovered, such as
23 fact, largest known, solar
24 times greater, largest volcano
25 Being, dangerous, harm, ways
26 get hurt, may lose
27 may, destoryed, be threatened
28 have serious effects on
29 shoots, preventing, reaching, disturbing
30 Deadly Volcano
31 active volcano, island, erupted
32 eruption, more than, residents
33 caused, unusually, around, following
34 What volcanoes, humans, however
35 soil, volcano, good, farming
36 Volcanoes, great tourist attraction
37 Looking, scenery, millions, tourists
38 be used, produce electricity
39 for, turns, volcanoes', into
40 ways, harmony, hopeful, found

01 Power, Volcanoes
02 have in common
03 islands, of course
04 fact, volcanic eruptions
05 are named after

06 make big islands appear, destory
07 should be studied and understood
08 how many volcanoes there are
09 According to, about, above sea level
10 underwater, hard to locate
11 a large number of, so far
12 are located along
13 home to, active volcanoes
14 alone, since, lies on   15 where, occur
16 Sudden
17 Working, something surprising
18 appeared overnight, flat cornfield
19 grow, within
20 kept growing, stopped growing
21 can be found
22 have been discovered, such as
23 the largest known, solar system
24 100 times greater than that of
25 do harm to, in many ways
26 get hurt
27 may be destoryed, can be threatened
28 have serious effects on
29 shoots, into, preventing, from reaching, disturbing
30 Deadly Volcano
31 active volcano, erupted   32 eruption, more than
33 unusually, following year
34 What volcanoes do, not always
35 is good for   36 tourist attraction
37 Looking for, millions of   38 can be used
39 turns, into electricity
40 greater harmony with, will be found

본문 TEST Step 3   p.14~15

1 화산의 힘
2 제주도, 시칠리아, 하와이의 공통점은 무엇일까?
3 물론, 그것들은 섬이다.
4 사실, 그것들은 모두 화산 분출에 의해 형성된 섬이다.
5 화산은 매우 강력한 힘을 가지고 있어서 로마의 불의 신, 불카누스에게서 이름을 따왔다.
6 화산은 큰 섬이 생겨나게 하거나 폼페이 같은 도시 전체를 파멸시킬 수도 있다.
7 그러므로 화산은 연구되고, 이해되어야 한다.
8 세계에 얼마나 많은 화산이 있는지 누구도 정확히 알지 못한다.
9 과학자들에 따르면, 해수면 위에 대략 1,500개의 활화산이 있다.
10 더 많은 화산이 해저에 존재하는데, 그것들은 정확한 위치를 파악하기가 어렵다.

11 그럼에도 불구하고, 과학자들은 지금까지 그중 많은 수를 발견했다.
12 지구상에 있는 많은 화산들은 태평양을 둘러싸는 '불의 고리(환태평양조산대)'를 따라 위치한다.
13 그 고리는 길이가 약 40,000km에 달하며, 전 세계 화활산의 약 75%가 여기에 있다.
14 인도네시아에만 120개가 넘는 활화산이 있는데, 이 나라가 '불의 고리'에 위치하고 있기 때문이다.
15 이 고리는 또한 전 세계 지진의 대부분이 발생하는 곳이다.
16 갑작스럽게 생겨난 화산
17 1943년 어느 날 옥수수 밭에서 일을 하다가 멕시코의 농부들이 놀라운 것을 발견했다.
18 밤사이에 평평한 옥수수 밭 위로 화산이 생겨난 것이다.
19 주민들은 그 화산이 일주일이 못 되는 사이 100m 넘게 자라는 것을 지켜보았다.
20 'Paricutin(파리쿠틴)'이라고 불리는 이 화산은 계속 자라났고, 1952년에 424m로 드디어 성장을 멈추었다.
21 화산이 지구에만 존재한다고 생각할지 모른다.
22 그러나 화산은 화성이나 목성 같은 다른 행성에서도 발견되어 왔다.
23 사실 화성에 있는 Olympus Mons(올림푸스 몬스)가 태양계에서 가장 크다고 알려진 화산이다.
24 그것의 부피는 지구에서 가장 큰 화산 Mauna Loa(마우나로아)의 부피보다 약 100배 더 크다.
25 매우 강력하고 위험하기 때문에, 화산은 여러 면에서 사람들에게 해를 끼친다.
26 때로는 사람들이 다치기도 하고, 집을 잃기도 한다.
27 작물이 파괴되거나, 항공 교통이 위협받을 수도 있다.
28 화산은 또한 세계 날씨에 심각한 영향을 미치기도 한다.
29 화산 분출은 다량의 화산재와 먼지를 공중으로 내뿜어, 태양 광선의 일부가 지구에 도달하는 것을 방해하고 그리하여 정상적인 기상 패턴을 깨뜨린다.
30 목숨을 앗아 가는 화산
31 인도네시아 Sumbawa(숨바와) 섬에 위치한 활화산, Tambora(탐보라) 산이 1815년에 분출했다.
32 분출은 주민 1만 명 이상을 죽음에 이르게 했다.
33 또한 이듬해 전 세계에 비정상적으로 추운 여름을 초래했다.
34 그러나 화산이 인류에게 항상 나쁜 것만은 아니다.
35 화산 인근의 토양은 농사에 좋다.
36 화산은 또한 매우 훌륭한 관광 명소이다.
37 환상적인 경관을 찾아 매년 수백만 명의 여행객들이 제주도의 한라산, 시칠리아의 Etna(에트나) 산, 하와이의 Diamond Head(다이아몬드헤드)를 방문한다.
38 화산은 또한 전기를 생산하는 데에도 이용될 수 있다.
39 예를 들어, 아이슬란드는 적극적으로 화산의 열에너지를 전기로 바꾼다.
40 오늘날 전 세계에서 사람들이 화산과 더 조화롭게 살 방법을 연구하고 있으며, 더 많은 방법이 곧 발견될 것으로 기대하고 있다.

1 The Power of Volcanoes

2 What do Jejudo, Sicily, and Hawaii have in common?

3 They are islands, of course.

4 In fact, they are all islands made from volcanic eruptions.

5 Volcanoes are very powerful, so they are named after Vulcan, the Roman god of fire.

6 They can make big islands appear or destroy entire cities like Pompeii.

7 Therefore, they should be studied and understood.

8 Nobody knows for sure how many volcanoes there are in the world.

9 According to scientists, there are about 1,500 active volcanoes above sea level.

10 Many more are underwater, and they are hard to locate.

11 Still, scientists have discovered a large number of them so far.

12 Many of the volcanoes on Earth are located along the Ring of Fire that circles the Pacific Ocean.

13 The ring is about 40,000 kilometers long, and it is home to around 75% of the world's active volcanoes.

14 Indonesia alone has over 120 active volcanoes since the country lies on the Ring of Fire.

15 This ring is also the area where most of the world's earthquakes occur.

16 A Sudden Volcano

17 Working on a cornfield one day in 1943, farmers in Mexico found something surprising.

18 A volcano appeared overnight on a flat cornfield.

19 Residents watched the volcano grow over 100 meters tall within a week.

20 The volcano, called Paricutin, kept growing, and it finally stopped growing at 424 meters in 1952.

21 You may think volcanoes can be found only on Earth.

22 However, they have been discovered on other planets, too, such as Mars and Jupiter.

23 In fact, "Olympus Mons" on Mars is the largest known volcano in the solar system.

24 Its volume is about 100 times greater than that of Mauna Loa, the largest volcano on Earth.

25 Being very powerful and dangerous, volcanoes do harm to people in many ways.

26 Sometimes people get hurt, or they may lose their houses.

27 Crops may be destoryed, and air traffic can be threatened.

28 Volcanoes can also have serious effects on world weather.

29 A volcanic eruption shoots lots of ash and dust into the air, preventing some of the sunlight from reaching Earth and thus disturbing usual weather patterns.

30 A Deadly Volcano

31 Mt. Tambora, an active volcano on the island of Sumbawa, Indonesia, erupted in 1815.

32 The eruption killed more than 10,000 residents.

33 It also caused an unusually cold summer around the world the following year.

34 What volcanoes do is not always bad for humans, however.

35 The soil near a volcano is good for farming.

36 Volcanoes are also a great tourist attraction.

37 Looking for fantastic scenery, millions of tourists visit Mt. Halla in Jejudo, Mt. Etna in Sicily, or Diamond Head in Hawaii every year.

38 Volcanoes can be used to produce electricity, too.

39 Iceland, for example, actively turns its volcanoes' heat energy into electricity.

40 Today people around the world are studying ways to live in greater harmony with volcanoes, and they are hopeful that more ways will be found soon.

My Speaking Portfolio Step 1

1. electricity, out

2. caught on fire

3. got stuck

4. burned my finger

5. fell down, broke

After You Read Details

1. volcano, comes from

2. the world's active volcanoes are located along

3. stopped growing

4. The eruption, brought about an unusually cold summer

My Writing Portfolio

1. Perfect Storm

2. saw, last weekend

3. came out, was directed by

4. about, in the Atlantic Ocean, in danger

5. because the scenes were exciting, realistic

6. good acting of the leading actor

7. learned, natural disasters like storms, dangerous

구석구석지문 TEST Step 2   p.22

My Speaking Portfolio Step 1

1. The electricity is out.

2. The pan caught on fire.

3. I got stuck in the elevator.

4. I burned my finger in hot water.

5. I fell down the steps and broke my arm.

After You Read Details

1. The name "volcano" comes from the Roman god of fire. - Mila

2. 75% of the world's active volcanoes are located along the Ring of Fire. - James

3. The volcano Paricutin in Mexico stopped growing. - Lucy

4. The eruption of Mt. Tambora brought about an unusually cold summer in 1816. - David

My Writing Portfolio

1. The Perfect Storm

2. I saw the movie *The Perfect Storm* last weekend.

3. The movie came out in 2000, and it was directed by the German director Wolfgang Petersen.

4. It is about a big storm in the Atlantic Ocean that put a fishing boat in danger.

5. I liked the movie because the scenes were exciting and very realistic.

6. Also, I liked the good acting of the leading actor George Clooney.

7. From the movie, I learned that natural disasters like storms can be very dangerous.

단어 TEST Step 1   p.23

01 이루다, 달성[성취]하다

02 확신하는, 자신만만한   03 현수막

04 심사, 테스트   05 난처한, 걱정[근심]스러운

06 침착한, 냉정한   07 수도   08 제의, 제안

09 기회   10 일생[평생]의   11 쫓다, 추적하다

12 보호   13 ~할 가치가 있는   14 완전히, 전적으로

15 짜증 난, 참지 못하는   16 연결하다

17 아주 기뻐하는   18 규칙

19 구하다, 절약하다, 저축하다   20 심각한, 진지한

21 표현하다   22 무서워하는, 겁먹은

23 기분 좋은, 즐거운 24 후회하다   25 도전적인

26 설립하다   27 상상, 상상력

28 향상시키다, 개선하다   29 수리하다

30 포함하다   31 잘못 알고 있는   32 결정, 판단

33 나머지, 휴식   34 기량, 기술   35 고장 나다

36 ~했을지도 모른다   37 ~을 다루다

38 발발[발생]하다   39 (과거에) ~이었다[했다]

40 ~을 부끄러워하다

41 ~에 지원하다, ~을 신청하다   42 ~와 시간을 보내다

43 반복해서

단어 TEST Step 2   p.24

01 confident   02 improve   03 banner

04 completely   05 include   06 lifelong

07 achieve   08 calm   09 express

10 connect   11 found   12 cheerful

13 delighted   14 chase   15 practice

16 regret   17 capital   18 tryout

19 protection   20 challenging   21 impatient

22 opportunity   23 worth   24 imagination

25 repair   26 skill   27 decision

28 save   29 scared   30 serious

31 mistaken   32 rest   33 pick

34 quite   35 go by   36 over and over

37 break down   38 must have p.p.

39 be ashamed of   40 break out

41 hang out with 42 deal with   43 apply for

단어 TEST Step 3 p.25

1 found, 설립하다   2 connect, 연결하다   3 rest, 나머지
4 create, 만들다, 창조하다   5 read, ~라고 적혀 있다
6 opportunity, 기회   7 impatient, 참지 못하는
8 decision, 결정, 판단   9 challenging, 도전적인
10 tryout, 심사, 테스트   11 banner, 현수막
12 include, 포함하다   13 serious, 심각한, 진지한
14 league, 리그, 연맹   15 regret, 후회하다
16 worth, ~할 가치가 있는

대화문 TEST Step 1 p.26~27

Listen - Listen & Answer Dialog 1

What / drawing cartoons, preparing for / are, when /
On, left / How's, gojng / It, to draw what, to express,
should have practiced / worry, make it

Listen - Listen & Answer Dialog 2

to meet, do well on, drawing exam / sure, did my
best / What made, apply for / (I')ve, loved, since, little
child / cartoon artist / quite right / What, think, most
important skill / I'd say, completely

Speak - Talk in pairs.

matter / hungry, saved / Don't, share, with

Listen - Listen More

to see / I'm afraid, be late / hate to be late for /
should have set / happens a lot, tired / What made,
late / got up, it took, do my hair / We're stuck in,
traffic jam, get off / you're mistaken, stay on /
terribly

Wrap Up 6

when, grow up / with / interested in making / that's,
quite right, repair / why / Because, think

Wrap Up 7

has viruses / How / shouldn't have done / were you,
I'd get, right now

대화문 TEST Step 2 p.28~29

Listen - Listen & Answer Dialog 1

B: Hi, Sora. What are you doing?

G: I'm drawing cartoons. I'm preparing for the exam
for Mana Animation High School.

B: Oh, are you? When is the exam?

G: On Friday, so I only have two days left.

B: How's it going?

G: It's not easy to draw what I want to express. I
should have practiced more.

B: Don't worry! You can make it!

G: Thanks.

Listen - Listen & Answer Dialog 2

M: Nice to meet you, Sora. Did you do well on the
drawing exam?

G: I'm not sure, but I did my best.

M: Okay. Let's start the interview. What made you
apply for Mana Animation High School?

G: Well, I've really loved drawing cartoons since I was
a little child.

M: So, you want to be a cartoon artist?

G: That's not quite right. I want to be a game
designer.

M: I see. What do you think is the most important
skill a game designer needs?

G: I'd say imagination. A good designer should create
a completely new world in a game.

M: Sounds good.

Speak - Talk in pairs.

A: What's the matter?

B: I feel hungry. I should have saved food for the
winter.

A: Don't worry. I'll share my food with you.

B: Thanks.

Listen - Listen More

G: Hi, Jiho.

B: Hi, Amber. It's nice to see you on the bus.

G: Yeah, but I'm afraid we're going to be late.

B: Yeah. I hate to be late for the school festival.

G: Me, too. I should have set my alarm. I forgot.

B: I understand. That happens a lot to me when I'm
tired, too.

G: How about you? What made you late?

B: Well, I got up early. But it took me some time to
do my hair.

G: Oh, I see. We're stuck in a heavy traffic jam. We
should get off and run.

B: No, you're mistaken. The traffic is starting to
move again. Let's stay on.

G: Okay. I just hope we're not terribly late.

Wrap Up 6

B: What do you want to do when you grow up?

G: I want to work with robots.

B: Are you interested in making robots?

G: No, that's not quite right. I want to repair robots.

B: I see. But why?

G: Because I think it'll be a good job in the future.

Wrap Up 7

G: My computer has viruses.

B: How come?

G: I opened an e-mail from a stranger. I shouldn't have done that.

B: If I were you, I'd get help from a computer service center right now.

---

01 GRANDMOTHER'S BASEBALL DREAMS

02 used to, cook, near

03 work anymore, delicious, which

04 one, that connect us

05 What connects, strongly, however

06 When, weekends, exciting, back

07 must have loved   08 listen to, over and

09 says, Go after what

10 afraid, something new, challenging

11 Don't, ashamed of failing

12 In, Professional, was founded

13 created, because, were fighting

14 there would, local tryouts

15 What would, like, finals

16 imagined, hanging, which included

17 explained, suit, serious, unkind

18 thought, wearing, made, impatient

19 On, for hours, other   20 excited to go after

21 About, later, found, mailbox

22 It, from, worked for

23 read, had, main tryouts

24 As, went by, worried

25 traveling, which, far away

26 tryouts, too afraid to

27 spent, rest, regretting, decision

28 watches, should have gone

29 worth chasing, even, few

30 Never miss, opportunity

---

01 GRANDMOTHER'S, DREAMS

---

02 used to be a cook, near

03 anymore, enjoys making, which

04 one, that connect us

05 What connects, strongly, is

06 on weekends, exciting stories, back

07 must have loved

08 listen to, over and over   09 Go after what

10 afraid of, something new or challenging

11 Don't be ashamed of   12 was founded

13 was created, were fighting

14 there would be local tryouts

15 What would it be like, the finals

16 imagined, hanging, which included

17 were explained, in a suit, serious

18 wearing a suit, might have made, impatient

19 for hours, other, women   20 to go after

21 later, found a letter   22 It was from

23 It read, had been invited, league's main tryouts

24 As, went by, worried

25 worried about, which, far away from

26 main tryouts, too, to   27 has spent, regretting

28 should have gone

29 are worth chasing, even if

30 Never miss, opportunity

---

1 할머니의 야구 꿈

2 우리 할머니 Helen은 Indiana주 South Bend 근처 작은 마을에 있는 식당의 요리사였다.

3 할머니는 더 이상 일을 하지 않지만 여전히 맛있는 음식을 즐겨 만드시고, 나는 그 음식들을 무척 좋아한다.

4 음식은 우리를 연결하는 많은 것 가운데 하나이다.

5 하지만 우리를 가장 강하게 연결하는 것은 바로 야구이다.

6 주말마다 할머니 댁에 가면, 할머니는 종종 과거 1940년대의 야구 경기에 관해 흥미로운 이야기를 내게 들려주신다.

7 그녀는 야구를 무척 좋아했던 게 분명하다.

8 나는 이 이야기들을 몇 번이고 듣는다.

9 그녀는 항상 "네가 원하는 것을 이루려고 노력하렴, Sarah.

10 새로운 것이나 도전적인 것을 시도해 보기를 두려워하지 말거라.

11 실패하는 것을 부끄러워하지 마라."라고 말씀하신다.

12 1943년, 전미 여자 프로야구 리그가 창립되었다.

13 미국의 청년 중 많은 사람들이 제2차 세계대전에 참전해 있었기 때문에 이 리그가 야구 팬들을 위해 만들어졌다.

14 Helen 할머니는 지역 심사가 바로 South Bend에서 있을 거라고 들었다.

15 그녀는 "야구 팀에 들어가서 고향을 위해 결승전까지 진출한다는 건 어떤 기분일까?"라며 궁금해했다.

16 그녀는 Helen Baker라는 이름이 포함된 큰 현수막이 야구장에 걸려 있는 것을 상상했다.

17 심사 당일 모든 규칙이 정장을 입은 나이 든 남자에 의해 설명되었는데, 그는 무척 진지하고 불친절하게 들렸다.

18 뜨거운 태양 아래 정장을 입고 있는 것이 그를 짜증나게 만들었을지도 모른다고 그녀는 생각했다.

19 그날, Helen 할머니는 다른 젊은 여성들과 함께 몇 시간 동안 야구를 했다.

20 그녀는 자신의 야구 꿈을 좇아가게 되어 신이 났다!

21 일주일쯤 지나, Helen 할머니는 우편함에서 편지 한 통을 발견했다.

22 그것은 시카고에 있는 여자 야구리그에서 일하는 사람들이 보낸 것이었다.

23 그 편지에는 그녀가 시카고에서 열리는 리그의 본심사에 초청되었다고 적혀 있었다!

24 하지만 하루하루 갈수록, Helen 할머니는 심사에 떨어질까봐 걱정되었다.

25 그녀는 또한 시카고까지 혼자 여행하는 것이 걱정되었는데, 시카고는 집에서 멀리 떨어진 곳이었다.

26 본심사가 있는 날이 되었을 때, 그녀는 너무 두려워서 갈 수 없었다.

27 할머니는 남은 인생을 자신의 결정을 후회하며 보내셨다.

28 텔레비전에서 야구 경기를 볼 때, 그녀는 종종 "난 시카고에 갔어야 해.

29 너도 알겠지만, 모든 꿈은 추구할 가치가 있단다, 비록 일부만 이루게 되더라도 말이야.

30 절대 기회를 놓치지 마라."라고 말씀하신다.

1 MY GRANDMOTHER'S BASEBALL DREAMS

2 My grandmother Helen used to be a cook in a restaurant in a small town near South Bend, Indiana.

3 She does not work anymore, but she still enjoys making delicious food, which I love so much.

4 Food is one of the many things that connect us.

5 What connects us most strongly, however, is baseball.

6 When I visit her on weekends, my grandmother often tells me exciting stories about playing baseball back in the 1940s.

7 She must have loved the sport very much.

9 I listen to these stories over and over.

9 She always says, "Go after what you want, Sarah.

10 Don't be afraid of trying something new or challenging.

11 Don't be ashamed of failing."

12 In 1943, the All-American Girls Professional Baseball League was founded.

13 This league was created for baseball fans because many of America's young men were fighting in World War II.

14 Helen was told that there would be local tryouts right in South Bend.

15 She wondered, "What would it be like to be on a baseball team and to make it to the finals for my hometown?"

16 She imagined a large banner hanging at the baseball field which included the name Helen Baker.

17 On the day of the tryouts, all the rules were explained by an old man in a suit, who sounded very serious and unkind.

18 She thought that wearing a suit in the hot sun might have made him impatient.

19 On that day, Helen played baseball for hours with many other young women.

20 She was excited to go after her baseball dreams!

21 About a week later, Helen found a letter in the mailbox.

22 It was from people who worked for the girls' baseball league in Chicago.

23 It read that she had been invited to the league's main tryouts in Chicago!

24 As the days went by, however, Helen became worried that she might fail.

25 She also became worried about traveling alone to Chicago, which was far away from home.

26 When the day of the main tryouts came, she was too afraid to go.

27 My grandmother has spent the rest of her life regretting her decision.

28 When she watches a baseball game on TV, she often says, "I should have gone to Chicago.

29 You know, all your dreams are worth chasing, even if you catch only a few of them.

30 Never miss an opportunity."

After You Read Graphic Organizer

1. broke out
2. so much
3. was, sure of, was afraid of traveling alone
4. founded
5. joined the local tryouts
6. main tryouts

My Writing Portfolio

1. MOTHER OF CHIMPANZEES
2. was born in London, England
3. Her interest in, when she first read
4. has been studying, since her twenties
5. has, been working, protection of chimpanzees
6. received, for protecting whild animals
7. Thanks to her lifelong study, come to know
8. one of the greatest scientists

Words in Action

1. are winning, are singing a cheerful song
2. If, stays calm, catches
3. misses
4. make two runs, game continues
5. looks ashamed, nervous
6. going wild, while, look scared, worried

7. Thanks to her lifelong study, we have come to know a lot about chimpanzees.
8. Jane Goodall is one of the greatest scientists in history.

Words in Action

1. The Cheetahs are winning the game, and their fans are singing a cheerful song.
2. If Jason stays calm and catches the ball, the game ends.
3. Oh my! He misses the ball!
4. The Ducks make two runs, and the game continues.
5. Jason looks ashamed and nervous.
6. The Ducks fans are going wild, while the Cheetahs fans look scared and worried.

After You Read Graphic Organizer

1. The Second World War broke out.
2. She loved baseball so much.
3. She was not sure of her success. Also, she was afraid of traveling alone.
4. In 1943, the All-American Girls Professional Baseball League was founded.
5. She joined the local tryouts in South Bend.
6. She didn't go to the main tryouts.

My Writing Portfolio

1. JANE GOODALL, MOTHER OF CHIMPANZEES
2. Jane Goodall was born in London, England, in 1934.
3. Her interest in chimpanzees began when she first read about Tarzan.
4. She has been studying wild chimpanzees in Africa since her twenties.
5. She has also been working for the protection of chimpanzees.
6. In 1995, she received the Hubbard Medal for protecting whild animals.

14 manager, 경영자, 관리자   15 record, 기록

16 whisper, 속삭이다

단어 TEST Step 1   p.42

01 외치다, 소리[고함]치다   02 안도, 안심

03 안전 제품   04 실제(로)는, 사실은

05 고통을 주다, 아프다   06 교훈

07 자전거를 타다   08 ~ 내내, ~ 동안 쭉

09 흙, 먼지   10 입구, 입장   11 그러나, 그래도

12 나무로 된, 목재의 13 숨 쉬다   14 입구, 관문

15 석고붕대, 깁스   16 경영자, 관리자   17 쿵쾅거리는

18 열린 구멍, 창(窓), 구멍, 틈   19 특별한

20 ~하곤 했다 (과거의 불규칙적 습관)   21 기록

22 비명   23 두터운, 빽빽한   24 속삭이다

25 어느 때처럼   26 출발하다   27 대답으로

28 (손·팔·다리 등을) 뻗다   29 매일

30 조금씩   31 얼마 후에   32 나란히

33 ~하자마자   34 처음에는   35 다시 말해서, 즉

36 갑자기   37 간신히 ~하다   38 ~ 덕분에

39 ~하곤 했다   40 ~가 …하는 것을 막다

단어 TEST Step 2   p.43

01 wooden   02 safety product 03 would

04 cast   05 though   06 scream

07 cycle   08 dirt   09 entrance

10 throughout   11 lesson   12 manager

13 opening   14 gateway   15 particular

16 record   17 thumping   18 hurt

19 whisper   20 relief   21 shout

22 actually   23 breathe   24 thick

25 at first   26 reach out   27 inch by inch

28 stop ~ from -ing   29 thanks to

30 set off   31 after a while   32 side by side

33 day in and day out   34 in other words

35 as soon as   36 in reply   37 as usual

38 manage to   39 all of a sudden 40 used to

단어 TEST Step 3   p.44

1 breathe, 숨 쉬다   2 cycle, 자전거를 타다

3 dirt, 흙, 먼지   4 entrance, 입구

5 thick, 두터운, 빽빽한   6 scream, 비명

7 relief, 안도, 안심   8 gateway, 입구   9 flood, 홍수

10 throughout, ~ 내내, ~ 동안 쭉   11 lesson, 교훈

12 particular, 특별한   13 thumping, 쿵쾅거리는

본문 TEST Step 1   p.45~48

01 Keep Out   02 used to go, coast

03 place, stayed at, same

04 stay, swimming, walking, little

05 other words, anything, happened

06 At the time of

07 particular, as, had, since

08 throughout, shone, in, out

09 But, loved, heat, sun

10 ride, further, away from

11 decided, ride, along, take

12 as usual, set off

13 easy, follow, cycled, by

14 while, thicker, behind, other

15 was ahead

16 toward, darker, formed, roof

17 stopped suddenly, ahead, shouted

18 to, wooden, across, opening

19 a tunnel, said

20 Keep Out, gate, replied

21 have a look inside

22 Actually, not want, inside

23 little, sudden, back into

24 answered, moved ahead

25 left, gate, climbed over   26 entered, cool tunnel

27 air inside, heavy

28 Above, sound, grew louder

29 called out

30 Keep, down, move on

31 Don't, fast, called after

32 meant, leave, behind, so

33 loud, thumping, express, scream

34 shouted, up, hear, reply

35 Speak, Tell, what's happened

36 toward where, been, dirt

37 reached out, something wet

38 were closed, breathing weakly

39 whispered, get, out

40 broken, hurts, get help

41 replied, get, out, safety

42 moving away, dirt, with

43 felt calm, in control

44 took, clear away, covering

45 Finally, managed to free

46 Holding, backward, toward, entrance

47 seemed, ages, able, out　48 look too well, though

49 stop, from crying out

50 found, brought, water bottles

51 get help, quick as

52 In reply, simply pressed

53 raced back, until, nearest

54 past, gate, washing, dishes

55 Thanks, taken, put, cast

56 soon, arrived, with relief　57 Let, be, lesson

58 lesson, *out, Stay, trouble*

59 manager, produces, safety products

60 am, fire fighter

39 get you out

40 (I')ve broken, go and get help

41 get you out of here　42 moving away

43 felt calm, in control

44 clear away, covering　45 managed to free

46 Holding, inch by inch, tunnel entrance

47 to take ages, out of　48 look too well, though

49 stop, from crying out, crying out

50 two water bottles

51 go and get help, as quick as, can

52 In reply, pressed my hands

53 raced back, the nearest farmhouse

54 ran past, washing some dishes

55 Thanks to her, where, put, cast

56 As soon as, with relief　57 Let that be a lesson

58 lesson, *Stay out of trouble*

59 other safety products　60 fire fighter

본문 TEST Step 2　p.49~52

01 Keep Out　02 Every, used to go

03 stayed at, guesthouse

04 stay for, swimming, walking

05 In other words, anything special

06 At the time of　07 had had

08 throughout, shone day in and day out

09 the heat

10 further and further away from

11 take us

12 to follow, as usual, set off

13 cycled along side by side

14 grew thicker, one behind the other

15 ahead

16 grew darker, formed a roof

17 Look ahead, shouted

18 next to him, black opening

19 a tunnel　20 Keep Out

21 have a look　22 Actually, go inside

23 all of a sudden, go back into

24 moved ahead　25 left, climbed over

26 entered　27 inside, heavy

28 grew louder and louder　29 called out

30 Keep, down, moved on

31 Don't go, called after　32 leave, behind

33 loud noise, thumping, like an express train, scream

34 what's up, reply　35 what's happened

36 where Ron had been

37 reached out, something wet

38 were closed, breathing weakly

본문 TEST Step 3　p.53~56

1 들어가지 마시오

2 여름마다 나의 가족은 해안으로 휴가를 가곤 했다.

3 우리는 항상 같은 곳에 가서 똑같은 작은 게스트하우스에 묵었다.

4 우리는 2주 가량 머물며 바다에서 수영하고 작은 마을 주위를 돌아다니곤 했다.

5 다시 말해서, 그런 휴가에서 우리는 특별한 일을 하지 않았고 정말 아무 일도 일어나지 않았다.

6 이 이야기는 내가 12살 때 일이다.

7 관측 이래 영국이 겪은 가장 더운 여름이었기 때문에, 대부분의 사람들은 이 특별한 여름을 기억할 수 있나.

8 6월과 7월 내내 비가 오지 않았고 태양은 연일 쨍쨍했다.

9 하지만 Ron과 나는 그 더위와 태양을 사랑했다.

10 매일 우리는 게스트하우스에서 조금씩 먼 곳으로 자전거를 타고 가곤 했다.

11 어느 날, Ron은 낡은 철로가 우리를 어디로 데려다줄지 알아보려고 그 철로를 따라 자전거를 타기로 결정했다.

12 난 늘 그랬듯 Ron을 따르는 게 즐거웠고, 아침 식사 후에 우리는 출발했다.

13 처음에는 철길을 따라가는 게 어렵지 않아 우리는 나란히 자전거를 타고 갔다.

14 한참 후, 풀이 점점 우거져서 우리는 한 사람이 앞서가고 다른 사람이 뒤에서 가야 했다.

15 Ron이 앞서가고 있었다.

16 철길은 숲으로 이어졌고 나무가 높이 자라 철길 위로 지붕을 형성하며 점점 더 어두워졌다.

17 Ron이 갑자기 멈췄다. "앞을 봐!"라고 그가 외쳤다.

18 나는 그의 옆에 멈춰서 캄캄한 입구를 가로지르는 흰색 나무문을 보았다.

19 "터널이네." 내가 말했다.

20 "맞아. 그리고 문에 '들어가지 마시오'라고 적혀 있어." Ron이 대답했다.

21 "안을 보고 싶니?"

22 사실, 난 안으로 들어가고 싶지 않았다.

23 갑자기 나는 한기를 살짝 느꼈고 햇빛 속으로 되돌아가고 싶었다.

24 그렇지만 나는 "물론이지."라고 답하며 앞으로 움직였다.

25 우리는 문 앞에 자전거를 남겨 두고 넘어갔다.

26 우리는 서늘한 터널로 들어갔다.

27 안의 공기는 묵직했다.

28 우리 머리 위로 점점 더 커지는 소리가 났다.

29 "저게 뭐야?"라고 내가 소리쳤다.

30 "박쥐야." Ron이 말했다. "머리를 숙여." 그러고 나서 그는 계속 움직였다.

31 "너무 빨리 가지 마." 나는 그를 부르며 뒤쫓았다.

32 '나를 두고 가지 마'라고 말하고 싶었지만, 나는 그렇게 말하지 않았다.

33 그다음 내가 들은 것은 바로 앞에서 나는 큰 소음이었는데, 그것은 마치 고속열차 같은 쿵쾅거리는 소리였다. 이어서 비명이 들렸다.

34 "Ron!" 나는 외쳤다. "Ron, 무슨 일이야? 내 말 들려?" 아무 응답이 없었다.

35 "Ron, 나에게 말해 봐. 무슨 일이 생겼는지 말해 줘."

36 나는 천천히 Ron이 있던 곳으로 걸어갔고 흙과 작은 자갈만을 발견했다.

37 손을 뻗었을 때 나는 축축한 무언가를 느꼈다. Ron의 얼굴이었다!

38 그의 눈은 감겨 있었고 약하게 숨을 쉬고 있었다.

39 "괜찮아, Ron." 나는 속삭였다. "내가 꺼내 줄게."

40 "다리가 부러진 것 같아. 정말 아파. 그냥 가서 도움을 요청해, Ben."

41 "안 돼." 나는 대답했다. "우선 안전한 곳까지 여기에서 형을 꺼낼 거야."

42 나는 손으로 흙과 자갈을 치우기 시작했다.

43 나는 침착했고 내가 잘할 수 있다고 느꼈다.

44 Ron을 뒤덮은 흙을 치우는 데에 오랜 시간이 걸렸다.

45 드디어 나는 그의 몸을 자유롭게 할 수 있었다.

46 팔 밑으로 그를 안고서 그를 터널 입구 쪽으로 조금씩 뒤로 끌어당겼다.

47 오랜 시간이 걸린 듯했지만 결국 나는 Ron을 터널 밖으로 데리고 나올 수 있었다.

48 그는 별로 좋아 보이지 않았다.

49 그의 얼굴은 창백했고 울음을 터뜨리지 않으려고 몹시 애쓰고 있었다.

50 나는 우리 자전거를 찾아서 Ron에게 물병 두 개를 가져다주었다.

51 "여기, 이거 마셔." 나는 말했다. "내가 가서 도움을 구할게. 최대한 빨리 올게."

52 대답으로 Ron은 그저 내 손을 꽉 잡았다.

53 나는 자전거를 타고 왔던 철길을 따라 달려, 마침내 가장 가까운 농가에 도착했다.

54 대문을 지나 달려가 나는 부엌에서 설거지를 하고 있는 부인을 발견했다.

55 그 부인 덕분에 Ron은 병원으로 이송되었고, 병원에서 다리에 석고붕대를 했다.

56 부모님이 병원에 도착해서 우리를 보자마자, 어머니는 안도감에 울음을 터뜨리셨다.

57 하지만 아버지가 하신 말씀은 "이 일이 너희에게 교훈이 되기를 바란다."가 전부였다.

58 그래서 교훈이 무엇이었을까? 그것은 '들어가지 마시오'라는 말은 '곤경을 멀리하라'는 뜻이라는 것이다.

59 Ron은 지금 안전모와 여러 안전 제품을 생산하는 큰 회사의 관리자이다.

60 그럼 나는? 나는 소방관이다.

본문 TEST Step 4 - Step 5
p.57~64

1 Keep Out

2 Every summer, my family used to go on holiday to the coast.

3 We always went to the same place and stayed at the same small guesthouse.

4 We would stay for two weeks, swimming in the sea and walking around the little town.

5 In other words, we never did anything special, and nothing ever really happened on these vacations.

6 At the time of this story I was twelve years old.

7 Most people can remember this particular summer, as it was the hottest summer England had had since records began.

8 It did not rain throughout June and July, and the sun shone day in and day out.

9 But Ron and I loved the heat and the sun.

10 Every day, we would ride our bicycles further and further away from the guesthouse.

11 One day Ron decided that we should ride our bikes along the old train tracks to see where they would take us.

12 I was happy to follow Ron, as usual, and we set off after breakfast.

13 At first, the tracks were easy to follow, and we cycled along side by side.

14 After a while, the grass grew thicker, and we had

to ride one behind the other.

15 Ron was ahead.

16 The tracks went toward the woods and it grew darker as the trees stood tall and formed a roof over the tracks.

17 Ron stopped suddenly. "Look ahead!" he shouted.

18 I stopped next to him and saw a white, wooden gateway across a black opening.

19 "It's a tunnel," I said.

20 "Yes, and it says, 'Keep Out' on the gate," replied Ron.

21 "Do you want to have a look inside?"

22 Actually, I did not want to go inside.

23 I felt a little cold all of a sudden, and I wanted to go back into the sunlight.

24 But I answered, "Sure," and moved ahead.

25 We left our bikes at the gate and climbed over.

26 We entered the cool tunnel.

27 The air inside was heavy.

28 Above our heads there was a sound that grew louder and louder.

29 "What's that?" I called out.

30 "Bats," said Ron, "Keep your head down." Then he moved on.

31 "Don't go so fast." I called after him.

32 I meant, "Don't leave me behind" but I didn't say so.

33 The next thing I heard was a loud noise right above us, a thumping sound like an express train and then a scream.

34 "Ron!" I shouted. "Ron, what's up? Can you hear me?" No reply.

35 "Speak to me, Ron. Tell me what's happened."

36 I slowly walked toward where Ron had been and found only dirt and small rocks.

37 As I reached out my hands, I felt something wet — Ron's face!

38 His eyes were closed, and he was breathing weakly.

39 "It's okay, Ron," I whispered. "I'll get you out."

40 "I think I've broken my leg. It really hurts. Just go and get help, Ben."

41 "No," I replied. "I'll get you out of here to safety first."

42 I started moving away the dirt and rocks with my hands.

43 I felt calm, and I felt in control.

44 It took a long time to clear away the earth

covering Ron.

45 Finally, I managed to free his body.

46 Holding him under the arms, I pulled him backward, inch by inch, toward the tunnel entrance.

47 It seemed to take ages, but finally I was able to get Ron out of the tunnel.

48 He didn't look too well, though.

49 His face was white, and he was trying hard to stop himself from crying out from crying out.

50 I found our bikes and brought the two water bottles to Ron.

51 "Here, drink these," I said. "I'll go and get help. I'll be as quick as I can."

52 In reply, Ron simply pressed my hands.

53 I got on my bicycle and raced back along the tracks until I got to the nearest farmhouse.

54 I ran past the gate and found a woman washing some dishes in the kitchen.

55 Thanks to her, Ron was taken to the hospital, where his leg was put in a cast.

56 As soon as our parents arrived at the hospital and saw us, my mother cried with relief.

57 But all my father said was, "Let that be a lesson to you."

58 And what was the lesson? It was "*Keep out* means *Stay out of trouble*."

59 Ron is now the manager of a big company which produces helmets and other safety products.

60 And me? I am a fire fighter.

MEMO

적중100

영어 기출 문제집

정답 및 해설

천재 | 이재영